National Curriculum: National Disaster?

The function of the National Curriculum is to realise the aims of the Education Reform Act to 'promote the spiritual, moral, cultural, mental and physical development of pupils at school and of society, and to prepare pupils for the opportunities, responsibilities and experiences of adult life' (ERA 1988). But does it achieve this?

In *National Curriculum: National Disaster?* Rhys Griffith proposes that the aims of the National Curriculum cannot be translated into practice because the National Curriculum in operation enforces a limited academic course restricted to the rote learning of subject-specific knowledge. This, he claims, is a form of school-based learning that is demonstrably inappropriate to the likely nature of citizenship in the future. To substantiate his claim, he presents his own research and fascinating examples of observed classroom practice, plans of classroom layout and copies of worksheets used by pupils.

National Curriculum: National Disaster? looks beyond the classroom and discusses the way in which the infrastructure of school codes of conduct, the physical environment of school sites and the hierarchy of human resources within schools impact on the aims and reality of the National Curriculum. An alternative skills-based educational programme is also outlined which may be more likely to fulfil the expectations that many parents now hold for the education of their children.

Dr Rhys Griffith is a writer, researcher and in-service training provider with many years of teaching experience. His previous publications include *Educational Citizenship and Independent Learning* (1998).

National Curriculum:
National Disaster?

Education and citizenship

Rhys Griffith

ROUTLEDGE / FALMER
Taylor & Francis Group

London and New York

First published 2000
by RoutledgeFalmer
11 New Fetter Lane, London EC4P 4EE

Simultaneously published in the USA and Canada
by RoutledgeFalmer
29 West 35th Street, New York NY 10001

RoutledgeFalmer is an imprint of the Taylor & Francis Group

© 2000 Rhys Griffith

Typeset in Galliard and Gill by
Keystroke, Jacaranda Lodge, Wolverhampton
Printed and bound in Great Britain by
St Edmundsbury Press, Bury St Edmunds, Suffolk

British Library Cataloguing in Publication Data
A catalogue record for this book is available from the British Library

Library of Congress Cataloging in Publication Data
Griffith, Rhys.
    National Curriculum– national disaster?/Rhys Griffith.
       p.   cm.
    Includes bibliographical references and index.
    ISBN 0-7507-0957-X (hc.) – ISBN 0-7507-0956-1 (pbk.) (alk. paper)
    1. Education–Great Britain–Curricula–Case studies. 2. Politics and education–Great
  Britain–Case studies. 3. Education and state–Great Britain–Case studes. I. Title.

LB1564.G7 G76 2000
379.1'55'0941–dc21   99-088317

ISBN 0–7507–0957–X (hbk)
ISBN 0–7507–0956–1 (pbk)

To Mu and Sara
For their example, their encouragement and their
enlightenment
and to
Josie, Emily and Harry:
Twentieth century learners, twenty-first century citizens.

Our object is to provide education which will not
produce a standardized or utility child, useful only as
a cog in a nationalized and bureaucratic machine, but
will enable the child to develop his or her responsible
place, first in the world of school, and then as a
citizen. (Conservative Party Manifesto, 1945)

Above all, let us remember that the great purpose of
education is to give us individual citizens capable of
thinking for themselves. (Labour Party Manifesto,
1945)

Our place in the world will depend on the character
of our people and on minds trained to understand and
operate the complex technical achievements of the
modern world. (Liberal Party Manifesto, 1945)

Contents

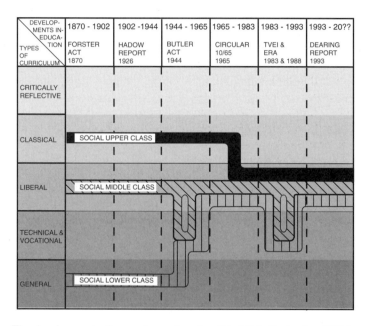

DEVELOP-MENTS IN EDUCA-TION TYPES OF CURRICULUM	1870 - 1902 FORSTER ACT 1870	1902 -1944 HADOW REPORT 1926	1944 - 1965 BUTLER ACT 1944	1965 - 1983 CIRCULAR 10/65 1965	1983 - 1993 TVEI & ERA 1983 & 1988	1993 - 20?? DEARING REPORT 1993
CRITICALLY REFLECTIVE						
CLASSICAL	SOCIAL UPPER CLASS					
LIBERAL	SOCIAL MIDDLE CLASS					
TECHNICAL & VOCATIONAL						
GENERAL	SOCIAL LOWER CLASS					

The development of secondary education (11–16) in England and Wales

Illustrations

FIGURES

TABLES

Acknowledgments

I wish to thank the following publishers for permission to reprint material in which they hold the copyright:

The Mini Enterprise in Schools Project/School Curriculum Industry Partnership for permission to reproduce extracts from *The Enterprising Classroom: Case Studies in English* (1991); Hodder and Stoughton in association with The Open University for permission to reproduce two pie-charts from *Education in the UK: Facts and Figures*, revised edition (1996); Jessica Kingsley for permission to reproduce an extract from *Educational Citizenship and Independent Learning* (1998).

Definitions and descriptions

For the purposes of this book, the following phrases have the following meanings:

Global citizenship: a construct of citizenship considered to be appropriate to the third millennium. The global citizen is not merely aware of her rights but able and desirous to act upon them; of an autonomous and inquiring critical disposition; but her decisions and actions tempered by an ethical concern for social justice and the dignity of humankind; therefore able, through her actions, to control and enhance 'the trajectory of the self' through life, whilst contributing to the commonweal, the public welfare, with a sense of civic duty to replenish society.

Educational citizenship: a concept of education based upon the premise that similarities between the qualities of the educated person and the global citizen indicate a symbiotic relationship between education and global citizenship. From this premise, it is argued that pupils of all ages should be accorded citizens' rights throughout their education, both to prepare them for full and active democratic citizenship and to improve the educational provision of their state schooling.

Independent learning: the pedagogical construct intended to translate a policy of educational citizenship into effective practice. Pupils have the independence to choose how they will learn, and through the development of the qualities of global citizenship, have the opportunity to learn to become independent in their making of decisions, both as pupils and as citizens.

Dependent learning: the pedagogical construct in which pupils are dependent upon others for their learning, and through the suppression of the qualities of global citizenship, learn to become dependent upon the decisions of others, both as pupils and as citizens.

Introduction

NATIONAL CURRICULUM: NATIONAL DISASTER?
AN INTRODUCTION

There will be few parents with children at secondary school who will not recognize the
following exchange:

Parent: What did you do at school today?
Child: Nothing.

An extended – but no more informative – dialogue will also be familiar:

Parent: What did you do at school today?
Child: Oh, you know.
Parent: Well, no, you tell me.
Child: Well, just, you know, the same old thing.
Parent: So it was OK then?
Child: Yeh, yeh. I s'pose.
Parent: Well, wasn't it OK?
Child:(exasperated) Yes, yes, it was fine. Now can I watch Neighbours/Home and
   Away/Brookside/Corrie/Eastenders?
Parent: Have you done your homework?
Child: Yesss!/We didn't have any/It hasn't got to be in till Thursday.

I expect that one explanation for these monosyllabic responses is that children, consciously
or subconsciously, resent adults intruding into their world, questioning them. But what I
find disturbing, saddening, about the way in which children speak about their secondary
school experience is the common tone that most use; a tone not of rebellion, or contempt,
hatred or even despair – but of passive acceptance, of resignation, of stoic endurance. It
seems to me, as someone who has been professionally involved in the state educational
system for 25 years and is a father of three children in state schools, that, on most occasions,
our children are not deliberately stonewalling, they are simply telling us the truth as they
perceive it: that during the school day – or to be more accurate – during school lessons,
nothing happens to them. There is no interaction, no stimulus, no new experience that
changes them in any way. Nothing happens to them.
   So maybe, as parents and teachers, as employers and citizens, we should start taking
our children's comments at face value and worrying a little bit more, being a little less

complacent. Because we can be sure of this: if pupils think that nothing happens to them while they are at school, day in, week out, year on year on year, then several things are certainly happening: their creative and intellectual and social resources are atrophying; their potential to develop as independent thinkers is being retarded; their opportunity to be participants and agents is being diminished; their capacity to engage with the world in which they presently live, and over which they may later hope to exercise some control, is being eroded.

It is the premise that children are telling the truth when they say that nothing happens to them in lessons that impelled the writing of this book. The research was undertaken between 1988 and 1998, at first when I was the Head of an English Department in a comprehensive school, then as the LEA Senior Advisory Teacher for English responsible for supporting the introduction of the National Curriculum and the Technical and Vocational Educational Initiative (TVEI) in secondary schools, and latterly as a freelance educational consultant, researcher and author. The research period spans the first decade of the 1988 Education Reform Act (ERA) that established the National Curriculum in British schools. During that time, I conducted a five-year fieldwork study that involved 7000 pupils and 250 teachers. Lessons were observed in 97 primary, secondary and tertiary educational establishments, and term-long teaching projects were conducted in each of the 33 secondary schools of one shire LEA, Greenshire, as were year-long projects with groups of schools across the LEA. Further research took place on a nationwide basis. Thus, this is a book very much based on educational practice as well as educational theory.

The main authorities to whom I refer are not academics, philosophers or politicians, but the pupils and teachers in whose classrooms I worked. The research findings are about the practical reality of ideology and legislation as experienced and perceived by pupils and teachers on a daily basis. This is the location at which either something or nothing happens – not in the cloisters of academia or the lobbies of Westminster – but in the classrooms where our children spend such an important part of their lives.

The function of the National Curriculum is to realize the aims of the 1988 Educational Reform Act 'to promote the spiritual, moral, cultural, mental and physical development of pupils at school and of society, and to prepare pupils for the opportunities, responsibilities and experiences of adult life' (ERA, 1988). A shorthand for this admirable intention might be: the function of the National Curriculum is to prepare pupils for citizenship and the workplace. This book examines the disparity between the purpose of the National Curriculum and its actual practice within Key Stages 3 and 4 (eleven to sixteen year-olds). My research suggests that the enlightened (some might say, inflated) purpose of the National Curriculum is not apparent in the typical school experience of most secondary school pupils.

From my classroom research, I analyse how the product of the National Curriculum (the accumulation of factual knowledge for a series of tests of memory) influences the process of schooling (curriculum, timetable, lesson-structure, the construction of institutional behaviour) so that the National Curriculum effectively defeats its own well-intentioned aims. Extensive examples of observed classroom practice are used to illustrate this analysis, as are quotes from teachers, pupils and educational observers, and the statistical results of qualitative and quantitative research into the behaviour during lessons of teachers, and girl and boy pupils. Photocopied examples of worksheets used by pupils, the written responses of pupils, and plans of classroom layout and pupils' seating are incorporated into the text. Chapters 2, 3, 4, 5 and 6 report the post-ERA classroom through the eyes of the pupils themselves, using their own words to describe what they want from their education. I also look beyond the classroom and discuss the ways in which the infrastructure of school codes of conduct, the physical environment of school sites, and the hierarchy of human resources within schools impact upon the aims and the reality of the National Curriculum.

I conclude that the aims of the National Curriculum are not translated into practice and suggest that they cannot be, because the aims are dissonant with the content of the National Curriculum; that is, that the aims imply an education typified by experiential learning and whole-person growth, whereas the National Curriculum, in operation, enforces a limited academic course restricted to the rote-learning of subject-specific knowledge so that pupils may perform well in written tests of memory. It is my contention that this knowledge-based, assessment-driven curriculum demands didactic drill-training to ensure examination success; and that such a pedagogy suppresses the development of a critical disposition, so that the school leaver becomes a passive serf or discontented outlaw rather than an emancipated citizen and productive worker.

This overview of the book is broken down into separate chapters. Chapter 1 seeks to show that, since Platonic Greece, there has always been a connection between a state educational system and citizenship. Traditionally, it has been the schools' role to prepare individuals to enter the social niche determined for them so that they may best contribute to the existing society. The historical development of a liberal philosophy of education as the preferred model for the state system in the United Kingdom is outlined. The anomalies and anach-ronisms of this model are identified and it is suggested that the inherited system has been redundant for some time. I claim that as contemporary society holds a less clearly defined and commonly agreed concept of citizenship, so schools find themselves in a state of flux. I suggest that the traditional role of the compliant and complaisant citizen, pledging an unquestioning allegiance to a monocultural, national identity, is inappropriate for the future and argue that post-millennial global citizenship will be characterized by individual autonomy of thought and action within a collective framework of ethical relativism and supranational economic and cultural relationships.

I question whether schools' legal responsibility to prepare pupils 'for the opportunities, responsibilities and experiences of adult life' (Education Reform Act, 1988) can be fulfilled by existing National Curriculum subjects or through bolt-on programmes of civic instruction, personal and social education, and technical and vocational education. I advocate a concept of educational citizenship that may be more likely to fulfil the aims of the 1988 Education Reform Act. The concept of educational citizenship is based upon the premise that pupils need to be educated as citizens in all lessons, and that the rights and responsibilities of citizenship should permeate all the activities of the school day. I identify certain markers – the twelve factors of independent learning – that may allow an observer to record whether pupils' school experience of the National Curriculum is preparing them for such citizenship.

I introduce the idea of a case study – tracking a typical pupil in a typical comprehensive school through a typical week – as a valid research method for assessing opportunities for educational citizenship. I maintain that case studies are an effective way of gathering data, and that it is possible to generalize from individual case studies – particularly with a statutory National Curriculum which requires all state schools to conform to similar syllabuses, methods of assessment and pedagogical styles. I contend that the documentary technique of the case study, with its cumulative dynamic, presents to the reader the reality of typical classroom experience in a way far more powerful and illuminating than quantitative research into public examination results can do (a major part of the government approach to monitoring the National Curriculum).

Chapter 2 comprises a case study of the school week of Josie, a fourteen-year-old, Key Stage 3 comprehensive school pupil: a lesson-by-lesson account, illustrated with photocopies of Josie's reading and writing, diagrams of classroom layouts, and transcripts of conversations. Each lesson is commented upon by myself, each day summarized and the total experience evaluated in terms of the opportunities for educational citizenship that are offered within the National Curriculum, via its predominant form of presentation, the subject-specific class lesson.

Chapter 3 comprises a case study of the school week of Emily, a fifteen-year-old, Key Stage 4 comprehensive school pupil, and follows the same pattern as Chapter 2. The chapter concludes by drawing upon the common experiences of Josie and Emily and makes the case that the present construction and timetabling of the National Curriculum, as practised in virtually all state secondary schools, is not only ineffective in fostering the attributes of citizenship, but actively represses their development. To reiterate the point made earlier, in practice the National Curriculum contrives to defeat its own well-intentioned aims as stated in ERA.

Chapter 4 comprises a case study of the progress of one collaborative group (called The Outfit) during an independent learning project in which pupils were encouraged to devise their own courses of study. Essentially, independent learning projects were pilot studies in educational citizenship that illustrated how the transition from a knowledge-based to a critically-reflective curriculum may be made via the National Curriculum. This chapter seeks to show that independent learning appears a natural activity but that teachers and pupils often do not recognise the learning that is taking place. I argue that, even at its most unstructured, independent learning is much more likely to develop the attributes of post-millennial citizenship than is the conventional presentation of the National Curriculum. I use the twelve factors of independent learning as a tool of analysis to identify the learning experiences of The Outfit.

In Chapter 5, I describe some successful independent learning projects and offer analyses of these projects, again using the twelve factors of independent learning.

In Chapter 6, I briefly review the practical and ethical difficulties of collecting data from young people. I make the point that, once appropriate steps had been taken to ensure that data collection methods were uncontaminated, common responses were recorded by pupils of both sexes, across the age and ability range in all the secondary schools of one LEA. The consensus was that the presentation of the National Curriculum in 'ordinary lessons' was boring and that the content of the National Curriculum bore little relationship to the lives, interests and concerns of pupils. Conversely, when pupils were given the opportunity, in term-long independent learning projects, to devise their own courses of study, the consensus was that learning was more stimulating, more active and more relevant. Teachers and other educational observers commented that the quality of work produced by pupils during these projects, the enthusiasm and commitment shown by pupils, and their general standards of behaviour, were significantly higher than in conventional National Curriculum lessons. The evidence demonstrates that, freed from the strait-jacket of a subject-specific National Curriculum and its concomitant method of presentation, the didactic class lesson, pupils not only have more opportunities to fulfil the aims of the National Curriculum, but they take these opportunities willingly and responsibly.

Having presented typical National Curriculum classroom practice and independent learning projects through the eyes and opinions of pupils (Chapters 2 to 6), Chapter 7 returns to the discussion of Chapter 1 and develops the examination of how an educational system that is manifestly failing its own stated intentions seems to be gaining an ever tighter stranglehold. I offer a critique of the philosophy of liberal education that underpins the knowledge-laden National Curriculum. I suggest that it is inappropriate that the school state system continues to promulgate the anachronism of a hierarchy of knowledge as the one tactic for achieving the strategy of equipping the schoolleaver with the sophisticated social and technical skills that are required of the contemporary citizen and worker. I look at postmodern understandings of what constitutes knowledge and argue that the acceptance epistemology of the National Curriculum must be superseded by an educational system that promotes a critically reflective epistemology. I give examples of the politicization of education and argue that a more objective forum must be created, in which educational debate is distanced from politically determined viewpoints and their accompanying rhetoric.

I conclude by offering some brief suggestions for how a process might be initiated to enable the positive transition from a knowledge-based to a critically reflective curriculum, so that a child's education aids, rather than inhibits, the aims of the National Curriculum 'to promote the spiritual, moral, cultural, mental and physical development of pupils at school and of society, and to prepare pupils for the opportunities, responsibilities and experiences of adult life'.

1 Educational citizenship and the National Curriculum

In the opening section of this chapter, I offer a brief review of the history of secondary education in the United Kingdom from 1864 to the present and then discuss some points arising, the principal one being that I see no significant change in the curriculum, organization and purpose of secondary education during this period.

The state always has a vested interest in the education of the population. That interest is self-preservation. Plato considered the social impact of education, and outlined a policy that has remained unchanged for two millennia: that one of the central purposes of a state educational system is to preserve and pass on the values of that system's society (Carr, 1991). The school is seen as a microcosm of the social macrocosm, and education as a process in which different groups absorb the social values and technical skills that, in theory, will best equip them to succeed in their personal and working lives and, via their assimilation into various predetermined social strata, to contribute to either the perpetuation of the status quo, or the development of the state. In effect, every nation that sponsors a state-maintained educational system imposes a national curriculum. This perennial policy can clearly be identified in the United Kingdom since the inception of a system of secondary education.

Between the 1840s–60s, pressure grew upon the British government to establish a national system of state-maintained secondary education. This pressure came from two sources: those who felt that education should offer the moral guidance to the individual that was required to maintain the fabric of society; and those who lobbied for a more educated workforce to improve capitalist production. In essence, the attempt to satisfy both these factions and to provide an educational service that balances the attributes of citizenship with the skills of the workplace is the history of state secondary education in the United Kingdom.

The Taunton Commission of 1864–9 recommended a tripartite system of schools based upon social class and the planned occupation of the pupil as adult worker. Grade One schools for the upper-class sons of the landed ancien-riche would offer a classical education with a curriculum based upon Latin and Greek, mathematics, modern languages and science. Grade Two schools for the middle-class sons of the commercial nouveau-riche would offer a liberal education with a curriculum based upon English, arithmetic, modern languages and natural science. Grade Three schools for the sons of an emergent social group on the cusp between the proletariat and the bourgeoisie (tenant farmers, small traders, skilled craftsmen), would offer a general education with a curriculum based upon literacy and numeracy.

From this model can clearly be seen the development of the public, grammar and secondary modern school system that was to dominate national education for the next hundred years, a model that was built upon the twin cultural and economic foundations of democratic capitalism in Great Britain: social class and wealth (occupation-derived or inherited). Grade One schools were intended to prepare the upper class for rule; Grade Two schools to prepare the middle class for management; Grade Three schools to prepare the working class for labour. It should also be noted that education was perceived as the study of certain discrete subjects, with a hierarchy of knowledge-as-power that fitted the existing social hierarchy of class-as-power (Grade One: mathematics and classical literature; Grade Two: arithmetic and English literature; Grade Three: numeracy and literacy). This is the view of a knowledge-based curriculum comprising selected areas of knowledge, to be studied at different levels by different groups of pupils, that informs the current National Curriculum.

The Elementary Education Act of 1870 (the Forster Act) did not pass legislation to compel the introduction of the grade schools suggested by the Taunton Commission, although the Commission's ideas, whilst not prescriptive, were to exert considerable influence upon the establishment of secondary education. The Forster Act made schooling compulsory (but not necessarily free) from the ages of five to thirteen. Despite a series of exemptions, the 1870 Act did seek to extend the educational franchise so that all working class children had the chance of a general education, and not just those whose parents had a trade, as the Taunton Commission had suggested for its Grade Three schools. Informed by the Taunton Commission and impelled by the Forster Act, a national system of secondary education began to develop, sporadically, and in piecemeal fashion, over the next quarter of a century (p. viii: illustration, column 1).

In 1895, the Bryce Commission criticized the lack of any coherent development, citing great variations across the country and recommending the creation of separate 'secondary' schools under one central authority. The Education Act of 1902 (the Balfour Act) put into law these recommendations, requiring the provision of county secondary schools, to be administered by local education authorities under the aegis of a national Board of Education. Nearly another quarter of a century passed before the next major government-commissioned investigation into secondary education. The Hadow Report (1926) recognized that two distinct types of secondary schools had developed and gave names to them. The 'grammar' school, offering a liberal education, was as clearly the offspring of the Grade Two school of the Taunton Commission as was the 'modern' school, offering a general education, of the Grade Three school. The tradition of a Grade One classical education for the sons of the rich remained the preserve of the great fee-paying public schools such as Eton, Harrow, Winchester and their less illustrious imitators. Whilst recognizing the differences in curricula, the Hadow Report emphasized the parity of esteem that the modern schools should share with the grammar schools.

The Spens Report of 1938 also stressed the need for parity of esteem (specifically staffing, facilities, class sizes and the abolition of fees for grammar and technical schools). The Report recommended raising the school leaving age from fourteen to sixteen. It considered various ways in which to redress the common feeling that modern schools were inferior to grammar schools, even mooting the establishment of what would later be called comprehensive schools, under a policy of 'multilateralism'. The committee drew back from advocating the building of multilateral schools but retained the ideal of multilateralism in three separate types of school: grammar, technical and modern schools. Here can be seen a further development of the tripartite system suggested by the Taunton Commission. In the state-supported educational system (which still had fee-paying components) the grammar schools became the Grade One schools, mimicking the public schools in manner but offering more of a liberal than a classical education, whilst the modern schools continued to offer the general education of the Taunton Grade Three schools. A demographic shift in pupil intake can also be discerned. The upper classes were effectively absent from state schools: public schools catered for their needs. Middle-class pupils predominated in grammar schools as did working class pupils in secondary modern schools. But whilst class distinctions were still evident, they were not as rigid as before. The cultural forces of democracy (including a universal educational franchise) and the economic forces of capitalism (particularly the increased use of technology in the workplace) had blurred the lines between the lower middle class and the upper working class. As industry adapted to the mechanically complex Fordian techniques of production, a need was created for a new kind of worker, and therefore a new kind of school. The technical schools were intended to provide an appropriate education for an emergent social and occupational group: workers with middle management expertise and technological skill, a buffer between the boardroom and the factory floor (Figure 1, p. vi, column 3). A clear parallel can be seen between the technical schools and the original intention of the Grade Three schools of the Taunton Commission.

In 1943 the Norwood Report consolidated the recommendations of the Spens Report, particularly the tripartite system of grammar, technical and modern schools, the raising of the school leaving age and parity of esteem between the three types of school. Also in 1943, a government white paper (published by a wartime national coalition government) supported the major recommendations of Hadow and Spens. It was upon these Reports that the Education Act of 1944 (the Butler Act) was based. In the 80 years since the Taunton Commission was formed, there had been an incremental improvement in the provision and administration of secondary education, but the underlying social and educational philosophy – a different type of education for different class strata of society – had not changed at all. The Butler Act introduced free, compulsory education and raised the school leaving age to fifteen, with a remit by an Order in Council to raise it to sixteen as soon as practicable. However, the notion that secondary education was free was often more formal than substantive. Some – possibly a majority of – working-class families whose children passed the eleven-plus examination could not afford the costs of uniform and travel to the nearest grammar school. Another complicating factor was that, whilst grammar school placement may have been free, some families could not afford the economic loss to the family unit of a fifteen-year-old wage-earner. Because of the cultural grip of the class system a number of discomfited working-class children did not feel free to take up the grammar school places they had won for themselves – my father-in-law was one of these pupils.

Despite the laudable innovations proposed by the Butler Act of 1944, its implementation consolidated a class-based tripartite system of education. At the age of eleven, children would take tests (the eleven-plus examination) which would determine whether they would have a liberal (grammar school), vocational (technical school), or general (secondary modern school) education. This selection process would have the strongest influence on the middle-class career (grammar), upper-working/lower middle-class trade (technical) or working-class job (secondary modern) prospects of each cohort.

The Crowther Report (1959) noted that the expected proliferation of technical schools had not occurred – there were fewer technical schools at the time of the Report than there had been when the school leaving age was raised to fifteen in 1947. Crowther recommended raising the school leaving age to sixteen and introducing stimulating, personally relevant and socially oriented 16+ examination courses for secondary modern schools. The Newsom Report of 1963 reiterated these recommendations.

By the early 1960s it was clear that the Butler Act's intended tripartite system of grammar, technical and modern schools providing liberal, vocational and general education to sectors of the school population decided by written tests of pupils at the age of eleven had not been realized. Without the capital investment required to build technical schools, the concept of a vocational education was left suspended for two decades until the Technical and Vocational Initiative of the 1980s, when government reawoke (as it had done in 1864 and 1944) to the need for an educated workforce located in the gap between management and labour. There can be little doubt that the demise of the technical schools was a major factor in the steady decline of British industry, which reached its nadir in the early 1980s with a national loss of competitive production, and consequent bankruptcies, mass un-employment and recession. Thus the lack of investment required to build technical schools in the 1940–50s (Marshall Aid funds were used instead to shore up stirling on the gold standard in a hopeless attempt to maintain Britain as an imperial world power) can be said to have had an *economic* impact upon capitalism. There was at least as powerful a *cultural* impact upon democracy, for by allowing the more socially integrated technical schools to wither, the distinction between the middle class (grammar school) and the working class (secondary modern) was sharpened. The Butler Act not only perpetuated but polarized the class differences of British society.

If there was a clear class distinction between the grammar and the secondary modern school, by the mid-1960s the same could no longer be said of the curricula that each offered. Well-intentioned notions of parity of esteem, dating back forty years to the Hadow Report (1926), led to both types of school offering virtually the same knowledge-based curriculum (p. viii: illustration, column 4) under the shared aegis of a liberal philosophy of education. An idea much put about during this time was that the difference between the grammar and the secondary modern was merely one of pace: children were benevolently guided at eleven into the type of school that would better allow them to work at their own speed, but essentially children at both schools were working to the same ends. This wasn't true. If it had been, why was comprehensivization to become such a contentious issue? By and large, grammar schools recruited university graduates (who needed to undertake no teacher training until 1973) whilst secondary moderns recruited from teacher training colleges (which did not offer degree courses in education until 1968). The majority of grammar school pupils left school at sixteen; until 1972, most secondary modern school pupils left at fifteen. Grammar school pupils sat GCEs; for 21 years after the Butler Act, there was no post-sixteen secondary modern examination until the introduction of the CSE in 1965. Per-capita spending was higher in grammar schools than in secondary moderns. Grammar school pupils wore blazers and caps and grammar school teachers often wore gowns. Dress codes were not a typical feature of secondary modern schools. The CACE Report, *Early Leaving* (Gurney-Dixon, 1954), had drawn attention to the clear relationship between grammar school success and social background, findings confirmed by the Crowther Report (1959), the Newsom Report (1963) and the Robbins Report (1964). The Robbins Report found that the proportions of upper-, middle- and working-class pupils going on to higher education had hardly changed in two generations (since the 1920s) and that a child from a middle-class background was twenty times more likely to go on to higher education than a child from a working-class environment. Bowles and Gintis (1976) claimed that 'the function of schools is to reproduce the class divisions of capitalist society' (Bowles and Gintis, p. 26, 1976).

Nevertheless, by offering the same kind of liberal education curriculum, an image of parity of esteem could be promoted. Thus, within 20 years of the Butler Act, the tripartite system of three different curricula for three separate school populations had disintegrated and the state educational system comprised a liberal education, albeit, in many secondary modern schools, at a diluted and under-funded level. By the 1970s, all state schools were offering versions of a knowledge-based curriculum, divided into subjects that were taught for short periods in specialist rooms, the guiding principle being that such an 'education' would broadly equip the pupil for life after school: connections between education and society and education and employment were intentionally implicit rather than explicit – the major recommendation of the Clarke Report of 1947.

As it became obvious that the curricula of both types of secondary school were virtually identical, it became harder to justify selection at the age of eleven, particularly as there was growing evidence that selection owed as much, if not more, to factors of class than to intelligence. Some local education authorities introduced middle schools, so that pupils were only divided at the age of fourteen to pursue GCE or CSE courses. Others introduced comprehensive schools that streamed pupils. A few LEAs went a stage further and promoted mixed ability classes within comprehensive schools.

During the 1950s, the Labour Party had committed itself to a policy in favour of comprehensive schools. In *Challenge To Britain* (1953) the Party made it clear that its policy was principally guided not by educational aims but by ideals of social equality and a dismantling of the British class system. This is not to say that there were not strong educational arguments in favour of comprehensivization, but *Challenge To Britain*, by emphasizing the powerful socializing effect of education, placed educational debate within a party political context in a way that had not happened before. The development of state education during its first hundred years had had common support from all the major political parties (Conservative, Liberal and Labour) that had formed or shared governments during this time. From the mid-1960s until the late 1970s, the social implications of education held an increasingly higher position on the agenda of the major political parties, with a widening political divide as education was absorbed into the different prevailing ideologies of the left and right. This politicization of education and polarization of ideology can be seen in the way in which a comprehensive policy was treated by the two parties of government during the 1960s and 1970s.

After 13 years of opposition, Labour formed a government in 1964 under the premiership of Harold Wilson. In the next two years, DES Circulars 10/65 and 10/66 were issued, requiring LEAs to submit plans for comprehensivization. In 1970, when Ted Heath became Conservative prime minister, Circular 10/70 rescinded the Labour Party initiative and allowed LEAs to determine whether to have selective or comprehensive schools. When Labour returned to office four years later, Circular 4/74 reaffirmed the Labour government's commitment to comprehensivization and required those LEAs that had not submitted plans to do so by the end of the year. When some – predominantly Conservative – LEAs continued to resist, legislation was introduced to force the issue, in the form of the Education Act of 1976. When the Conservative Party, now led by Margaret Thatcher, won the 1979 election, that year's Education Act repealed the 1976 Act. The 1980 Education Act created the Assisted Places Scheme, whereby the government paid, wholly or partly, for some pupils to transfer from the state sector to public schools.

Over the course of this stop-go wrangle can be seen the emerging and opposing ideologies of the Labour and Tory parties as applied to the national educational system. The Labour Party believed that government had a duty to the progressive development of society. Thus, it championed comprehensive schools as an instrument of social equality. The Conservative Party believed that government had a duty to control the pace of social change. Thus, it preferred to maintain the status quo of social power, of which selective entry to separatist schools was regarded as an important aspect. Labour had a collectivist, cooperative and linear view of society: equal opportunity was best served by all pupils attending the same type of school and receiving the same kind of education. The Conservatives had an individual, competitive and hierarchical view of society: equal opportunity was best served by children taking entrance examinations to determine which type of school would provide an education appropriate to the individual pupil's perceived academic abilities (or the parents' ability to pay). Labour's socially inclusive ideology was characterized by a commitment to a state-funded system of comprehensive schools and suggestions for the abolition of fee-paying private schools. The Tories' socially exclusive ideology was characterized by a commitment to grammar and public schools and the patronage of government-funded scholarships so that certain favoured individuals could be plucked from the barren ground of the state system and rebedded in the more fertile soil of the private sector. One viewpoint saw the Labour Party as caring – the Sex Discrimination Act (1975) and the Race Relations Act (1976) were intended to end unfair distinction, against pupils and teachers, on grounds of gender and ethnicity – and the Conservative Party as heartless – the Education (Milk) Act (1971) that abolished free school milk for primary school pupils, and the Education Act (1973) that abolished LEA discretionary grants for postgraduate education, appeared to disadvantage the less well-off.

A contrasting view of the same legislation portrayed Labour as obsessed with ideology and social engineering and the Conservatives as prudent accountants of the nation's finances. The politicization of education continued and the gulf between the two major parties widened. A left-wing view depicted the Labour Party as democratic and generous, wanting every pupil to be given the opportunity of a better education, and denigrated the Conservative Party as meritocratic and miserly and wanting only the privileged to have the best education. A right-wing position castigated the Labour Party as feckless and reckless, jealous of individual success and wishing to drag the educational system down to the level of the lowest common denominator, whereas the Conservatives were championed as the responsible standard-bearers of traditions of academic excellence and national heritage.

In the event, without prescriptive legislation, the vast majority of LEAs moved to comprehensive reorganization and by the early 1980s, this reorganization was about as complete as it was going to be, although it was not until the mid-to-late-1980s that grammar and secondary modern schools that had taken their first comprehensive cohort earlier in the decade had a fully comprehensive school population. Nearly a third of LEAs retained some form of selection. The long and weary political battle over comprehensivization had stumbled to an uneasy draw. Labour could claim the establishment of a comprehensive system, whilst the Conservatives could respond that a two-tier system had been retained where the local public had wanted selection and separatism. The implementation of comprehensive education, first suggested 60 years earlier on educational grounds, in the Spens Report of 1938, had been a battle fought on socio-political grounds for over 30 years. In 1998, comprehensive reorganization remains an uncompleted process rather than a concluded event.

In many ways this 30-year war has been futile. In terms of curriculum, timetabling, assessment, classroom pedagogy and school organization, comprehensive schools are little different from grammar or secondary modern schools. Moreover, because of a policy of segregating pupils by ability, either by streaming (distinguishing different bands of pupils by ability), or setting (a more precise form of streaming that distinguishes each subject by ability), there is not, within lessons, the degree of social levelling and mixing that the comprehensive ideal pursued. At its best, the two schools within a school – the grammar and secondary modern streams within the comprehensive system – coexist peacefully. At their worst, there is no interaction. One 'comprehensive' in which I taught very briefly in 1975 was created by removing the fence between the local grammar school and its secondary modern neighbour and changing the 'new' school's name. The headteacher of the former grammar school became the head of the comprehensive school and his heads of department became the new comprehensive heads of department (their secondary modern counterparts eventually losing their postholders' allowances). The comprehensive intake was divided into two streams that corresponded exactly to the old grammar and secondary modern cohorts, and they were taught on the old grammar and secondary modern sites. At lunchtimes, teachers retreated to the grammar or secondary modern staff rooms whilst pupils went to separate dining rooms before eying each other suspiciously at the demilitarized zone between the two schools where the the old boundary fence had stood.

Comprehensivization obviously offered some social and educational gains. Setting by subject allowed pupils who were strong in some subjects and weaker at others to find their own level of success. Although this was the rationale claimed for the separatist schools, the comprehensive system offered much greater range and flexibility than the crudity of selection that the eleven-plus exam enforced. Entry to the comprehensive school was open to all pupils at the age of eleven (except where there was a middle school system, when transfer was made at the age of thirteen) so there was no need for an eleven-plus exam, which, although intended as an assessment to allocate the child to the school that would best suit her, was publicly perceived as a test that the pupil either passed to ascend to grammar school glory or failed, to descend to secondary modern mediocrity. But, whether good or bad of their kind, comprehensive schools, in terms of the subject-specific liberal education that they provided, were little different from the grammar and secondary modern schools that they replaced – indeed that is the argument that those LEAs that have retained selection and separatism use: that both schools provide the same quality and equality of education, but on different sites. The reality was another loss of opportunity to provide a relevant educational service, as recognized by Denis Lawton, ex-director of the Institute for Education, London University:

> In practice, comprehensive schools found it very difficult to escape completely from the 'dead hand' of the grammar school. The curricula of most comprehensive schools has tended to be a watered-down version of the grammar school curriculum for the more able pupils and a sad neglect of the needs of the less academic.
>
> (Lawton, p. 20, 1992)

The long war over the comprehensives had been a socio-political issue of education and democracy. The Tory government educational reforms of the 1980s centred upon the econome-political issue of education and capitalism. The comprehensive debate had been about schools as agents of social reform and this had diverted attention away from the role that schools play in economic reform, principally by giving those pupils who will go directly from school to job the skills they require to be successful in the workplace, but also by developing the skills of those who would enter industry at a postgraduate managerial level. By the 1980s, the legacy of the demise of the technical schools and a predominant liberal education curriculum in all state schools (whether grammar, secondary modern or comprehensive) was alarmingly clear. Britain simply did not have the reservoir of technological expertise that was necessary for post-Fordian capitalist production. Other countries – particularly Germany and Japan (who had invested their Marshall Aid funds in developing, via education and industrial and management training, a sound technological skills base amongst its workers) – were much better placed to adapt their methods of production to automation and computerization. For too long the social debate about comprehensivization had obscured the need to consider the economic effects of state education:

> By the mid-1980s the secondary examination structure had evolved into a three-tier system for 16 year old pupils: General Certificate of Education Ordinary Level (GCE 'O' Level) for the most 'academic' 20 per cent of the population; the Certificate of Secondary Education (CSE) for the the next 40 per cent or so; and no school leaving examination or qualification for the supposed 'bottom 40 per cent' of the ability range. A system which 'failed' more than one third of its young people was – apart from any question of social justice – clearly inadequate for a society in which unskilled and semi-skilled jobs were in rapid decline.
>
> (Lawton, p. 119, 1992)

Leaders of business and industry were complaining that the liberal education experienced by all pupils did little to equip those who would enter the increasingly technological and fast-changing world of work rather than continue in higher education. These fair criticisms led to a shift in educational policy after the 1983 General Election, which had won the Conservative Party the second of four consecutive terms of office (1979–97). The policy of 'new vocationalism' (Pollard, Purvis and Walford, 1988) was led within government by three monetarist free-marketeers: Sir Keith Joseph, the Secretary of State for Education, David Young, Secretary of State for Employment (which, via the Manpower Services Commission instituted TVEI) and Professor Brian Griffiths, Head of the prime minister's Policy Unit. As the British economy went into recession in the mid-1980s, and unemployment soared to over three million, the Conservative government declared a new interest in vocational education, and launched TVEI – the Technical and Vocational Educational Initiative (p. viii: illustration, column 5). Other acronymic schemes quickly followed, such as MESP (Mini-Enterprise in Schools Project) and SCIP (School Curriculum Industry Partnership) and the founding of some CTCs (City Technology Colleges). The idea behind all these ventures was perfectly reasonable and educationally justifiable: to provide opportunities in all lessons for pupils to gain the skills and attributes of the post-Fordian worker and manager. Such skills were computer literacy, time-planning, problem-solving, the ability to plan and to communicate, to construct groups for specific purposes, and such attributes were flexibility, adaptability, reflexivity.

But, like the technical school initiative of 40 years earlier, these vocational initiatives foundered. The principal reason for their failure was not lack of funding (the TVEI pilot schools were very well-funded), nor was it intransigence on the part of teachers, nor was it that the initiatives were educationally unsound. The brick wall that these initiatives ran up against was the deeply entrenched tradition of a liberal education that saw education as to do with the accumulation of knowledge rather than the development of skills. The various vocational initiatives were designed to develop a high order of complex personal and social skills that embraced attributes of citizenship, rather than to inculcate a narrow range of factory-fodder skill-drills. It is fair to say that they exhibited a forward looking concept of life after school. It is also fair to say that these innovations were developed by teaching bodies involved in the early stages of TVEI and departed widely from the original utilitarian intentions of the Conservative government. To develop these skills and attributes required extended active, experiential courses of study in which pupils worked collaboratively and cooperatively to research, to resolve problems and to complete complex assignments.

Courses were often organized in modules that crossed traditional subject boundaries and incorporated forms of continuous assessment rather than terminal examinations. This critically reflective way of learning was diametrically opposed to the entrenched didactic pedagogy of a liberal education upon which the state secondary educational system had been founded. The typical state secondary school (as will be demonstrated in Chapters 2 and 3) has a knowledge-based curriculum, in which a corpus of knowledge is divided into specific subjects. This subject knowledge is imparted to passive pupils by benign but authoritative teachers, all specialists in their own subjects. During short lessons, pupils generally sit in silence, often copying notes from the blackboard, or from a textbook or worksheet, or from the teacher's dictation. The two styles of teaching and learning – the didactic and the critically reflective – could not possibly co-exist. For the second time in 40 years (the first being the under-funding of the technical schools following the Butler Act of 1944), there had been a chance to break away from an anodyne liberal education, and for a second time that opportunity was lost.

The prime minister, Margaret Thatcher, was reported to be privately furious with teachers and educationalists whom she believed were hi-jacking sensible, pragmatic reforms such as TVEI and then distorting them for their own left-wing agenda of social engineering (Baker, 1994). It was a time of confrontation, between two opposed groups each with strong convictions, in an increasingly fervid atmosphere. The Tory press expressed growing concern about supposedly falling educational standards (for which no authoritative figures have ever been produced), a rising youth crime rate was blamed on morally bankrupt teachers, there was a growing media myth that the state educational system was controlled by trendy lefties, the major teaching unions took extended industrial action, there was rising youth unemployment. All in all, it was easy to believe the tabloid headlines that screamed hysterically that the educational system – now recognized to have powerful social and economic influences – was on the verge of collapse, and that its collapse may very well undermine democratic capitalism itself.

Something had to be done and Margaret Thatcher did it. Having won her third successive general election in 1987, she decided that she had the mandate she needed to take on the educational establishment. She would bring order to what appeared to be an incoherent and incohesive national secondary school system that included comprehensive, grammar, secondary modern, single sex, co-educational, middle and special schools, all administered or supervised by politically disparate local education authorities. If order could not be brought through standardizing pupil groupings (as Minister of Education between 1970 and 1974 and Prime Minister since 1979, she was a veteran of the comprehensive versus selection war), then order should be brought by standardizing the curriculum for all state schools – a major departure from a long-established convention that government interest in the curriculum of schools was descriptive rather than prescriptive (see Callaghan's Ruskin speech of 1976). Thus was born the idea of a national curriculum, and in its train, national tests, and, inevitably under a free market political ideology, the publication of schools' performance in these tests so that direct comparisons could be made between individual schools and between types of school, ostensibly to encourage consumerism via freedom of parental choice.

The Education Reform Act of 1988 (ERA) established the National Curriculum, and greatly increased the centralized control of government over state schools – the Act gave over 400 new powers to the Secretary of State (somewhat anomalous with the Thatcherite ideology of individual choice). With control of the curriculum and its assessment, the politicization of education was nearly complete (a third element – pedagogy – is dealt with in Chapter 7). The Act was remarkable in its imposition of a narrow political ideology upon a state educational system. However well-intentioned were the aims of the Act, its consequences have been disastrous. The construction of a knowledge-based curriculum that does not cater for society's needs is one of the most obvious failures of the 1988 Act, but other components of the Act will possibly have a greater deleterious effect on educational development in the future. These are the aspects of the Act that have led to a political climate in which it is becoming harder and harder to discuss education sensibly, neutrally and consensually, or even to acknowledge defects in the National Curriculum.

The most significant of these aspects was the emasculation of local education authorities. For nearly a century (since the Balfour Act of 1902) LEAs had provided a filter between government and schools, being able in turn to interpret and apply government policies as appropriate to local areas, and also to provide a united voice for the majority opinion of school managers and to represent that voice to government. Most LEAs enjoyed a consensual relationship with their schools, advising and supporting rather than dictating and imposing. LEAs were also able to organize links between schools via in-service training courses, conferences for headteachers and heads of department and the provision of subject advisory groups. At its best, the LEA system operated in an atmosphere of trust and cooperation between neighbouring schools and LEA officers. I experienced both sides of this partnership, as a comprehensive school head of English for nine years and, in the same LEA, as the Senior Advisory Teacher for Secondary English for five years. A further five years as an independent researcher, consultant and writer have allowed a more distanced perspective that has done nothing to change my mind about the positive role that enlightened LEAs played.

Whole sections of the 1988 Education Reform Act undermined the LEA-schools relationship. Sections 26 to 32 dealt with open enrolment, effectively replacing overall LEA planning for school numbers by an unpredictable system of parental choice at local school level based more upon rhetoric than reality. Sections 33 to 51 introduced LMS – the Local Management of Schools, by which responsibilities and funds previously held by LEAs were to be devolved directly to schools, with funding on a per capita basis. This had the effect in many LEAs of the curtailing of central support systems such as advisory, inspection, child psychology and music services. Sections 52 to 104 dealt with GMS – the establishment of Grant Maintained Schools. GMS was a super version of LMS, with individual schools encouraged to opt out of the LEA to be funded directly from Whitehall. Had a significant number of schools taken this option, LEAs would have found it difficult if not impossible to formulate regional policy. Had a majority of schools opted out, this would have led to the effective dissolution of LEAs. Sections 120–155 dealt with higher and further education establishments, which were removed from LEA control. Of the 196 sections of ERA, only the first 25 deal with the establishment of the National Curriculum, whilst 113 sections deal with the disempowerment of local education authorities. One of the direct effects of this policy was to make individual teachers in individual schools feel exposed to the full glare of the burning sun of Thatcherite accountability (or perhaps more accurately, culpability). No longer could the LEAs provide the shade they had in the past. Schools became isolated from one another and then competitive against each other as open enrolment, LMS related to the number of pupils on roll, and the publication of league tables of National Curriculum tests began to bite.

ERA ended the educational partnership that had existed between schools and replaced it with competition in its crudest form – the dog-eat-dog excesses that characterize the very worst of the capitalist marketplace. In such a climate, it became very difficult for serving teachers to criticize the National Curriculum and its assessment procedures, in some cases deemed to be literally 'more than my job's worth'. The application of monetarism, market forces and consumer choice to education changed the whole way in which education was viewed, and the metalanguage of industry used to discuss education reflected this. Business-influenced planners began to use such phrases as 'curriculum audit', 'the delivery of the curriculum' and 'quality output'; on one course that I attended, the lecturer referred to the pupil as a PDU – a point-of-delivery unit. There was a glut of books written in the new techno-speak, such as *Marketing Your Primary School* (Sullivan, 1991) or *Total Quality Management and the School* (Murgatroyd and Morgan, 1993). The business jargon in the following quote typifies both the view that education is a commodity subject to the laws of industry, and the anger of a businessman that educationalists just can't grasp this obvious truth:

> Too many teachers are failing to educate adequately hundreds of thousands of young people. A significant percentage of the 'profession' is highly unionised, self-interested and performs at an unacceptably low level. Market demands are ignored, ever-increasing funding and status are expected. If many teachers live by the rule that performance and productivity are irrelevant, how can we expect our students to believe any differently?
>
> (White, p. 14, 1997)

After the bitter clashes over comprehensive schools, there was, perhaps curiously, little difference of political opinion over the constitution and administration of the National Curriculum. With the exception of the abolition of the Assisted Places Scheme (1997) Labour government education policy in 1998 is to continue Tory education policies since 1988. Prime Minister Tony Blair has pledged not to abolish grammar or secondary modern schools (his stance is that of the Tory DES Circular 10/70). He believes in forms of selection for those schools that wish it. He advocates streaming rather than mixed-ability teaching. He agrees with testing at the ages of seven, eleven, fourteen and sixteen and the publication of league tables. He has retained Tory-appointed Chris Woodhead as Chief Inspector of Schools with an enhanced contract. He approves of a 'chalk-and-talk' pedagogy, a 'back-to-basics' curriculum, and of a national curriculum for teacher training colleges that is likely to be as prescriptive of teaching style as the National Curriculum is of teaching content.

Private schools and City Technology Colleges are exempt from the National Curriculum, but because National Curriculum tests at Key Stage 4 comprise the GCSE examinations, private schools – which have of their own accord been adapting from a classical to a liberal education since the middle of the century – have found themselves drawn into the National Curriculum, at least for those pupils aged fourteen–sixteen who must study National Curriculum syllabuses to pass National Curriculum 16+ Tests (the GCSE examinations) in order to enter higher education.

The National Curriculum typifies earlier attempts at curriculum construction: it is essentially the curriculum of a liberal education as delineated by the Taunton Commission in 1869 for its Grade Two schools. There is obviously some recognition of the need to recover some of the ground lost over the last 40 years with the demise of the technical schools, and so Technology has been introduced, not only as a subject, but also as a cross-curricular dimension that should permeate all lessons (NCC, 1990a). Economic and Industrial Understanding has been introduced as a cross-curricular theme (ibid). An awareness of the social impact of education can also be detected in the cross-curricular themes of

Education for Citizenship and Environmental Education and the cross-curricular skills of personal and social education (ibid). There is some acknowledgment of the transferable skills of the worker and the citizen in calls called for adaptability and flexibility to be promoted (ibid). All very laudable, but the experience of TVEI has shown that the weight of a knowledge-based curriculum tends to crush peripheral concerns for skills and attributes. With assessment being used to create league tables to encourage parents to choose between schools, and school budgets being directly linked to the number of pupils on roll, then it was obvious that schools would concentrate on those parts of the curriculum that were to be tested (Hutton, 1995): and none of the more enlightened areas was subject to tests. As will be shown in Chapters 2 and 3, National Curriculum suggestions for lessons in citizenship, environmental education, personal and social education, industrial and economic awareness were not introduced into schools, or were justified by rhetoric rather than practice as cross-curricular initiatives, or became an option available to some pupils rather than an entitlement for all.

Figures 1.1 and 1.2 reveal that the National Curriculum has made no significant difference to the traditional course content of a liberal education that has characterized state secondary education from its beginnings in the middle of the nineteenth century.

Fourteen to sixteen-year-old pupils study the same subjects, in the same kind of timetabled lessons, as they did before the imposition of the National Curriculum. In 1984, pupils spent 13 per cent of their time studying English and maths, in 1993, 12 per cent. In 1984, pupils spent 16 per cent of their time studying science, in 1993, there is a small shift to 13 per cent. The time spent on studying technology (despite a huge focus of attention and funding) varies only by a single percentage. The time spent on learning a foreign language (despite European Union and the drive towards globalization) remains exactly the same. The apparently greater amount of discretionary time in 1993 will, for most pupils, be taken up by the humanities and arts subjects depicted in the 1984 model.

Despite all the disruptions and bitterness caused by the introduction of the National Curriculum, previous attempts at vocational courses, and the prolonged introduction of

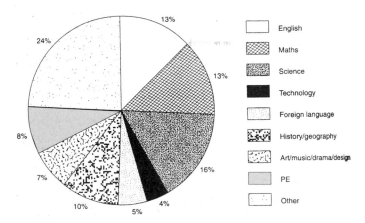

Figure 1.1 Percentage of time devoted to 'national curriculum' subjects by fourth and fifth year pupils (National Curriculum Key Stage 4) in England, 1984. Note: the National Curriculum category of Technology was not used in the DES 1984 survey; the figure for 'Craft-based CDT' has been used here in its place (Adapted from DES, 1987, Table 5)

Source: Mackinnon, D. and Statham, J. with Hales, M. (1996) *Education in the UK: Facts and figures*, London: Hodder and Stoughton

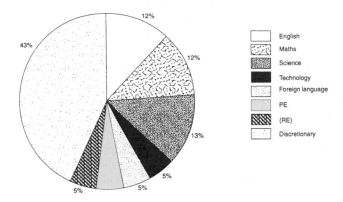

☐	English
▨	Maths
▨	Science
■	Technology
▨	Foreign language
▨	PE
▨	(RE)
☐	Discretionary

Figure 1.2 The Dearing Report's suggested minimum allocation of time to compulsory subjects at Key Stage 4, 1993 (Adapted from Dearing, 1993, Section 5)

Source: Mackinnon, D. and Statham, J. with Hales, M. (1996) *Education in the UK: Facts and Figures*, London: Hodder and Stoughton

comprehensive schools, curriculum content and pedagogy are essentially unchanged in the last century and a half. Thus, as we enter the twenty-first century, virtually every secondary school in Great Britain, whether state or independent, is offering the sort of liberal education that would have been familiar to the middle classes in the middle of the nineteenth century. Yet we no longer live in the nineteenth century – we barely live in the twentieth century. Contemporary society – and therefore citizenship – is characterized by flux rather than stasis. During the last 50 years, the previously established patterns of life (birth and socialization into a particular class, heterosexual courtship leading to the longevity of marriage, the companionship and support of the extended family, job security) have unravelled. There is less sense of any permanence to social structures, and less respect for the great institutions of state that were once the cultural touchstones of calmness and continuity: parliament, monarchy and the established church. The nature of citizenship has changed. As individuals we need to be more flexible, more adaptable, and more amenable to change and uncertainty; as a society we are less deferential, more demonstrative, and more willing to exercise our democratic rights and to challenge infringements upon them. We are more ready to accept, if sometimes unwillingly or somewhat begrudgingly, that we have a personal responsibility for the direction of our lives.

There is a conflict here with the ethos and administration of the educational institutions which will provide the new citizenry, for most schools, whatever the rhetoric promulgated in glossy prospectuses, are old-fashioned and hierarchical, demanding conformity and unquestioning obedience, stifling the development of a critical disposition and independent thinking, promoting individual competition and denigrating collaboration and cooperation as forms of cheating. This is rarely the natural inclination of the teachers and headteachers – or so my experience as a teacher, LEA adviser, educational researcher and in-service training provider leads me to believe. However, such conditions are the inevitable consequence of the expedient embrace of didactic teaching styles, subject-specific curricular organization and fragmented timetabling, which are commonly agreed to constitute the most effective pedagogy in training pupils in the rote-learning of factual material for timed examinations – as required by the National Curriculum and its assessment procedures.

So in attacking the National Curriculum, which this book certainly does, I am not seeking to score short-term party-political points but to question the tradition of a knowledge-based liberal education in this country, the latest manifestation of which is the National Curriculum, and to argue that it is ineffective, and quite inappropriate to the social and economic demands of democratic capitalism as we enter the third millennium. When we compare the modest changes in education since the Forster Act of 1870 with the incredible (to a Victorian) advances in just about any other area of life (transport, medicine, science, housing, entertainment) we cannot avoid asking ourselves, if everything else has changed so dramatically, can it really be right that education should have stood so still? Can we really justify an educational system, effectively unchanged in terms of philosophy and construction of curriculum and pedagogy since the middle of the nineteenth century, as an appropriate preparation for the citizens of the twenty-first century?

I began this review of state education with the Taunton Commission of 1864–69, which clearly envisaged a tripartite educational system for a tripartite social system (p. viii: illustration, column 1): a classical education for the upper class, a liberal education for the middle class and a general education for the lower class. In closing the review, I have claimed that all pupils, from whatever social class, now receive the same liberal education via the National Curriculum (p. viii: illustration, column 6). It may be argued that the homogeneity of curriculum is reflected in a homogeneity of class (or perhaps it is the other way around). Certainly, the distinctions between social classes, whilst still apparent, are less easily defined as we enter the third millennium. This cultural realignment will be an important factor when considering the curricular and citizenship demands of the twenty-first century, so it is worth giving some examples to illustrate the shift in class structure. Therefore, before discussing the educational implications of contemporary citizenship, I want to pay some attention to three areas of human activity – home and family, leisure and entertainment, and the world of work – in which traditional markers of class no long apply with the old surety and neatness.

Traditionally the upper classes inherited their homes, the middle classes bought their houses and the lower classes lived in rented or tied accommodation. The sale of council houses and the establishment of housing partnership schemes have obscured the distinction between the middle class home owner and the lower class tenant, whilst at the other end of the social scale, death duties and high maintenance costs have made it more likely that a National Trust manager rather than the rich man will live in the castle and that it will be the sightseer rather than the poor man at his gate. Moreover, the security of home-ownership has changed: council house tenants, requiring only small mortgages to buy at discounted prices the houses that they had previously rented, are less likely to have faced the problems of negative equity and repossession with which many middle-class owners have been confronted. White-collar redundancy, a general atmosphere of professional insecurity, and changes in the divorce laws in which property can form part of the settlement (that can also apply in 'palimony' cases) have all contributed to a breakdown of the class markers of home-ownership.

There have also been huge changes within the constitution of families, traditionally another clear marker of class division. The most marked of these changes have been forged by feminism. Old images are of the lower class matriarch, cooking and washing for an improbably large family, the middle-class organizer of fetes and church flower-arranging rosters (membership of the Mothers' Union and the Women's Institute obligatory) and the upper-class lady of the manor fulfilling her parochial duties as magistrate, school governor and chair of local good causes. The contemporary reality is that more women than men now work in some place of employment and that the family chores will be gender-shared. Social diaspora has also curtailed the extended family, which has been replaced by the nuclear family, a more compact unit, ready to move houses and regions in pursuit of work or a higher standard of living. The concept of family as comprising an adult heterosexual monogamous couple and their children is increasingly challenged. These changes are not distinct to a particular class but occur in, and affect, all.

There have been significant changes in leisure and entertainment that have also blurred old distinctions of class – and gender distinctions within classes. Traditionally, couples in the lower classes pursued separate leisure pursuits, whilst the middle classes spent their time together. On a Friday night working-class men went to the pub to play cards, darts and snooker, and the women went to bingo; whereas the middle-class couple went to the cinema or the theatre together. On Saturday afternoon, the working-class man went to a football match, whereas the middle-class couple gardened, went shopping or played golf. Today, football, once the preserve of the working-class male, is equally enjoyed by men and women of the chattering classes. Film and popular music, not so long ago regarded as ephemeral and of less cultural significance than stage drama and classical music, have been absorbed into The Arts. Pop stars from working- or middle-class origins enjoy multi-millionaire lifestyles in the polyglot company of monarchy, aristocracy, self-made business people and National Lottery winners. Cheap air fares and holiday packages have made foreign travel widely accessible and not the preserve of a particular class. Where once the choice in a provincial town was between a posh restaurant and fish and chips, now the range of cuisine and variety of restaurants that characterize a pluralist society have eroded class differences and promoted cultural diversity. It is particularly amongst the under-thirties that the greatest movement has been made. New laddism, girl power, and the influences of different ethnic minorities have broken down barriers so that members of different classes can partake of hobbies and interests that were once exclusive to a particular class, or gender within that class.

The world of work has seen three major changes: the erosion of the authority of office, the impermanence of the workforce, and the increased number of women in employment. The dwindling of the authority of office is, I suppose, an indicator of a more relaxed, equal and democratic workplace. Language and dress codes are less formal, and deference to the authority of institutional power is replaced by a personal regard (or disregard) for the present holders of authority (a transition epitomized by a shirt-sleeved prime minister addressing his first cabinet meeting with the words, 'Hi, call me Tony'). The impermanence of the workforce has been brought about by the privatization of nationalized industries and utilities, the weakened power of the unions to resist redundancies and the introduction of new codes of procedure, the uncertainty of consumer-driven global markets, and the constant need to update practices, replace machinery and retrain staff to maintain a competitive edge. More women are taking leadership roles so that traditional power structures and management practices are altering.

The expectation in many, if not most, families, that both adult partners will work has led to a rise in the general standard of living via dual incomes but is having far-reaching social and economic effects. There are now likely to be more potential employees than vacancies, thus strengthening the power of capitalist management and creating a sump of people, perhaps as many as a million, who will never work. This also has the effect of widening the gap in society between the affluent and the impoverished. Dual income families enjoy increased economic prosperity but at the cost of an unquantifiable personal and social impact upon family life, particularly the stability, the comfort and security of a home parent that many children now never know.

These changes are contributing to a new *zeitgeist* of democratic equality that is demanding meaningful recognition in all areas of human activity. The old snobberies are now recognized as ridiculous. Class as a phenomenon of social control still exercises a residual effect, but its power is waning. Increased personal wealth, throughout British capitalist society, allowing greater freedom of choice and autonomy of action, has broken the rigid conventions of social class. Increasingly, class may be considered less an external imposition of caste and more a matter of individual preference of lifestyle. This is not to say that class structure and differences will wither away, as in the Marxist prediction for nation states. I don't think they will: what I see changing is the inviolability of class as caste, an immutable social role defined at birth. I think that there will be more conscious blurring and crossing of class borders (for example, Tony Blair's use of estuary English when he appears on the Des O'Connor show or David Mellor's funambulism as a broadcaster: the highbrow music lover on his Classic FM show, and the blokish mate of football lads on his Radio Five Saturday phone-in) and less sense of a deterministic cultural hierarchy (in 1998, following a government-commissioned study directed by Professor David Rose of the University of Essex, the old typography of six levels spanning the working, middle and upper classes, dating from 1921, was replaced by seventeen new classifications of social class). This unlocking of the predominantly white class structure will be aided and accompanied by changing ethnic patterns of demography. There will continue to be a move away from traditional Anglocentrism towards greater democratic diversity at expanding circumferences: our own pluralistic society within the United Kingdom, the European Union and the global community.

In the same way that class is becoming a matter of choice, so is national identity. In the 1966 World Cup, the predominant flag waved by English supporters was the Union Jack. In 1998 it is the cross of St George. The myriad ethnic and racial groups that inhabit the British Isles are rejecting the overlordship of white Anglo Saxon supremacy, and its attempts at the assimilation of different cultures, and asserting their own identities. In 1983, Norman Tebbit's test of national identity (for black British cricket fans to support the West Indies team when they played against England was the brand of a traitor) apparently saw patriotism as a Pavlovian response. But globalization leads to different emphases. I can offer my own post-Tebbit reference to nationality and sport in support of the idea that nationality, like class, is becoming a more flexible identification. I am Welsh when Wales are involved in international football (or Celtic if I am supporting Scotland or Ireland) whilst my neighbour is Afro-Carribean when Jamaica are playing, but we were both British when we sat together to watch (on TV) England play in the 1998 World Cup, European when France contested the World Cup Final and global citizens in the joy we felt at the predominantly peaceful coming together of football fans from all over the world, who, with colourful costumes, face paintings, dance and music, transformed a sporting event into a world celebration of cultural diversity. With devolved political power in the United Kingdom and localized budgets (not just to the Celtic regions, but to urban and ethnic communities via a mayor for London and the state funding of Muslim schools), so different ethnic or regional groups identify more with similar groups rather then some concept of Britishness based upon privilege and patronage, monarchy, Christian worship and unquestioning jingoism.

How might these demographic changes in class and ethnicity affect schooling in the pluralistic citizenship of the United Kingdom? Few would disagree that school-leavers need to be reflexive, adaptable and resourceful to claim their place as participants, decision takers and policy makers in the era and culture of high modernity. Yet the general public's perception of a good educational system is characterized by a nostalgic view of schooling that has more to do with the last, rather than the next, century: of neatly and uniformly dressed pupils sitting attentively in orderly rows, listening obediently to the didactic presentation of a clearly defined area of factual knowledge, given by an authoritarian, albeit benign, teacher. This type of national curriculum may well have been in harmony with the simple citizenship of the first half of the twentieth century, when people knew their place and felt comfortable in that knowledge and that place, but it is dissonant with the complex form of citizenship that has been developing since the mid-1950s, which prevails today, and is likely to be the template for the next half-century.

Gazing into the future it is possible to see in the near distance, a young figure, a school-leaver on the threshold of post-millennial, global citizenship. She is uncertain of her future, of herself. 'Who am I?' is the great postmodern question, and the search for self the postmodern quest. An ill-defined sense of identity that can no longer rely on the traditional markers of class and nationality makes this a difficult question for the figure to answer. She is confused. She does not know in which direction to take her first step. 'What is The Good?' was the great classical question and the search for morality the philosopher's quest. But to this young figure right and wrong, good and bad are cloudy issues, for in a diverse world all values appear relative, there is no firm ground upon which to take that first step into the world, into the void. She hesitates. Not knowing herself, how can she know others and how can they know her? Not knowing right from wrong, how can she make decisions, how can she act? She pauses. How can she make a path for herself when there are no signs and she has no map? She cannot go forward and she can never go back. She sits and she waits, not knowing for what she waits. The mists roll over her.

Through a patch in the mist we see another figure, another school-leaver. She too faces the same doubts, the same questions, the same journey. Who is she? She is who she is today. She may be someone else at another time or in other place or with other people. She is all these selves, or rather she is confident and comfortable to reveal different facets of a multi-self, and to recognize that she is capable of changing one or some, but not all, of these facets as her will and circumstances change. What is right and wrong, good and bad? She has the confidence to know that she is not sure, that the answers may differ in different circumstances, or two answers may seem equally applicable in one circumstance. How can she be confident? Because knowing herself, she can think for herself and she trusts her judgments to be considered and appropriate. The mists begin to close in and the way seems dark, but she steps out briskly.

What characteristics has this second figure that enable her to face a complex and uncertain future with equanimity? I suggest this definition of the global citizen. The global citizen is not merely aware of her rights but able and desirous to act upon them; of an autonomous and inquiring critical disposition; but her decisions and actions tempered by an ethical concern for social justice and the dignity of humankind; therefore able, through her actions, to control and enhance 'the trajectory of the self' through life, whilst contributing to the commonweal, the public welfare, with a sense of civic duty to replenish society. (For an extended development of this thesis, see Griffith, 1998.)

If we accept this definition as appropriate to the citizenship of postmodernity, of the new millennium, then there are significant implications for a state educational system that claims that, via the National Curriculum, it is preparing pupils for citizenship. Can a traditional liberal education, with a knowledge-based curriculum, subject-specific lessons, a didactic pedagogy and an assessment procedure based upon tests of memory develop the qualities of the global citizen? Or should we be looking to a form of education that actively encourages the development of these qualities, a form of education that I have named educational citizenship? Educational citizenship is a concept of education based upon the premise that pupils of all ages should be accorded citizens' rights throughout their education, both to prepare them for full and active democratic citizenship and to improve the educational provision of their state schooling. A policy of educational citizenship would emphasize the process of learning rather than its product, which a liberal education, as characterized by the National Curriculum does. The process of learning would require the development of the attributes of global citizenship, attributes we would also recognize in an educated person. The aims of state education might then be: the development of a critical disposition, so that the citizen-learner is able to question the world around her rather than accept it unquestioningly; the development of a sense of ethics, so that the citizen–learner becomes increasingly able to make critical decisions within a moral context; the development of social awareness – that global decisions affect local people and their cultures; the development of autonomy, the ability to act for the benefit of oneself, balanced by the development of a sense of obligation to community and agentive social justice – the commitment to act on behalf of others.

Few would disagree with these aims and most schools claim that they pursue them, but it is my contention that these aims should be embedded in every lesson, should be the core of the child's learning experience. For this to happen, it would be necessary to establish a pedagogical construct intended to translate a policy of educational citizenship into effective practice. Such a pedagogy I have called independent learning. Pupils have the independence to choose how they will learn, and through the development of the qualities of global citizenship, have the opportunity to learn to become independent in their making of decisions, both as pupils and as citizens. The following factors of independent learning were identified during my research as a combined result of the literature search and classroom observation and practice: the provenance of the factors lies both in the theory and the practice.

1 **Collaborative groupwork**: a group of between three and five pupils, preferably mixed gender and self-selected, working in partnership to research a subject chosen by the group;

2 **Cooperative groupwork**: non-competitive agreements and exchanges between the collaborative groups; the cooperative group to encompass all involved in the project including adults;

3 **Individual responsibility**: to contribute, and adhere, to the formulation of codes of practice for both groups above;

4 **Pupil-designed tasks**: each collaborative group should define its own project tasks and the range of outcomes;

5 **Pupil-designed assessment**: each collaborative group should decide what aspects of its work should be assessed, at what stage of the project, to what criteria and by whom – multiple assessors should be encouraged (e.g.: a peer, a teacher, adult other than teacher);

6 **Pupil-negotiated deadlines**: pupils should be entitled to plan the progress of their own project;

7 **Pupil-initiated research**: pupils should have the opportunity to interview and conduct questionnaires, to use databases, to communicate directly with living authorities, to access information centres off the school campus, to make site-visits;

8 **Pupil-use of a range of language technology**: (synthesizers, cameras, audio and video editing and recording equipment): pupils should have the opportunity, by creating their

own media artifacts, to experience and interpret the effect of language in a post-literary, audio-visual, high-tech society;

9   **Community involvement and use of the environment**:
Community: education should be seen as relevant to real life; by allowing pupils to make a choice of topical social issues for their collaborative topic and by relating the work of all groups to the community of humankind, pupils may be encouraged to see global society as a series of concentric cooperative groups (starting with the cooperative group undertaking the project);
Environment: taking the learning experience beyond the classroom walls (where it must be taken voluntarily by the learner if learning is to continue after the strictures of a statutory state education); a stimulus to experiential learning in the environment in which the local community lives; an awareness of a shared global environment.

10   **A sense of audience**: lending purpose to the project and shaping its presentation differently for different audiences, thus encouraging the critical awareness that messages can be put across more effectively if directed with a specific audience in mind; a way of giving something back to the community;

11   **Presentation in various forms**: for a curriculum to be accessible for all, a wider range of project presentation than the traditional pupil's manuscript is desirable; for pupils to develop their ability to read the world, their own opportunity to create media artifacts is helpful in developing a wider literacy;

12   **Reflexivity**: the sense of a personal stake in one's education, and the development of the capacity for critical and self-critical reflection.

It is not claimed that these factors are exclusive to independent learning, but, if opportunities for some or all of them are available within a pupil's lessons, irrespective of subject content, then, according to the thesis of this book, educational citizenship is more likely to be developed than if the factors are not present – because they are intended to support a learning environment of global citizenship. An 'ethical concern for social justice and the dignity of humankind' is engendered as pupils work together in small groups yet are aware of a responsibility both to the larger society of the class within which they operate, to the larger societies in which the school is located, and to the self (Factors 1, 2 and 3: collaborative and cooperative groupwork and individual responsibility). The development of 'an autonomous and inquiring critical disposition' is fostered in these citizens of the classroom as they become decision-takers and policymakers by designing their own tasks, undertaking their own active research, having some control over the time and pace of their work, and being involved in any assessment of the worth of their labour (Factors 4, 5, 6 and 7: pupil-designed tasks and assessment, pupil-negotiated deadlines and pupil-initiated research). Through presenting their research and opinions in the way in which news and opinions about the world are presented to them (via television programmes, newspapers, magazines, public meetings), they learn how the media always has a point of bias. Thus, by creating their own media artifacts, they learn 'to read the world' (Jones, 1990) (Factor 8: pupil-use of a range of language technology). These citizens are encouraged to realize that their actions have a wider consequence and relevance by placing their work in the context of the real communities and environments, whether local, national or global, within which they live (Factor 9: community involvement and the use of the environment). By presenting their work to a wider audience, they are encouraged to see that groups within society can inform others with a view to bring about change (Factor 10: a sense of audience). A variety of styles of presentation allows the efforts of all pupils to be communicated to a wider audience and to be seen as having intrinsic value, thus promoting self-worth and a desire to participate (Factor 11: presentation in various forms). Cumulatively, the factors are intended to nurture a capacity for self-critical reflection, an attribute of the postmodern citizen, as identified in Giddens' (1991) phrase 'the reflexive project of the self' (Factor 12: reflexivity). Different factors have different emphases, but in sum they are intended to stimulate the active development of the pupil as global citizen, as defined above. More detail about the organization of independent learning projects is given in Chapter 5.

Independent learning is the pedagogy of a critically reflective model of education (educational citizenship). The antithesis of independent learning is dependent learning, a pedagogical construct in which pupils are dependent upon others for their learning, and through the suppression of the qualities of global citizenship, learn to become dependent upon the decisions of others, both as pupils and as citizens. This is the pedagogy of the National Curriculum.

If the definition of the global citizen is accepted as a paradigm of likely citizenship in the early part of the next millennium, then that is the kind of citizenship that those involved in the state educational system should have in mind when they consider how to implement the aim of the Education Reform Act of 1988 'to prepare pupils for the opportunities, responsibilities and experiences of adult life' (ERA, 1988). How effective the National Curriculum is in realizing that aim is the subject of Chapters 2 and 3. The method of research that I chose to gather data was to follow two pupils, one from Key Stage 3 and one from Key Stage 4, through all their lessons for one week.

During classroom research, I had been looking for a more structured way than occasional observation of lessons in different schools to gather information about the curriculum that flowed around the various pupils and teachers with whom I had been involved in term-long independent learning projects. The tracking of individual pupils in each key stage gave finer detail to the brushstrokes of the broad picture that I had gained via other classroom observation, discussion with teachers and pupils, and the scrutiny of data such as school prospectuses, departmental syllabuses, and pupils' timetables and workbooks. It also offered a pupil's eye view of teaching and learning styles.

The purpose of the tracking, then, was to make some assessment of the typical curriculum and timetable of eleven to sixteen-year-old pupils; and to see what opportunities were offered for the promotion of educational citizenship. Thus, the case study is of a curriculum rather than an individual. Josie (see Chapter 2) and Emily (see Chapter 3) represent typical Key Stage 3 and 4 pupils in a typical comprehensive school: they are the lenses through which the researcher observed the week's lessons. I accompanied them to all their lessons. I did not often sit beside them, but instead chose a position from which I could observe all their actions and hear all they said, either in conversation with other pupils or with teachers. Each case study is structured as a chronological narrative. I have presented the data in this way as I consider it the most authentic form of presentation of the organic nature of the research process.

To illustrate the content and style of lessons, examples of the writing, reading and talking of the pupils, as well as illuminative charts and diagrams, are embedded within the text. Chapters 2 and 3 could have been shorter had such material been excised from the text. But I believe that in its present form, the evidence of what pupils actually do in lessons is given its most appropriate forum: speaking powerfully from centre stage, rather than whispering off-stage, relegated to distant appendices. What you see is what they get: the reality of the National Curriculum in the classroom.

The intense study of the curricular experience of a pupil throughout an entire timetabled week appeared to offer the possibilities of generalizability in a variety of ways. If a school was chosen that had a five-day timetable cycle, then the curricular work of one week would demonstrate certain consistencies for the whole school year, or key stage. Unless the pupil who was tracked was aberrant in some way, then her curricular experience would be shared, although not exactly duplicated, by others within her class, National Curriculum Year and key stage. If the school demonstrated practices that were known to be typical of others (for instance, the teaching of the National Curriculum, the division of the curriculum into discrete subjects, the teaching of subjects in discrete lessons, a timetabled day of six 50-minute lessons), then findings may be transferable to similar institutions. In short, both the shadowed pupil and the school could be regarded as particular rather than unique, and a case study could illuminate a wider field of pupils and schools.

It has been maintained that such a study can offer the 'fittingness' of generalizability in a variety of ways (Goetz and LeCompte 1984; Golby 1994; Guba and Lincoln 1982; Schofield 1993; Stake 1978; Wolcott 1973, 1990; Yin 1989). External validity is strengthened if the case study can be shown to offer typicality, if there is detailed description and if research is conducted on multi-sites. I now prepare for Chapters 2 and 3 by offering data of typicality, detailed description and multi-site research.

Josie Leigh was a fourteen-year-old girl in Year 9 of Key Stage 3 when the week's tracking took place at Tiverdale School in the mid-1990s. Emily Jay was a fifteen-year-old girl in Year 10 of Key Stage 4 when the week's tracking took place at Forestmead Community School, four weeks after Josie's tracking. Both pupils were regarded by their form tutors, their teachers and their heads of year as typical, that is, socially well-adjusted pupils of average academic ability. Both pupils followed a weekly timetable in which lessons were taught in 50-minute periods. The six daily periods were divided by a 15-minute break between lessons two and three; and by a dinner-break between lessons four and five. Josie and Emily regarded the week of their tracking as typical of their timetabled school week. They were asked (by myself) every day if this or that lesson was normal, ordinary, 'the kind of thing you usually do', and they said that it was.

Both were pupils in comprehensive schools that were regarded by me as typical of other comprehensive schools in their presentation of the National Curriculum. My opinion was primarily based upon four years' experience as the County Senior Advisory Teacher for Secondary English, during which time I had supervised independent learning projects in every comprehensive school in Greenshire, had attended departmental meetings in every comprehensive school and had organized residential in-service training courses attended by English teachers from every comprehensive school. I had also attended regional and national courses (Southampton, York, Swansea, London, Manchester, Leicester, Plymouth, Chester, Exeter) which had given me the opportunity to meet teachers and to visit schools across the country.

Secondary data suggesting typicality were provided by my attendance at annual heads of English conferences in Greenshire, as a head of English, between 1979 and 1988; and my experience as one of the two county teaching representatives to the South West Examinations Board (English), and as a CSE Examinations Moderator between 1976 and 1982, during which time I represented and visited many secondary schools in the south-western counties of England. Further data of typicality were provided by a scrutiny of GCSE results achieved by comprehensive schools in Greenshire and nationally, a comparison of the school prospectuses of the LEA's comprehensive schools, one-to-one meetings with each secondary headteacher in Greenshire, and opinions expressed by the senior management teams of Tiverdale and Forestmead schools.

The second criterion of the generalizability of case studies is detailed description. The full text of the two case studies comprises 52,000+ words of lesson-by-lesson commentary and analysis, photocopies of all of the pupils' reading and writing for the week, and diagrams of seating arrangements for every lesson. A description of the schools' management systems is given, of how introductory contact was made with the schools, and the way in which the case studies were initiated. It is an edited version of this text that comprises Chapters 2 and 3. The full text resides in my research archive and is available to educational researchers.

The third criterion of generalizability is that case study research should be conducted on multi-sites. The week-long pupil tracking took place with four different pupils (one tracking for each National Curriculum key stage) in three schools (although only the Key Stage 3 and 4 trackings are reported in this book). This intensive study followed lesson observation in 74 schools – including every comprehensive school in Greenshire – between 1988 and 1996.

The case studies were conducted with due concern for the ethics of research. Teachers and pupils participated voluntarily. They were informed of the purpose of the tracking and that the researcher (myself) was a post-graduate, part-time student at Exeter University. Teachers and pupils were aware that material gathered or photocopied, and data collected, may later be published in some form. Teachers and pupils were shown the forms I used for data collection. Questions asked of me were answered honestly. Arrangements for the tracking were made with the headteachers and senior management team of the two schools, but the tracking would not have taken place without the consent of the full staff, whom I addressed at staff meetings before both trackings. The parents of the two tracked pupils gave their permission. The trackings took place four weeks apart (Josie first and Emily second) sometime in the mid-1990s.

It is possible that, as the case studies were undertaken several years ago, some readers may question whether they are typical of current educational practice. They are. I continue to visit both primary and secondary schools regularly as a parent, a researcher and an educational consultant. Classroom observation and discussions with pupils, teachers, governors, inspectors, advisers and parents leave me in no doubt that had the case studies taken place this week, the style of lessons would have been as described in Chapters 2 and 3. My conclusions are just as relevant now as when the case studies were conducted. If anything, because of the increased intensity of pupil testing, teacher appraisal and school inspection, today's lessons are even more sterile than those experienced by Josie and Emily.

Confidentiality and anonymity have been observed. All names, other than my own, are pseudonyms. It should not be assumed that Greenshire, the LEA in which I locate Tiverdale and Forestmead schools, is a pseudonym for the LEA in which I worked as an advisory teacher, nor that Tiverdale and Forestmead schools are situated in that LEA. During the establishment of TVEI and the National Curriculum, there was a great deal of liaison between the advisory services of different south-western LEAs and I had the opportunity to work with colleagues in Cornwall, Devon, Dorset, Somerset, Avon, Gloucestershire, Wiltshire and Berkshire. Tiverdale and Forestmead could be in any of these counties. It might be best to think of Greenshire as a conceptual LEA, much as Thomas Hardy's Wessex was a conceptual south-western county.

2 Josie Gets Taught A Lesson

A National Curriculum case study at Key Stage 3

Monday: staff briefing (0830 – 0845)

As a result of attending or directing in-service training courses throughout the South West, I had met some of the staff at Tiverdale, mostly those who taught in the English department and those in senior management. The headteacher, Bill York, had been an advisory teacher and I had known him then, later when he was a deputy headteacher at Saltair and in his present job. My first approach concerning the possibility of tracking a Key Stage 3 pupil had been a telephone call to Sally Parton, one of the deputy heads, whom I had known for about ten years, as she had been head of English at Gannelford School. She was immediately enthusiastic about the idea and, after discussion with the Senior Management Team, confirmed that the tracking could take place during the first week of February. The arrangements were made over the 'phone and Sally asked me to arrive by eight-thirty on the Monday morning to introduce myself at the staff briefing. She stressed that, whilst the school senior management team were keen to cooperate, access to classrooms could only be at the invitation of teachers whose lessons would be observed.

I arrived at Tiverdale School on Monday, just after quarter past eight, and presented myself at Reception where I was asked to sign the daily visitors' register, stating my name and business, while one of the secretaries paged Jane Wendron, the head of Year 9. The atmosphere of the school was not in the least intimidating, although it was ordered, as was evident in corridor conduct, uniform, prefects, the way in which various support systems (secretarial, technician, kitchen staff) interacted with staff and pupils. There seemed to be a corporate spirit: despite the size of intake (approximately 1200 pupils), whole-year assemblies were held; and during my week there, all of Year 9 gathered to share each other's work in personal and social education. The organization required to move large groups of people in short times in a calm manner was characteristic of the orderly school atmosphere. During the week, I heard only one voice raised in anger – a young teacher's, whose estimable self-control and patience were wearing thin with a group of giggling boys during a lesson. Staff were friendly towards me, although not always relaxed; but that I was allowed into lessons to do what I did indicates the openness and confidence of the school management.

Over the phone, Jane had told me that she would find a pupil and 'sort things out'. I didn't know what this meant. As I waited in the foyer, Bill, the headteacher, hurried by, recognized me and invited me to the staff briefing, talking quickly as we bustled along the corridor.

'Hello, Rhys, mate, course, you're in with us on this language thing, just for the day is it, oh, for the whole week, great, Jane fixed you up all right has she . . . what exactly are you doing . . . ?'

I gabbled inarticulate replies as we sped along. There was some confusion as to who was to speak at the briefing – him? Jane? Bill invited me to, when we met Jane on the stairs leading to the staffroom. The threeway conversation, with Bill making introductions over his shoulder, was conducted on the march.

As Bill strode into the staffroom ('Morning everyone, let's get to it!') nothing was decided. I sat down to await events. Bill began the briefing. Questions from staff were about uniform ('What rule is there about the length of girls' skirts?' 'There's no rule about length, only about colour'), smoking ('There's a whole group of them smoking down the lane before school. I saw them this morning.' 'Are they on the school premises?' 'No, but they're in school uniform . . .'), prefects ('What does a prefect look like?' 'I'm sorry, Jim, what point are you making?' 'Well, I was on duty on Friday and there's supposed to be prefects by the tennis courts and on the door. They just weren't there.').

The head of Year 7 gave a few points of information about pupil absence and then Jane stood up: 'As we discussed at the last staff meeting, Rhys Griffith is going to be here this week and he's going to be tracking a Year 9 pupil to look at their English in all their lessons, at what they read and write, so if you see him around or in your lessons, that's who he is if you don't know him, which some of you do, there he is over there and the pupil is Josie Leigh.'

There were no questions and people dispersed.

Monday: tutor period (0845 – 0850)

I accompanied Joan Ridge, Josie's tutor, to the tutor room and was introduced to Josie. I sat down at the table she shared with her group of friends. I said my name was Rhys and the girls told me their names: Sally, Layla, Nicki. They were self-conscious, understandably. I showed Josie an example of the forms I'd be filling in, and told her she could look at the file in which they were contained whenever she wished. (She never did, nor showed any interest in what I was writing.) She showed me her timetable (Figure 2.1), which confirmed what Sally Parton had told me in response to my question during our first phone conversation, that there were six fifty-minute lessons each day. After the first two lessons there was a 15-minute break, then another two lessons before the one-hour dinner break, and then two more lessons before the end of the school day. On a few occasions lessons were 'doubles', lasting for the full 100 minutes between breaks.

Monday: lesson one – English (0850 – 0940)

The first lesson of the week was English and we trooped along busy corridors, me trying to keep Josie in sight, not too difficult because she was tall and I could follow the progress of her fair-haired ponytail as she strode out, chatting to others in her circle. When we arrived at Room H2, the teacher, Patty, whom I knew, asked Josie to go and find the videotape of *Romeo and Juliet* because she wanted to show it during the lesson.

'I'll go with her, Miss,' announced Sara, linking her arm through Josie's.

'It doesn't need two of you,' said Patty, lamely.

Sara smiled vivaciously over her shoulder, 'Oh yes it does, Miss,' and the two of them hurried out, laughing.

Timetable for Josie Leigh

Registration Group 9 (K)
Teacher: Mrs Q
Baseroom: A23

DAY	1	2	3	4	5	6
Mon	E	H	G	S	M	F
	H2	C1	H1	L16	A49	A15
	PA	AB	PP	DC	MS	MT
Tue	M	PE	AD	DR	S	MU
	A49		B14	A22	L16	A4
	MS	LE	WA	JD	DC	BI
Wed	E	SE	RE	GM	DT	DT
	H2	A21	A2	A15	T33	T33
	VF	JD	GJ	MT	EL	EL
Thu	M	E	GM	PE	F	G
	A49	H2	A15		A15	H1
	MS	PA	MT	LE	MT	PP
Fri	M	DT	S	S	PE	H
	A49	T33	L16	L16		C1
	MS	EL	DC	DC	LE	AB

Tiverdale School session times:

a.m. 0845 to 1225
p.m. 1325 to 1530

Code	Subject	Set	Level	Teacher (s)
E	English	04		Mrs Anthony & Mrs Farrell
M	Mathematics	01		Ms Studleigh
S	Science	03		Mr Carter
DT	Design Technology	03		Mr Idwallendar
G	Geography	03		Mr Peters
H	History	03		Mrs Burton
RE	Religious Education	03		Mr James
AD	Art and Design	03		Mr Allen
DR	Drama & Theatre Arts	03		Mr Donnelly
MU	Music	03		Mr Larham
PE	Physical Education	02		Mrs Laity
GM	German	01		Mrs Thomson
SE	Personal & Social Ed.	05		Mr Donnelly
F	French	06		Mrs Thomson

Figure 2.1 Josie's timetable

With a rueful shrug to Patty, I followed the girls. They spent ten minutes going to various classrooms and asking the teachers if they had the tape. Eventually they found it in the cupboard that Patty had originally looked in.

This English lesson, the first of the six 50-minute daily lessons, was scheduled to start at 0850, but because the class were waiting for Josie and Sara to return, the first activity did not get underway until 0905. Homework was handed back. The homework had been for pupils to write the first draft of a diary that Benvolio might have kept (the class was studying the DFE prescribed Shakespeare text for Year 9, *Romeo and Juliet*), and pupils were asked to check for underlinings made by Patty, and to try and identify their mistakes. If they couldn't, they could ask a friend. Patty, having given out papers and instructions, stipulated silence until pupils had made their own efforts to correct errors: 'Right, no talking.'

This raised some interesting questions. Was individual, silent work seen as somehow a more rigorous and disciplined way of working than collaborative work? Was the chance to talk offered as the reward for maintaining silence for a certain time? Did it imply a distinction between different language forms: reading and writing were distinct activities, with different operating codes from talking?

The pupils I observed did not talk about their drafts; they scanned them for teacher's comments and then chatted societally, quietly, until the teacher signalled the end of this activity after seven minutes. Whilst the class had been occupied, Patty had wound the videotape through the opening credits to the first scene. The class turned their chairs so that all could see the screen and the blinds were drawn. Pupils were told that, whilst watching the video, they could take notes and, sitting in friendship pairs or groups, were allowed [sic] to exchange comments. Josie made no notes, nor did any other pupil I observed. It would have been difficult as the room was very dark. The class watched the video for 28 minutes, which turned out to be one of the longest activities, in academic lessons, of the week. The lesson ended when the bell rang, with Capulet in mid-sentence on the screen.

This first lesson was to prove a microcosm of the week's lessons. Superficially, there seemed to be a lot of good things. There was a balance between reading (pupils reading their own drafts, their peers', the teachers's annotations, the media text of Zeffirelli's *Romeo and Juliet*), writing (annotating their own and a peer's drafts, making notes during the video) and talking (about their drafts and the video). There was a balance between collaborative groupwork (the paired reading exercise, the opportunity to discuss the video with a partner), individual responsibility (the note-making whilst watching the video) and cooperative, whole-class work (the class watching of the video). There was a chance to interrogate a range of texts (own work, peer's work, teacher-annotations, the video). There was an interaction between the three aspects of English (pupils were reading their own writing and talking about it in preparation for a redrafting; their reading of the media text, and the chance to comment to a partner during that reading, gave more information about Benvolio that would assist the writing of the second draft). The relationships between pupils and their peers and the teacher were good in a placid kind of way: there seemed to be an easy-going acceptance that the pupils would do what they were told, but more or less at their own pace (the fact that some pupils had not yet handed in their homework of the Benvolio diaries, Sara accompanying Josie in the search for the video).

And yet it was all done at such a shallow level and in such an undemanding way, that I really didn't feel that learning (rather than training, instructing, indoctrination or child-minding) was taking place. Certainly, there was no real opportunity for any of the twelve factors of independent learning. During the seven minutes given to the handing back of the homework, it is true that pupils could point out each other's 'mistakes', and that the whole class had to keep more-or-less still and quiet whilst watching the video, but it is stretching things to really claim these as examples of collaborative and cooperative groupwork.

Monday: lesson two – history (0940 – 1030)

Josie's second lesson was history and as we walked to C1 I noted the orderly conduct of pupils in the corridors as, unsupervised, (teachers tended to remain in their rooms waiting for the next class) they moved from one lesson to another. Approximately 1200 pupils, in groups of about 25, got up, and walked amongst each other, most of them forming new groupings to attend a lesson that had no connection with the lesson that they had just left. About 80 teachers waited in their rooms for the next group to arrive. What connections did they feel linking their working day? Fifty minutes later the bell would ring and the migration to the next lesson would happen all over again.

English had been taught in a mixed ability group (although around 30 pupils in the year were extracted to form a 'top' set) but the history lesson was taught by tutor group. It took four minutes for the class to assemble, as pupils had to come from a range of lessons and rooms to form the tutor grouping for this lesson. Mrs Burton started by reiterating ('and do you remember from last time') some positive listening skills and then, with a rhetorical 'Everybody listening?' she introduced the topic of Russia. There was a 12 minute whole-class question-and-answer session about ethnic and religious groups before the class was given the following worksheet to complete (Figure 2.2).

Russia's industrial growth

Study the following groups of statistics about Russia in the years before the revolution:

SOURCE A: Population 1900 (in millions)

Russia	103	France	39
Germany	56	Great Britain	41
Austria-Hungary	45	Italy	32

SOURCE B: Railways – kilometres of track in 1900 (in thousands)

Russia	53	France	38
Germany	52	Great Britain	35
Austria-Hungary	36	Italy	16

SOURCE C: Coal production in 1900 (in million tonnes); figures in brackets refer to percentage increase in production since 1890

Russia	16 (170%)	France	33 (28%)
Germany	149 (67%)	Great Britain	225 (24%)
Austria-Hungary	39 (50%)	Italy	(0.5%)

SOURCE D: Steel production (in million tonnes)

	1890	1900		1890	1900
Russia	0.4	1.5	France	0.7	1.6
Germany	2.3	6.7	Great Britain	3.6	4.9
Austria-Hungary	0.5	1.2			

(Sources A, C and D from A.J.P. Taylor, *Struggle for Mastery in Europe, 1848–1918*, 1971)

a Which two countries, on the basis of Sources C and D, had the biggest industrial output?
b Of the five countries listed in both Sources C and D where would you rank Russia in terms of output?
c Which of the nations listed in Sources C and D was growing the most quickly in terms of output? Support your answer with evidence from the statistics.
d Source B shows Russia as having the largest railway network.
  i Why is this a misleading statistic?
  ii How does Source A put Source B and the other sources concerning Russia in a more accurate position?
e What do you think this exercise tells you about the dangers for historians of using statistics?

Figure 2.2 First worksheet given to Josie in history, Monday

As in later lessons, the tables at which pupils sat were positioned for groupwork yet the tasks set by the teacher were intended to be completed individually. However, because of their proximity, pupils naturally chatted, but as they were supposed to be working on their own, they rarely discussed their work – I suppose this might have been regarded as cheating. When pupils did talk about their work, it was usually in an aside during a conversation about something else:

Sally: '. . . yeh, but not as good as last week [*discussing this week's episode of Blind Date*]. Is it Great Britain or Germany [*referring to one of the questions*]?'
Josie: 'Germany – '
Sally: ' – where they had that couple – '
Layla: ' – oh yeah!'

This led me to make a distinction between the social and societal chat of pupils. The buzz of conversation that pervaded individual 'silent' work could have been pupils talking sociably about their work. It hardly ever was. The conversation was actually societal: pupils discussing the customs and events of the social community to which they belonged, whilst simultaneously engaged in some subject-based lesson task.

Josie worked quickly but assiduously, taking little part in the general chat. She finished the worksheet before anyone else on her table and put her hand up to signal the teacher, who commented upon the quality of her answers and then gave her another worksheet to start (Figures 2.3 and 2.4).

The teacher asked the class to pack away at 1026, after thirty minutes of the worksheet activity and the bell for morning break rang at 1030.

Russia, 1900–17

● **Russia in 1900**

In 1900 Russia was a nation with great troubles. Many of the people were poor peasants with little political freedom. For example, they had no vote and could not own land freely. Thus they were years behind most of the other inhabitants of western Europe.

Much of the control of Russia lay in the hands of one man – the Tsar. He was an emperor who was treated by his people almost like a god and his word was law. Tsar Nicholas II had come to the throne in 1894 and believed firmly that he should be a father-figure for his nation, deciding its policies at home and abroad with the advice of a small group of ministers.

However, during the last twenty years of the nineteenth century, industries had developed quickly in some parts of Russia. Factories were built to produce iron and steel, railways, cotton and other manufactured goods. Their workers were not peasants living in the countryside and they wanted rights. They were seeking the vote, higher wages and the freedom to belong to trade unions.

To achieve their aims they formed political parties, like the Social Revolutionary Party (later split into the Bolsheviks and the Mensheviks), the Liberals and the Social Democratic Party. Soon there were strikes, but the Tsar's government sent in secret agents to find the leaders.

1.a) Who was the Tsar and what power did he have?

b) How was Russia changing in the late 19th century?

c) What did the Russian people want?

● **The ideas of Karl Marx**

Some of these 'underground' politicians believed in the ideas of Karl Marx. Marx (1818–83) was a German Jew who lived in Paris, Brussels and London, where he wrote books setting out his ideas. He divided society into two classes. First came the capitalists, who were owners of factories, land and wealth. Second were the workers (the proletariat) who were employed by the capitalists.

Marx claimed that capitalists controlled governments for themselves. They set out to use workers to make money, while paying them little. One day, he said, workers would rebel, abolish capitalism and share out wealth. This would be communism and he claimed that all would benefit.

A keen follower of Marx's ideas was Vladimir Ulyanov, known as Lenin, a member of the Social Revolutionary Party. In 1900 he left Russia to live in Switzerland and waited for the day when he could bring his ideas back to his native land.

2.a) Who was Karl Marx ?

b) What were some of the ideas that Marx believed ?

Figure 2.3 Second worksheet given to Josie during history, Monday

● Bloody Sunday

On Sunday 22 January 1905, while the war was still on, thousands of people marched in a procession to the Tsar's Winter Palace in St Petersburg (later called Petrograd; later still Leningrad). Led by a priest, Father Gapon, they were protesting for better working conditions and more political freedom.

They were met by a hail of bullets from soldiers protecting the Palace. Scores of people were killed or wounded. The incident led to great anger among the workers and a greater determination to gain reforms.

● The Duma

Under pressure, the Tsar agreed to call a Duma (Parliament) and some wage-earners were given the vote. However, over the next few years the Tsar paid little attention to what his parliament wanted. If he did not like their suggestions he could dismiss them. Some voters and candidates were imprisoned if they did not agree with government policies.

So by 1914 ordinary Russians did not have much control over the running of their country. Thousands of them disliked the Tsar and his supporters.

● Russia at war, 1914–17

When Russia went to war in 1914 it was with the largest army of any nation taking part. It was expected that the Russian 'steamroller' would flatten Germany from the east. But bad leadership and organization soon led to disasters. The 'steamroller' went into full retreat.

There were shortages of everything except men, who became 'cannon fodder' in the early campaigns. The Russian soldiers showed great bravery, but suffered terrible casualties. Their mass attacks against German and Austrian positions were often devastated by enemy artillery fire. Yet, because of shell shortages, their own guns were sometimes limited to firing only five rounds per day!

There was trouble also for civilians at home in Russia. There, the shortages of food and everyday goods meant that many people suffered badly. Many Russians became angry with a government that appeared unable to govern.

The Tsar appointed himself as Commander-in-Chief of his army in an effort to put matters right, but things only got worse. In 1916, after heavy Russian attacks, the Austrians were very weak, yet the Russians lacked the leadership to carry them to victory.

Inside the nation, the Tsarina (the Tsar's wife) was given a strong hand in governing the country. But she was under the influence of a strange monk, or 'holy man' named Rasputin. He claimed that he could cure her son who was suffering from a rare blood disease. So the government was filled with corruption and ordinary people had little faith in their leaders. The stage was set for a great change.

Copy and complete these sentences using the words in the **word list**.

3. (a) In 1900 Russian people had little political. . . .
   (b) The . . . was the most powerful man in Russia.
   (c) The Tsar's wife, the . . . , was under the influence of a monk called. . . .
   (d) . . . . . . divided society into capitalists and workers.
   (e) After the 1905 Revolution the Tsar agreed to call a. . . .

word list: Karl Marx; Tsar; Duma; Rasputin; Tsarina; freedom

4. (a) Imagine you are a Russian officer in 1916. Write a list of reasons why your country should stay in the war against Germany.
   (b) Imagine you are a Russian woman in 1916. Write a list of reasons for *not* staying in the war.

Figure 2.3 continued

Monday: morning break (1030 – 1045)

I hurried across to the Elliot hut, used for English and general purpose lessons, that I was to make my base during the week. Between the two classrooms was a staffroom with electric kettle and easy chair. I wanted to check some of the statements of attainment for English for each of the attainment targets, Speaking and Listening, Reading and Writing (NCC, 1990). As Josie had not contributed in any discussion, her speaking and listening opportunities had not risen above Level 1: 'respond appropriately to simple instructions given by a teacher'.

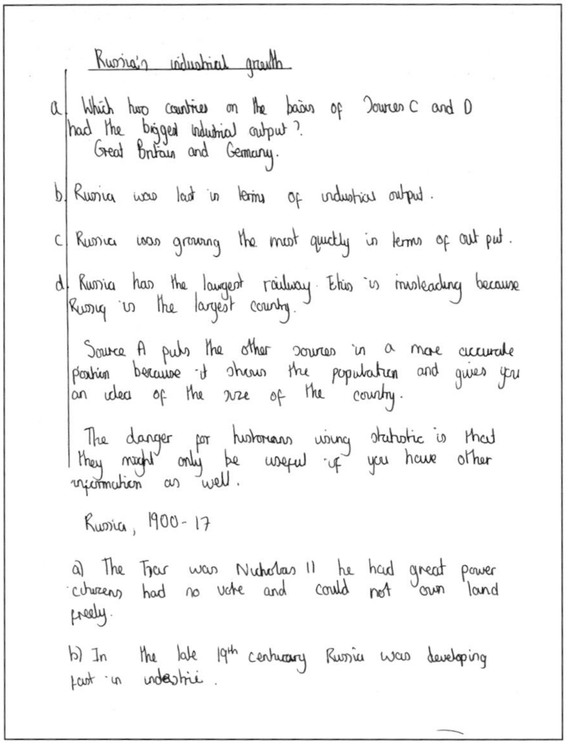
Russia's industrial growth

a. Which two countries on the basis of Sources C and D had the biggest industrial output?
Great Britain and Germany.

b. Russia was last in terms of industrial output.

c. Russia was growing the most quickly in terms of out put.

d. Russia has the largest railway. This is misleading because Russia is the largest country.

Source A puts the other sources in a more accurate position because it shows the population and gives you an idea of the size of the country.

The danger for historians using statistic is that they might only be useful if you have other information as well.

Russia, 1900-17

a) The Tsar was Nicholas II he had great power citizens had no vote and could not own land freely.

b) In the late 19th century Russia was developing fast in industrie.

Figure 2.4 Josie's answers to the worksheets in history, Monday

As she had neither talked nor written about the video, she showed no evidence of the Media strand. The comprehension exercise did not meet the criteria of the study skills strand for reading, which requires pupils to select their own materials, before making appropriate selections relevant to their research from within these materials. For writing, only the structure and organization strand applied and that only at Level 2. The average end-of-Key Stage 3 pupil (and Josie was supposed to represent that vexed paradigm) should be working at Level 6. Level 2 represents the average performance of a seven-year old.

Although none of the activities that Josie had so far undertaken could be charted on to the levels for reading in the National Curriculum for English, a reading of the actual texts (video and worksheets) required sophisticated comprehension skills. But the associated writing task for the worksheet in history was not consistent with the reading age needed to access and interrogate that text. The written response required short-phrase or simple-sentence answers to factual questions – a fairly low-level demand on pupils. In short, to successfully complete the preparatory reading task, a pupil would need significantly more highly-developed literacy skills than for the writing task that was consequently made. This led me to coin Josie's Paradox: if a pupil is able to read the text, she'll be bored by the written task; but if the written task is appropriately challenging, the pupil won't be able to do it, because she'll find the text too difficult to read.

Monday: lesson three – geography (1045 – 1135)

The next lesson started within a minute of the bell for the end of break. The lesson was taken by Bill York. The geography lesson was held in a non-specialist room (one of those in the Elliot Hut) and Josie was with the same class as for the last lesson, her tutor group, and seated, as in the last lesson, with her friends. The first 14 minutes of the lesson were given over to whole-class discussion, in which Bill took the class through the worksheet up to the task on six-figure references (Figure 2.5).

It was the same style of introduction as Mrs Burton had used, although Bill's approach was more focused. His questions were specific rather than the generalities of 'Does anyone know anything about Russia?' Bill also tried to personalize the worksheet by telling of his own experiences with a group of pupils on the Brecon Beacons. However, as with the other lessons of the day, there was no attempt to explain the purpose of the lesson, or why it may be relevant to the pupils. Josie, again, made no spoken contribution. Once again she sat in an all-girl group. Once again tables were arranged for groupwork, but the activities were either whole-class or individual. The first written task took six minutes and Josie wrote the response shown in Figure 2.6.

Five minutes of whole-class discussion then followed, although this is a euphemism as the discussion did not involve the whole class; pupils were selected by the teacher to answer a shut-ended question: 'What have you got for that one? Yes, Rick . . . yes that's right'. I decided to define this type of spoken interaction as 'teacher-led talk', a phrase more accurate than 'whole-class discussion'. The pupils then spent 11 minutes on the Brecon Rescue task (Figure 2.7) and there followed seven minutes of teacher-led talk checking the answers.

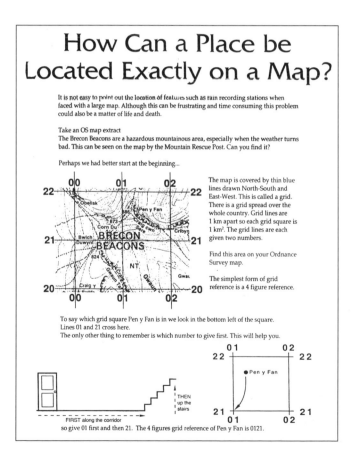

Figure 2.5 Worksheet used in geography, Monday (continued overleaf)

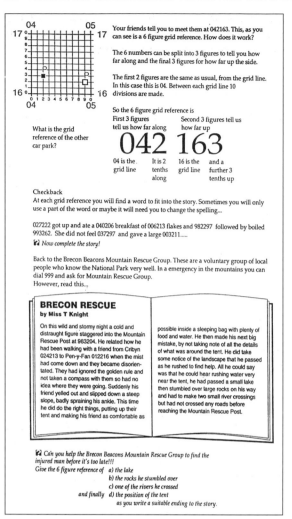

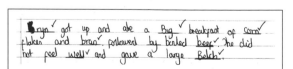

Figure 2.5 (continued)

Figure 2.6 Josie's answers to first geography worksheet exercise, Monday

Figure 2.7 Josie's answers to second geography worksheet exercise, Monday

Then the pupils read from the chapter 'A Walk in the Mountains', page 77 of the *Ordnance Survey Map Skills* book. The 49 minute lesson had contained six activities, all related to the same worksheet. The longest time pupils spent on a task was 11 minutes.

Monday: lesson four – science (1135 – 1225)

The next lesson was science, which meant the third change of pupil grouping that morning, for Josie was in the top set for this subject. Two of Josie's tutor group chums, Nicki and Layla, were in the same set. Once again, tables were arranged for groupwork but the lesson required only whole-class or individual activities. Mr Carter introduced a new topic, 'Things that attack your body'. The first seven minutes was the by-now familiar 'whole-class' discussion; the next 13 minutes had an added element: pupils copied notes from the board as they emerged from the discussion (Figure 2.8).

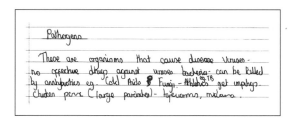

Figure 2.8 Notes copied from blackboard in science, Monday

No-one in Josie's group contributed to the discussion, preferring to chat quietly in between periods of copying from the board. Any reference to the subject of the lesson tended to be anecdotal: 'My mum had a virus on her chest,' said Nicki to Josie and Layla as the three of them doodled on the back page of Layla's science exercise book. The class was then to watch a video, but there was a problem with the electricity supply and then the programme was not the one the teacher wanted, so it took ten minutes before the class settled to watch a video about microbes for the last 15 minutes of the lesson.

Monday: dinner break (1225 – 1325)

So ended the morning session. Back to the sanctuary of the Elliot hut to do some quick sums based on the activity forms I had been using. The four lessons were each supposed to last 50 minutes, giving a total of 200 minutes of lesson time. However, moving from one lesson to another, the taking of a register at the beginning of every lesson, the general business of settling at the start of a lesson and packing away at the end, had reduced this to 162 minutes; of this a further 58 minutes consisted of teacher-led talk in which Josie took no part. Of the remaining 104 minutes (52 per cent of the timetabled lesson time) 43 were devoted to watching videos, 47 to comprehension exercises and 7 to reading (a geography textbook).

In terms of language across the curriculum, as defined by National Curriculum English criteria, this was not a rich seam of language development. Josie had yet to speak in discussion, so her Speaking and Listening skills (English Attainment Target 1) could still only be assessed at Level 1. The opportunities for Reading (Attainment Target 2) had been limited. There had been little evidence of Range (videos and worksheets) and none for Response to Literature. As the TV watching was an essentially passive experience, pupils were not asked to 'show in discussion or in writing that they can recognize whether subject matter in non-literary and media texts is presented as fact or opinion, identifying some of the ways in which the distinction can be made' – the lowest level in the Non-Literary/Media strand of English. The comprehension exercises involved reading and writing, but could only possibly apply to the study skills or non-literary strands of reading and the structure and organization strand of writing. On examination, however, only one question (on the second history worksheet) could meet the non-literary criteria and no lesson activity applied to study skills, which require pupils to select their own research or resource materials. There had been no explicit teaching of Knowledge About Language, although implicitly pupils might have absorbed some understanding that different types of language exist and are used to convey different meanings.

Whatever else Josie might have been doing, she wasn't doing English. If this pattern continued, the comfortable notion that pupils are taught English in all lessons because all lessons are taught in English would be strongly challenged:

> Schemes of work in all subjects provide opportunities for pupils to meet attainment targets in English.
>
> (NCC, p. 12, 1990a)

It should be noted that I used the rubric of the original English Orders for the National Curriculum of 1990 for this analysis and not the condensed Orders which were informed by the Dearing Report of 1993, and introduced, for English, in August of 1995 for Key Stage 3 and in August of 1996 for Key Stage 4.

At dinnertime I read the school prospectus which claimed that some of the aims of the school were to develop individuality, to extend intellectual skills, to cultivate a love of learning and an inquiring disposition in pupils and to create a learning ethos that was lively and enthusiastic. I have no doubt that such aspirations, which are reiterated in every school prospectus that I have ever read, are well-intentioned and sincere. Such statements of intent are closely aligned to the concept of educational citizenship and could underpin a policy of independent learning. But I was beginning to wonder when I would see any evidence of these aims during lessons. Because if the aims of a school are not explicitly pursued through the curriculum, then when are they pursued? When do pupils get their entitlement to the very worthwhile aspirations to which emancipatory aims allude?

Nothing I had seen so far had allayed reservations about how difficult it was for a conventionally organized school to fulfil its laudable aims with a ten-subject curriculum, a six-lesson day, up to six different lesson groupings a day, no meaningful cross-curricular language development, lesson activities lasting about 10–15 minutes, a diet of comprehension exercises in unrelated lessons – all of this compounded by gender groupings and teaching styles that tended to encourage boys to participate more than girls.

Monday: Year 9 assembly (1325 – 1350)

All Year 9 pupils assembled in the gymnasium and sat cross-legged on the floor. Teaching staff stood around the walls. Senior staff sat on chairs on a raised dais, the headteacher in the middle. Year 9 was addressed by a Methodist about his religious convictions, how they applied to his professional life as a businessman and how a strong Methodist faith would help pupils with their work.

Monday: lesson five – maths (1350 – 1440)

The afternoon session usually begins at 1350, but pupils were late leaving the Year 9 assembly and the first of the two afternoon lessons, maths, got underway at 1400 hours. The class was taken by Ms Studleigh, a PGCE student on her teaching practice at Tiverdale. The desks were arranged in rows and pupils sat in pairs. This classroom conformed to the standard configuration in the school: a rectangular room, just large enough to take sixteen stacking tables, each table intended for use by two pupils, and leaving space at the front for the teacher's desk. On the wall behind the teacher's desk was a blackboard. One of the long walls was windowed along its length. The two other walls were available for display, and one of these walls was cupboarded to a work-surface height. Above this work surface were glass-fronted wall-mounted cupboards. The floor was carpeted. The door had a glass-panel and opened from the corridor. Variation between rooms depended on whether the walls were used for display (the maths room wasn't), how the tables were arranged, and the colour of walls, tables and carpet. There were also rooms that did not conform to this pattern. The English room was almost twice the normal size, but doubled as a canteen eating-area. H1, where the geography lesson took place, was in an Elliot hut, with two windowed walls and a linoleum floor. The science lab had sturdy dark-wooded tables and dark-wooded work-surfaces.

Ms Studleigh's opening words to the class were, 'Get your homework out without talking.'

The first five minutes were given to a whole-class marking of the homework. For the first time, in purported whole-class discussion, Josie spoke. Ms Studleigh asked her to give her answer for one of the sums set for homework, to which came the response: 'Sixty seven point four'.

This was a setted group, Set Two, and Josie was reunited with her English partner, Sara. I noticed that there were no mixed pairs, and then tried to deduce some pattern from the seating plan, in terms of boys nearest the front or whatever. I recalled that in the science lesson, the girls had occupied the tables at the back of the class, but couldn't remember for the other lessons. I decided to start keeping a plan of seating arrangements in lessons to see if any pointers emerged.

After the marking of homework, there followed a 15-minute activity in which pupils wrote notes copied from the board and other notes dictated by Ms Studleigh (Figure 2.9):

> Copy the title from the board: 'Using Pythagoras Theorem' . . . in triangle ABC, A with a little hat on top equals ninety degrees, AB equals seven centimetres, AC equals . . . equals six centimetres. Find BC . . . we need to find BC not BC squared so what is it on your calculators? . . . **Everybody in tomorrow lunchtime. Maybe then you'll learn not to talk in my lessons** . . .

Josie was asked by Ms Studleigh for another answer and I recorded her second and final whole-class utterance of the day: 'AC squared minus BC squared equals AB squared'. In 82 minutes of teacher-led talk, Josie had spoken for less than five seconds, and then in fluent geometric, not English. Assuming an average class size of 25, and assuming that somehow

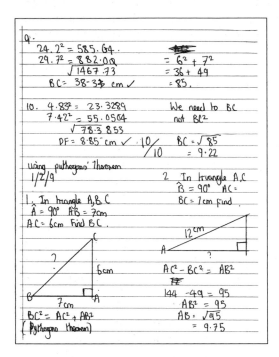

Figure 2.9 Josie's record of notes dictated by the teacher in maths, Monday

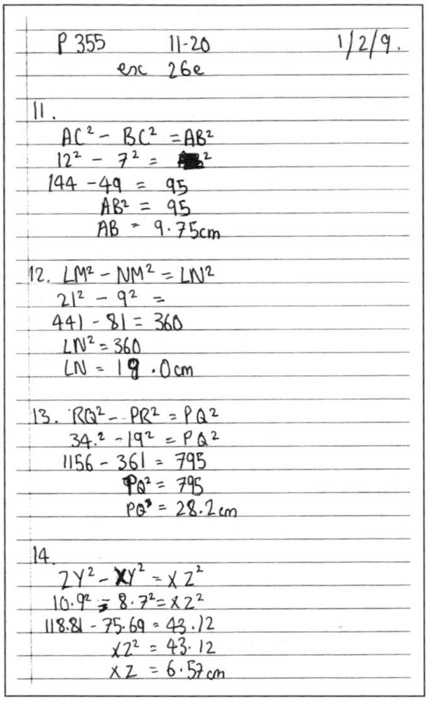

Figure 2.10 Josie's working of sums 11–20, *STP Maths 3B*, p. 355 in maths, Monday

each pupil, over the day had an equal speaking time, this would have given Josie a share of 3 minutes and 38 seconds; she only used 2 per cent of this time. Of course, this kind of number-crunching does not work because in teacher-led talk there is not an equal distribution: the lion's share of the time is taken by the teacher, then by boys. Considerations like a pupil's shyness, knowledge of the subject and relationship with the teacher are other factors that may limit a pupil's contribution to teacher-led talk.

Yet Josie is not a shy girl. She is confident in company – one of the reasons that she was chosen by the school to be the tracked pupil is because of her self-composed nature. This is not a girl who lacks subject knowledge. She is average or above average in all her subjects. Often I see that she knows the answers to the questions asked by the teacher: they are correctly written in her exercise book, or she mouths the answer to herself, or she murmurs it to a companion. This is not a girl who has relationship problems with teachers. She is confident and relaxed in dialogue with them. It should also be said that not once did I hear a teacher react sarcastically or negatively if a pupil gave an incorrect answer. Quite the opposite, in all the lessons throughout the week, teachers were supportive and kindly. Nevertheless, on this particular day, Josie spent 99.9 per cent of teacher-led talk time in silence.

After finishing the dictation, pupils were asked to do sums 11–20 on page 355 of their textbook, STP Mathematics 3B (Figure 2.10). They worked individually. Their use of calculators gave the first tick of the day in the independent learning section of the form: Pupil Use Of A Range Of IT (but this is only gathering evidence, not confirming it, because this factor refers to a *range* of technology).

As in all the previous lessons, this maths lesson seemed to show a sense of detachment from any social reality. Why have these pupils done this exercise? What is its relevance to their lives? Ms Studleigh made no attempt to explain any context in which the theorem might apply to the pupils. Similarly, no-one in the class asked why they were learning about the theorem. This activity lasted for 18 minutes and then pupils packed away in preparation for the bell that signalled the last lesson of the day.

Monday: lesson six – French (1440 – 1530)

The French room is at the other end of the school. The class was large (32 pupils), the room standard size. Extra chairs had to be brought from nearby classrooms. By the time Mrs Thomson, the head of modern languages, was able to start the lesson, ten minutes had passed from the end of the previous lesson, even though, on the timetable there is no indication of a break in learning time.

The pattern of the lesson was familiar: whole-class introduction, with pupils invited to contribute, in preparation for a written task. The variation between lessons tends to depend on the didactic skill of the teacher as front-of-house entertainer, the warm-up act who cossets the audience before introducing the night's star turn, usually that old favourite, Some Form Of Comprehension Exercise. Mrs Thomson was preparing the class for a survey on jobs. Her introduction lasted six minutes and the task, ten (Figure 2.11).

This was the second example during the day of small groupwork: pupils working in pairs as questioner and answerer. The contacts were very brief, each pair forming and breaking within a minute. There was a sense of cooperative work, for all the pupils in the class were involved. This was also the second time that pupils had actually been asked to use talk as part of the learning experience, other than in teacher-led discussion. There was certainly no pupil initiated research: the teacher had decided the focus of the research, chosen the categories for research and the terminology involved, and had devised the survey form. The data collection lasted ten minutes and then the lesson returned to teacher-led talk for 13 minutes.

I was beginning to realize that boys tended to answer much more frequently than girls. There has been a great deal of well-recorded research to claim this (AGIT, 1994; Herbert, 1992; Measor and Sykes, 1992; Riddell, 1992; Whyld, 1983), but I think I had assumed,

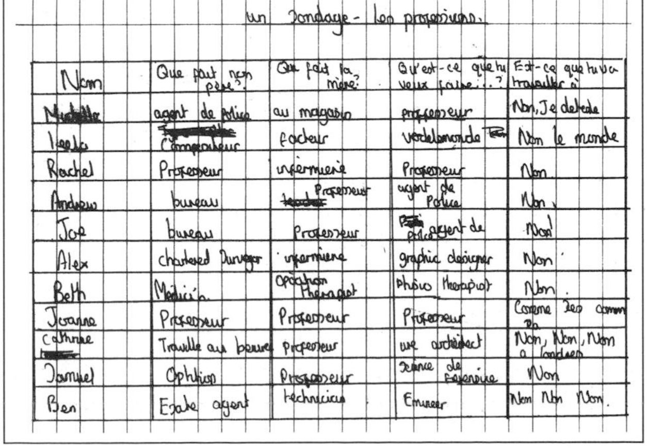

Figure 2.11 Josie's completed questionnaire in French, Monday

because we were aware of this tendency, that teachers had adopted strategies and tactics to redress the balance. Every school in Greenshire has an Equal Opportunities Policy that includes statements on the curricular entitlement of all pupils. Between 1988 and 1994 there was a County Advisory Teacher for Multicultural Education, and much of her work had publicized the socio-cultural differences in the way in which boys and girls are treated. One of the curriculum enhancement areas of the Technical and Vocational Education Initiative, well-established in Greenshire secondary schools, was Equal Opportunities: Gender. The Greenshire LEA has a county policy on equal opportunities and a standing committee to monitor practice in schools. Residential and school-based INSET had been provided by several of the advisory teams (including the English team). One of the National Curriculum cross-curricular dimensions, which are intended to permeate all lessons, is Equal Opportunities: Gender.

Nevertheless, in the Tiverdale classrooms, particularly in 'whole-class' discussion or when pupils were required to demonstrate some skill or practice, I gained the impression that boys got a disproportionate amount of time and opportunity. I wanted to become clearer about this gender differentiation so I determined, from the next day's lessons, to start recording how and when boys and girls spoke, as well as where and how they sat in classes.

For the last 12 minutes of the French lesson, pupils were asked to jot down answers to a comprehension exercise on page 38 of their textbook, *Tricolore 2*. The bell rang at 1530 and the first day of my week at the school ended.

Monday: summary

During the day's lessons, Josie has moved from English to history, geography, maths, science and French. Although her curriculum is divided into subjects, there is, as yet, no evidence to suggest that these subjects unite to represent a holistic body of knowledge. No connections have been made between any of the subjects. Their separatism is emphasized by different subject-specialist teachers, different purpose-specialist rooms and different criteria for grouping pupils. If there is no attempt to present a unified curriculum, there is also little or no effort made to relate discrete subject knowledge to the personal and social lives of the pupils in their myriad interactions with the multi-communities and environments within which they live. There is also no suggestion, as yet, that the acquisition of bits of knowledge in different subjects is seen as part of a process that develops learning skills that are transferable across subjects, and that transcend those subjects, so that learning how to learn is the holistic aim, rather than the *per se* accumulation of subject-based knowledge.

The curriculum is unified, not by content links, or cross-curricular skills, themes and dimensions, but by a common teaching and learning style. Lessons begin with an intro-duction by the teacher, pupils work individually on short exercises, the class 'discuss' their findings and the process is repeated. Although comprehension exercises may, as their name presumably suggests, exercise pupils' comprehension, they have not so far required the application of a critical disposition. In short, education appears to be a process in which knowledge is neutralized and reified and then transmitted to learners who are instrumen-talized by the transmission process. The accumulation of knowledge is purposeless and irrelevant to their daily lives.

There was very little in what I had seen during the day that would allow pupils to learn independently, in terms of the 12 factors. Pupils did not learn collaboratively (Factor 1), or did so only very briefly on minor tasks decided by the teacher. They did not work cooperatively (Factor 2), for the teacher's role was clearly external to the pupil body. There was no sense of individual responsibility (Factor 3). Pupils completed short-term individual tasks at the command of the teacher, but the rest of the class were engaged on exactly the same tasks. Completing these tasks involved no intrinsic responsibility; their completion was a matter of low-level self-convenience and expediency to avoid teacher-imposed sanctions. Pupils did not design their own tasks (Factor 4), or have any control over the time allocated for their completion (Factor 6) or any involvement in initiating research (Factor 7) – all tasks were from teacher-selected texts. Pupils had no voice in the assessment of their work (Factor 5). In English they could only comment on the teacher's assessment. In other subjects, 'answers' were always a matter of factual right or wrong, the decision made by the teacher or author of the textbook being used. The use of a range of technology (Factor 8) was limited to the use of calculators in maths. There was no suggestion that the content of lessons related to the community or the environment and certainly no movement into the local environment and community for pupil-initiated research (Factor 9). There was no sense of audience for the work (Factor 10), other than teacher as marker, and the range of presentation of work (Factor 11) was in only two forms: hand-written or spoken response during lessons (a form of presentation that seemed to favour boys). There was no evidence of reflexivity (Factor 12).

In the absence of a commitment to educational citizenship via the practices of independent learning, there was no evidence of any clear alternative philosophy that actually related to the observed practice. Instead, there was confusion and inconsistency that suggested an ambivalent, uncertain attitude to what the school was trying to achieve: English was taught in mixed-ability groups – but also had one fast-track top set; classroom furniture was arranged for groupwork, but only individual work took place; there were the juxtaposed messages of the school prospectus that attempted to embrace both pupil responsibility and adult control; there was the perceived need for different class-grouping criteria (peer, ability, gender and faith) for the same pupils for different subjects; teachers made knee-jerk calls for silence, but there was an acceptance of tolerable noise levels of societal chat during lesson tasks.

What of the school context in which these lessons were observed? Like individual lessons, at a quick glance, the macrocosm of the school system seemed efficient, for overlaying the actual practice (which may have been inefficient in achieving the stated aims of the establishment) was a veneer of apparent professionalism that was – at that quick glance – not merely plausible but nighwell inviolable of any criticism.

During the first day of observation there had already been many examples of this overpowering patina of monolithic certitude: institutional codes of address, of movement around the buildings, of performance (school teams, 'houses', photos and plaques in the foyer, a glossy prospectus with public examination results, music certificates awarded in assembly), of suppression of personal freedom via school rules, of the emphasis upon neatness and conformity that a school uniform requires. The power discourse could be most vividly read in the Year 9 assembly, with those ennobled adults at the apex of the hierarchy flanking their enthroned leader, who literally looked down on his young subjects as they sat at his feet.

The school regime was authoritarian, albeit benevolent in that paternalistic 'because I say so' and maternalistic 'we know what's good for you' authoritarianism. This ethos was evinced in its many rules aimed at conformity rather than individuality. This spilled over into the set-up of the lessons, where all decision making was controlled by the teachers, all activities were presented as worthwhile without explanation, and all learning was seen as accumulating factual information for no established or questioned purpose: coal output in

1910 in Russia, map references in the Brecon Beacons, pathogens in the bloodstream, triangles in ancient Greece.

However, there were indications that the potent authoritarian ethos of the school was superficial and that the pupil body, although lacking any officially recognized role in the power structure, was no downtrodden proletariat. Quite the contrary. In all of the day's lessons I sensed that pupils were really in control and that the teachers had to walk the fine line between overtaxing them and overboring them, in which case the pupils would withdraw their consent to the idea that the teachers were in charge and start to talk, mess around. The major impetus of the lessons seemed to accept this unspoken premise, with teachers entertaining and mollifying, keeping noise and movement down to some accept-able level. Given that the basic curriculum was uninteresting, then teachers seemed to adopt as a defensive mechanism, a series of short tasks, endlessly moving pupils on as soon as they became noisily bored with any particular activity. It appeared to be an unarticulated but accepted agreement that the teachers had some right to be heard if they struggled to impose their voice, but that they would soon shut up and give up and set another short, easy task which would allow pupils to chat quietly and societally for ten minutes or so as they completed the task.

It seems to me that such a basic notion of education – picking up bits of 'facts' at differentiated levels depending upon which set a pupil is in – is philosophically untenable, even though a regime can be constructed to accommodate it: subject lessons, hierarchical groups, micro-activities during short lessons, a behavioural code that discourages enquiry or individuality, the official disempowerment of the majority. The longevity of such a system relies almost totally on its perceived success, its credibility with those involved in the system: pupils, parents and practitioners. Much of this credibility is promoted by drawing attention away from the difficult areas (like the curriculum and its pedagogy) and towards various totems that have been artificially created as observable indicators of success: uniform, rules, punishment systems, homework, a spuriously impressive timetable, a glossy prospectus, public examination results and the other trappings of Institution. To maintain this credi-bility, a climate is created in which the rightness of Institution becomes unquestionable: parents don't ask why their children need to be segregated by ability, teachers don't ask why their classes' weekly lesson time has to be scatter-shot across the timetable, pupils don't ask why they are doing what they're doing in a lesson. This is a climate of indoctrination in which members of all three groups – parents, practitioners and pupils – collude in their own oppression.

Tuesday: lesson one – maths (0850 – 0940)

The first lesson on Tuesday was Maths, which followed the same format as yesterday's lesson. Ms Studleigh dictated to the class, putting some phrases or formulae on the board for the class to copy (Figure 2.12). Today's subject was 'Special Right-angled Triangles':

Ms Studleigh: 'Any triangle in this ratio, colon, three to four to five, comma . . .'

Josie made her first voluntary utterance of the week when she politely called out, 'You've put three times three equals fifteen', drawing attention to a mistake Ms Studleigh had made on the board. 'Glad someone's awake,' said Ms Studleigh. The dictation/copying lasted 20 minutes and then for the 20 minutes until it was time to pack away, the class carried on with yesterday's sums. Those who finished them began the next exercise (Figure 2.13).

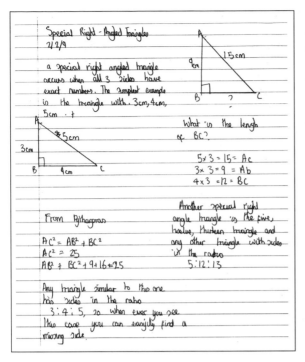

Figure 2.12 Josie's record of dictated notes made in maths, Tuesday

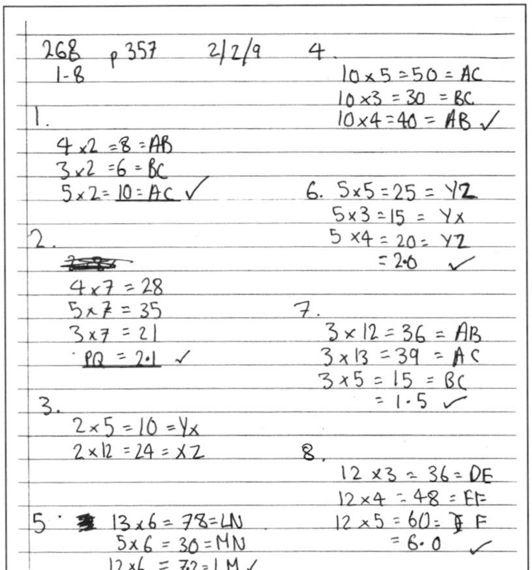

Figure 2.13 Josie's working of Exercise 26F, *STP Maths 3B*, p. 357, maths, Tuesday

Josie worked competently and quietly (she is in the second of eight ability sets for maths), occasionally asking a question of Ms Studleigh, who was walking around the class, checking work and giving advice. Josie asked Ms Studleigh for some help to decipher a section of the text in her dog-eared textbook: 'Miss, is that a Q in the corner there? I can't read it.'

Later, on completing the first exercise, she turned to Sara: 'What one do we do when we finish?'

Sara shrugged, so Josie called Ms Studleigh: 'For number two, do you have to do this three, four, five?' Ms Studleigh came to help her and Josie responded to Ms Studleigh's questions as follows: 'Um, seven . . . seven fours? Twenty eight . . . um, twenty one . . . two point one.' Later she asked Ms Studleigh for further clarification: 'Um, for LM, I can't work out whether it's three, four, five; or five, twelve, thirteen'. As Ms Studleigh explained, Josie responded with monosyllabic responses: 'Yeh . . . mm . . . mm . . . yes.'

Of the final five minutes of the lesson, three were given to writing in homework diaries and two to packing away.

Once again, the general goodwill was evident: the calm manner of the teacher, the industry of the pupils. I feel a sense of betrayal in writing critically of a well-intentioned young woman who had willingly offered me the hospitality of her classroom, but this was a depressing lesson, particularly as Ms Studleigh was a university graduate undertaking her PGCE year. If this was the kind of practice that was going to take school mathematics into the middle of the twenty-first century, it seemed to me that it was obsolescent – as I had felt identical lessons to be when I was a fourteen-year old pupil not that long after the middle of the twentieth century. Is this the type of maths endorsed by schools of education and teacher training colleges? Or do young teachers feel bound to follow the lead of the department they find themselves in (Schempp, Sparkes and Templin, 1993)?

Tuesday: lesson two – physical education (0940 – 1030)

The next lesson was the most striking example yet of how the putative 300 minute curriculum-time each day was eroded. In a 50-minute physical education lesson, 18 minutes were spent playing netball. The rest of the lesson (32 minutes or 64 per cent of the time) was given to changing into PE kit, walking to the netball courts, putting up the posts, putting on team bibs, choosing opponents, putting the equipment away, returning to he changing rooms and changing back into school uniform.

The PE teacher's opening comment to the class, once they had gathered on the all-weather court was, 'Listen!'.

Tuesday: lessons three and four – art (1045 – 1225)

The first words spoken by the teacher were, 'Be quiet!' The teacher who introduced this double lesson was not taking the class, but was a member of the art department. The classteacher was away and the head of music was covering the double period. The class (Josie's tutor group) was told to continue painting 'Dolly Vardens', which are the decorative knots used in the wrapping of Christmas presents. Societal chat was allowed throughout the 97 minutes of the lesson, with the cover teacher occasionally asking two different groups of boys to stop messing around.

So ended the second morning. It seemed a wasted opportunity that there was not some way of linking the physical/aesthetic lessons of PE, art and, in the afternoon, music. However, there was no connection, and, before the music lesson, there were 50 minutes of science.

Tuesday: lesson five – science (1350 – 1440)

The class was slow to settle to the science lesson after the dinner break, with perhaps the added difficulty of readjusting to an academic subject for such a short while, after a morning mostly spent in PE and art and before a return to another aesthetic subject, music. Added to this, there was a group of boys who were ragging Mr Carter. By 1404, 14 minutes into the lesson, the incredibly patient teacher had had enough and brought the tomfoolery to an end by shouting and punishing three of the boys (in what way I don't know: 'You three, see me at the end of the lesson!').

The next seven minutes were devoted to a whole-class question and answer session on yesterday's lesson. Today I noticed that only boys answered voluntarily. Josie sat doodling with Layla and Nicki. One girl, Samantha, was requested to speak in answer to a question from the teacher. Boys dominated the exchanges during class discussion, and were seated closer to the teacher, the girls contributing no voluntary responses and sitting at the back of the class.

The class then turned to Section 1.21 'Viruses and Bacteria' from the distributed textbook, *Science Kaleidoscope*. The teacher read through the text, clarifying points, asked

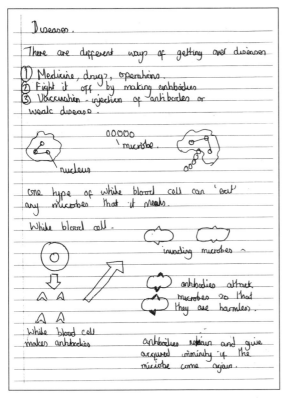

Figure 2.14 Notes and diagrams copied by Josie from the blackboard and her textbook in science, Tuesday

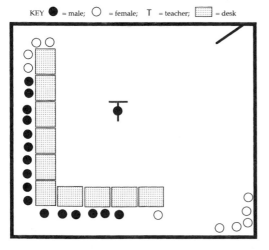

Figure 2.15 Plan of music room, showing seating arrangements, Tuesday

the class to copy some notes he had written on the board before the start of the lesson, and then to copy the diagram from the textbook (Figure 2.14).

Tuesday: lesson six – music (1440 – 1530)

The final lesson of the day repeated this pattern in its most obvious form yet. It was this lesson that first alerted me to the need to gather firm data, rather than just observations of gender bias. I use the word *bias* rather than *prejudice* because I take prejudice to be conscious, whereas I think the teachers were unaware of the way in which they discriminated against girls in some lesson activities. Figure 2.15 shows the seating arrangements. From his position, Mr Larham was effectively facing a class of boys. His eye contact and vocal delivery were to this group. At the edges, sat two groups of girls. The five girls away from the L-shape of the tables were actually sitting on the floor – a poignant symbol of gender supplication? The first half-hour was a teacher-led discussion about the American Civil War (about soldiers . . . about men).

In 29 minutes, boys spoke 71 times. Girls spoke five times. Such was the high level of voluntary contributions from the boys that it was not necessary to ask for a response, but Mr Larham did ask a boy to contribute on four occasions. Such was the low level of voluntary response from the girls that one might have thought that he would have encouraged the girls to contribute on many occasions. Mr Larham did not ask a girl to contribute throughout the 29 minutes. When he wanted pupils to demonstrate a drumbeat, he chose two boys. The remaining eight minutes of the lesson were given to a class singing of *When Johnny Comes*

Marching Home, a sentimental song about a boy-hero returning from war that contains the lines: 'The men will cheer, the boys will shout, the ladies they will all turn out'. The class singing was led by the teacher on piano, and the two chosen boys on drums.

I don't want to appear as if I am pillorying Mr Larham. This was a very entertaining and interesting lesson, one in a series concerning the historical impact of music upon society. Perhaps today's subject – warfare – was of its nature more male-oriented, and other lessons redressed this gender imbalance. I don't know. Mr Larham may well have been surprised at the amount of attention that he gave to the boys at the expense of the girls. It is not something that is that apparent, until you start to look for it. Mr Larham might also have rightly claimed that the boys were more responsive and more eager to be involved and to answer questions. I am sure that the reasons for the pattern of this lesson (which, although more marked, were to be revealed as typical of all lessons) are much more complex than a simple matter of deliberate favouritism.

Tuesday: summary

So far this week, Josie has attended lessons in ten different subjects (each in a different part of the school) and been in six different teaching groups, for which four different grouping systems have been used. A third of the lessons (but half the day's lesson-time) today have not been taken by the usual teacher (maths and art).

Over the first two days of this week, the timetabled 600 minutes of lesson-time have actually been 479 minutes, a loss of just over an hour a day, or 20 per cent of curricular time. One hundred and twenty-seven minutes (21 per cent of lesson-time) have been spent on teacher-led talk, with Josie making seven seconds' contribution. The next highest timescore is for non-academic activities: 123 minutes (18 – PE; 97 – art; 8 – singing = 20.5 per cent). In lessons, pupils have spent 85 minutes doing comprehension exercises (14 per cent), 57 minutes watching videos (9.5 per cent), 51 minutes copying notes (8.5 per cent), and 19 minutes reading textbooks in geography and French (3 per cent). The remaining 17 minutes (3 per cent) have been collaborative group talk (discussing teacher's annotations to homework in English, filling in the questionnaire compiled by the teacher in French).

So, at the end of the second day, certain themes are emerging:

- the loss of curricular time between lessons;
- the boy/girl quota of teacher attention – and possibly the way in which lesson content is influenced by the presence of boys in a class (music);
- the lack of opportunity for, or acknowledgment of, independent learning;
- the lack of any unifying feature between subjects in terms of cross-curricular content or context, other than didactic teaching style;
- the reiteration of the value of silence as a normal working procedure;
- the lottery of what lesson will happen when (science sandwiched between PE, double art and music);
- the low expectations that teachers and pupils appear to share of individual lessons contributing to a holistic curriculum of either a content or a skills-based nature.

Wednesday: lesson one – English (0850 – 0940)

Wednesday's first lesson was English, but not with the same teacher as Monday. Because of timetable difficulties, the class has a different English teacher on Wednesdays, Mrs Farrell.

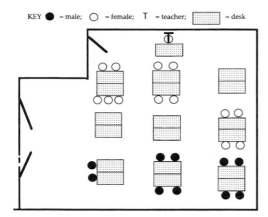

KEY ● = male;   ○ = female;   T = teacher;   ▨ = desk

Figure 2.16 Plan of English room, showing seating arrangements, Wednesday

Thus, the class never have the same English teacher for consecutive lessons. There were 13 girls and 10 boys in the class and in the one-minute whole-class question and answer session to review Act One of *Romeo and Juliet* as far as the class had watched on video, boys answered four times, girls two times, despite the fact that all the boys were seated to the rear of the room, furthest from the teacher. There were no mixed gender groups (Figure 2.16).

The week's observation so far seemed to indicate that boys tended to offer to answer more often than girls (signalling by voice or gesture), and teachers tended to pick boys more. This may have been rewarding their eagerness. Another reason might have been to encourage the boys' involvement, at the expense of the girls, as a form of crowd control; for it was the boys who became more unruly than the girls when not involved. Possibly, because girls did not signal their willingness to answer as often as boys, teachers were trying to be sensitive in not picking a girl whom they felt might be shy or give the wrong answer and feel exposed.

For the next 14 minutes pupils read, in groups, Act One, Scene Five of *Romeo and Juliet* and were asked to prepare a synopsis. Josie and Sara joined with Ruth and Emma and chose their speaking parts. They then read the text with no show of understanding. They did not pause to discuss meaning. By the time they were finished, the teacher called an end to the activity, so the girls were unable to prepare a synopsis. A brief (four minutes) session was given to whole-class discussion, with Mrs Farrell asking questions that directed pupils' attention to character ('What's the nurse's attitude to this? How does she react?') and imagery ('What's all that about pilgrims? Who's the pilgrim?') Boys responded four times, girls five.

Mrs Farrell introduced Act Two, concentrating on the introductory Chorus speech and then asking three of the groups to prepare it for a reading to the class and three of the groups to prepare a summary or explanation of it. Josie's group read the piece in silence. No-one spoke until a minute before the activity ended, and then it was societal chat about making a T-shirt in the next lesson. From Mrs Farrell's introduction to when she called the class together eight minutes elapsed. The presentation and explanation took up another eight minutes. In the discussion, boys spoke seven times, girls not once.

There was a final four-minute activity: a 'class' reading of Act Two, Scene One. This scene only has male characters, all of whose lines were read aloud by boys. Mrs Farrell broke into the dialogue to explain what it was about. The girls sat silently. The bell went. The lesson ended.

The pattern of micro-activities within short, discrete lessons is shown again in this lesson. There may be several reasons for this, two of which have often been expressed to me by teachers. Firstly, there is a feeling that pupils can't concentrate for more than a few minutes on any one activity. Secondly, teachers say that they feel pressured into moving quickly from one topic and activity to another because there's an imposing empirical body of knowledge that must be rushed through in each National Curriculum subject syllabus.

Wednesday: lesson two – personal and social education (0940 – 1030)

The next lesson was PSE: Personal and Social Education. This aspect of education (upon which the curriculum is based according to the aims of the school) is viewed as another discrete subject and distilled into a single weekly lesson (i.e. about 3 per cent of a pupil's education). One of the potential problems of this approach is that if PSE is regarded as a subject, then the responsibility for personal and social education is more likely to be seen as a particular department's specialist responsibility and therefore not the responsibility of all other subject teachers. This tends to reinforce the idea of a subject curriculum consisting of supposedly value-free knowledge: knowledge is extant from a personal and social context. This might well be one of the reasons why teachers don't question the endless diet of whole-class discussion and comprehension: they really don't see any responsibility for PSE so wouldn't think of structuring their lessons (let alone restructuring the timetable) to accommodate the kind of pedagogy that encourages personal and social education – the practices associated with independent learning.

Having said that, the PSE lesson was the most imaginative and, at face value, educative of the week – because it was about personal and social education. The week before, the entire Year 9 cohort, in their tutor groups, working in friendship groups of four or five pupils, had been given the brief of designing and making a T-shirt from paper materials, each shirt to represent a theme or issue to which each small group wanted to give publicity. The seating arrangements for Josie's tutor group during the making of the T-shirts shows that only one of the collaborative groups was mixed gender – a trio of two boys and a girl (Figure 2.17).

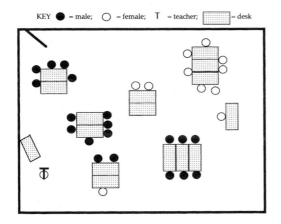

KEY ● = male;   ○ = female;   T = teacher;   ▨ = desk

Figure 2.17 Plan of tutor room, showing seating arrangements for personal and social education, Wednesday

The first 22 minutes of today's lesson were given to hurriedly finishing the shirt, before the eight tutor groups assembled in the drama hall to be an audience for each other's work. A catwalk had been erected by GCSE Drama pupils and a public address system provided by GCSE Music pupils. Each group had nominated a pupil-model to show their creation. Two teachers (head of maths and head of creative arts, but in their capacity as Year 9 tutors) were the comperes. This worked well, given the short timescale, for the teachers, in role as the comperes, were able to direct the assembly of 200 excited pupils without recourse to authoritarian traffic-control.

It was a very colourful occasion, a community occasion, with generous cheering and clapping, no booing or catcalling. Josie, the girl who has so far spoken for seven seconds this week, hammed it up as a Madonna clone, complete with conical-breasted T-shirt bearing the slogan 'No! to animal tested cosmetics'. Green, welfare and health issues predominated: in 25 minutes, to the accompaniment of the comperes' commentary and a techno-funk backbeat, a panoply of socially-aware and personally confident pupils came together to celebrate their project. Without making a head count, I would say that the models representing each group were split pretty evenly between boys and girls.

For the first time during the week's tracking, there was simultaneous evidence of some of the factors of independent learning: collaborative and cooperative groupwork, individual responsibility, pupil-designed tasks, assessment and research, community and environmental involvement (in that the lesson required an awareness of the outside world, but not in the involvement of the community or the use of the environment in the lesson), a sense of audience (pupils' peers to whom the work was presented), presentation in a medium which did not exclude some sections of the community. This could have been a combined design, English, media studies, drama, movement and art project, informed by work in the sciences. Instead, teachers and pupils in those subjects, because of the timetabled notion of PSE as a discrete subject, were prevented from collaborating and cooperating in an exciting project; and from seeing how their lessons could be enlivened and strengthened by a more active and effective approach to the corpus of knowledge within their own specialist subject.

Wednesday: lesson three – religious education (1045 – 1135)

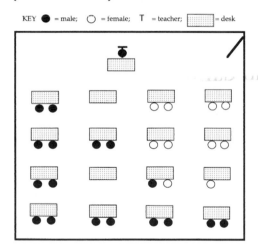

KEY ● = male;   ○ = female;   T = teacher;   ▦ = desk

Figure 2.18 Plan of religious education room, showing seating arrangements, Wednesday

After break, the week's RE lesson. The class of 27, 10 girls and 17 boys were grouped as in Figure 2.18.

The first 20 minute activity was a whole-class reading and discussion of a passage on Islam. Mr James set the lesson in the context of previous work the class had undertaken on other major world religions. He had grouped the desks so that the class was facing him in pairs. Thus, he had cut down the likelihood of inattention and societal muttering. He was sensitive to the reading level of the text, checking for potential difficulties before asking a pupil to read a paragraph. In discussion, boys spoke 21 times. No girl spoke. In choosing readers, I think Mr James tried to redress this balance: he asked three girl readers and one boy, and one girl offered to read and he accepted her offer. For nine minutes, the pupils then made notes based on the text they had read and discussed. Mr James asked the pupils to work individually and silently and they did (Figure 2.19).

During this time, Mr James set up a video about Islam and for nine minutes the class watched and took notes. The teacher used the pause control to enforce points. Boys spoke four times; no girl spoke. For the final six minutes pupils were asked to redraft their notes (Figure 2.20).

I thought that, of its kind this was (apart from the boy/girl ratio in discussion) an excellent lesson: it was well-paced, it was set in a context of continuing learning, it used written and media texts, it encouraged note-taking rather than note-copying, it encouraged the pupils to do something with their notes (redrafting). The atmosphere was

introduce
baby is Islamic birth- happens immediately to their
washed 1st call to prayer in right ear and faith
Command to worship in left ear
to symbolise and stay
pently Shave hair off and cover
bury head in olive oil, weight of hair
hair is given to the poor in pounds.
Male babys circumsised soon after birth.
Goat or sheep are sacreficed 2/3 to
relatives rest to poor.

Bismillah
4 years 4 months 4 days, new clothes
and sweets after child goes to Madrasah
regulery taught to pray and read Arabic.

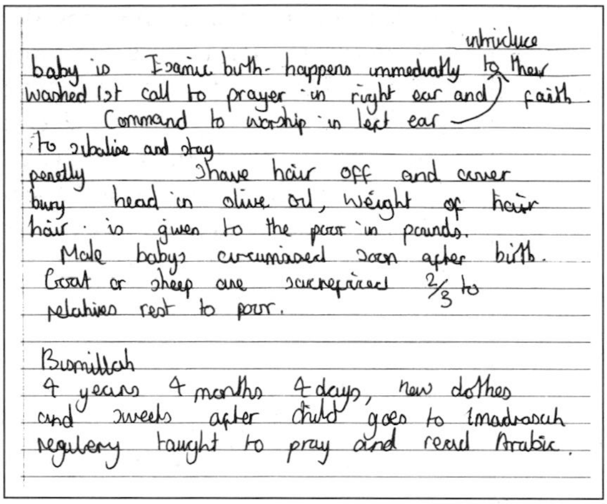

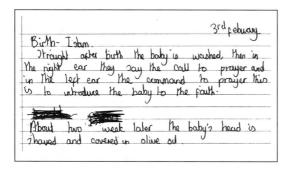

Figure 2.19 Notes made by Josie based on the textbook reading in religious education, Wednesday

3rd febuary
Birth- Islam.
Straight after birth the baby is washed, then in the right ear they say the call to prayer and in the left ear the command to prayer this is to introduce the baby to the faith.

About two week later the baby's head is shaved and covered in olive oil.

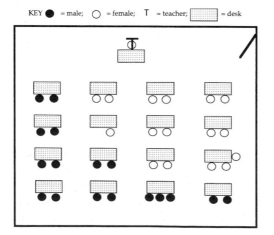

Figure 2.20 Josie's redrafted RE notes, Wednesday

Figure 2.21 Plan of the German room showing seating arrangements

purposeful. But it was only good of its kind. It was essentially the same as most lessons: teacher-led talk, pupils writing individually and (where it could be enforced) silently. I think this teacher had extended the professional limits of competence within this teaching style, but I also think he had extended the pupils' learning only fractionally more than any other lesson. That is to say, that the quality of presentation of this kind of lesson may vary much more widely than the quality and range of learning within it. So, even when there is an experienced and capable practitioner (like geography and music) this way of working doesn't engage and empower pupils in the way that the type of learning encouraged in the PSE lesson can.

Wednesday: lesson four – German (1135 – 1225)

The last lesson of the morning session was German (also Josie's twelfth different subject of the week). German was taken by Mrs Thomson, the head of modern languages, and the German group comprised the pupils who were in the top set for French. To take German, they must miss other lessons. Josie misses a PE lesson and a lesson she is not in the top set for (English) to do German, but then misses her second German lesson of the week to have violin tuition. There were 33 pupils in the class (the same 33 as for Josie's French group), 16 girls and 17 boys. They sat as they did for French (Figure 2.21).

Mrs Thomson explained that the pupils were going to listen to an audiotape in German. She pointed out some phrases that she had

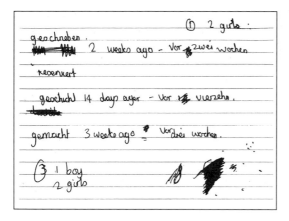

Figure 2.22 Notes made by Josie whilst listening to an audiotape in German, Wednesday

written on the board and that she particularly wanted the class to listen out for. The pupils listened to the tape twice, making notes (Figure 2.22). Then Mrs Thomson replayed the tape to the whole-class and asked for responses. Boys answered on six occasions, girls twice, and once she asked a girl for her answer.

Wednesday: lessons five and six – design and technology (1350 – 1530)

After lunch, Josie had a double lesson (the rest of the school day) of design and technology. The class (ten boys and ten girls) worked individually. They were making small boxes to a common pattern, although they were encouraged to bring their own ideas to the design: the edges could be barrelled or bevelled, the lid horizontal or sloping, drilled or plugged with a design, the bottom could have felt glued to it.

Work on the heavy machinery (drills, lathe, circular saw) was undertaken by Mr Idwallendar at a pupil's request and to the pupil's design. Pupils chatted societally as they glued and sandpapered.

Wednesday: summary

Today, Josie had twelve activities in her six lessons, (five of these in English and four in RE). Seventy-one minutes were spent in whole-class discussion (24 per cent), 49 minutes in groupwork (16 per cent). Forty-one minutes (14 per cent) were spent in room changes and lesson registration. Fifteen minutes (5 per cent) were spent writing (nine taking notes and six redrafting) and nine minutes (3 per cent) were spent watching a video. No time was spent on comprehension or individual reading (although in RE twenty minutes of whole-class time was based on the shared reading of a textbook). One hundred and fifteen minutes (38 per cent) were spent watching, or performing in, the fashion show and making little boxes.

Apart from the PSE lesson, there was no evidence of the factors of independent learning.

Thursday: lesson one – maths (0850 – 0940)

If people are more alert and attentive in the morning, then the maths department benefits more than any other subject: three of the week's four lessons are the first of the day. Ms Studleigh's lesson followed the usual pattern of the prevalent school pedagogy, although this morning she did not dictate notes. The pupils sat in the same places and the same single-gender pairs as in previous lessons – I know this because I checked with Josie and Sara (Figure 2.23).

The lesson started with a six-minute marking of the homework, with pupils putting up their hands to give the answer. Occasionally Ms Studleigh asked a pupil who had not put her (invariably her) hand up to answer. Ms Studleigh asked boys to answer 14 times, girls 4 times. I decided to adapt the data-collection form to allow me to collect these data more clearly: How many times do girls volunteer to contribute to whole-class discussion (by raising their hands) but are not picked in favour of a boy with his hand up? How many times do boys or girls pre-empt silent volunteering by calling out the answer unasked? (Boys seem to do this a lot, so that girls with their hands up have the chance to answer snatched away from them.) How many times are pupils who do not put their hands up asked to answer?

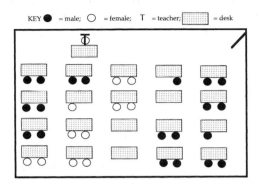

KEY ● = male; ○ = female; T = teacher; ▦ = desk

Figure 2.23 Plan of maths lesson showing seating arrangements, Thursday

After the homework was marked, Ms Studleigh spent four minutes explaining the task for the rest of the lesson: Exercise 26 G p. 359 *ST(P) Mathematics 3B*. The class then worked individually, in more or less silence for the next 26 minutes. Ms Studleigh moved around the desks, advising and assisting.

Thursday: lesson two – English (0940 – 1030)

The walk from the Maths room to H1, for English, is from one end of the school to the other (at least it is for those who are in Set Two for maths and Josie's group for English). Once again there was a gradual drifting in of pupils from various parts of the school. Pupils sat in the same places as the last English lesson. The register was taken and homework handed back to those who had done it on time and gathered in from those who hadn't, and arrangements made with a third group of pupils, those who still hadn't done their homework.

Thus, it was ten minutes into the lesson before the first activity took place, and considering the above, it was not that successful because it was, as in Patty's last English lesson, a pair sharing of the homework. Pupils were encouraged to comment on each other's work. Josie and Sara did this cursorily ('Yeh, it's good isn't it', 'Yours is good,') and then chatted until, after seven minutes Patty brought this activity to a close. Patty then asked the pupils to 'close your eyes and think of someone you really fancy'. Then pupils were to write down a list of words that described the object of their desire, individually, in silence. Then, if they wanted, they could show the list to a partner. This was not a very purposeful activity: the pupils are at a self-conscious age and took refuge in giggles and (the boys) ribaldry. Once again I was aware of the stipulation of silent, individual writing that can only be shared afterwards. Josie did write her list but wouldn't show it to anyone (later in the week she told me she had written 16 words).

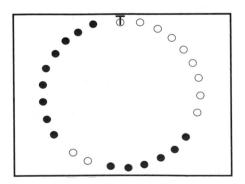

Figure 2.24 Plan of English lesson showing seating arrangements, Thursday

Patty then asked the class to draw up their chairs into a communal circle in the large space on one side of the room. The circle arranged itself as in Figure 2.24. Patty chose a girl to read the part of Juliet and a boy to read the part of Romeo. Until the end of the lesson (19 minutes) the two pupils read and Patty translated what they were saying. This was not the best of passages for a class reading, with only two speaking parts. It would have made a good passage for pair work.

Thursday: lesson three – English . . . German . . . violin (1045 – 1135)

The English lesson was to continue after break, but this was the English lesson that Josie missed to go to German. But it was also the lesson that Josie missed to go to her violin lesson – not quite true: she missed half of it. So to German, the usual settling down, register-taking and then ten minutes of oral pair work before Josie had to leave.

Thursday: lesson four – physical education (1135 – 1225)

The last lesson of the morning was girls' dance. As this was in the hall, there wasn't the loss of time in walking out to the pitches and the activity time was 25 minutes – half the lesson-time of 50 minutes.

Thursday: lesson five – French (1350 – 1440)

The first lesson of the afternoon was French, but those pupils in the top set for maths, about half the class, went to do a Maths Challenge, leaving eight boys and seven girls. Mrs Thomson took them to the library where the pupils read individually, silently, from French story texts they chose from a selection offered by the teacher from the *Bibliobus* series. This session lasted for 45 minutes, 30 of which were spent reading.

Thursday: lesson six – Geography (1440 – 1530)

The last lesson of the day was geography, this time in the computer room. Bill (the geography teacher and headteacher) was present, but the lesson was taken by Ms Costerdine, an English teacher who has a cross-curricular responsibility for information technology. Working to Ms Costerdine's precise instructions, the groups entered the information provided by Bill on to a simple database programme (Grass). There were 10 girls and 17 boys in the class, but only one mixed-gender group was formed at the computer consoles (Figure 2.25). The lesson lasted 45 minutes.

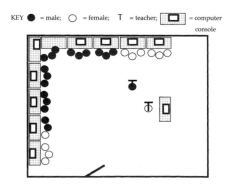

Figure 2.25 Plan of geography lesson showing seating arrangements, Thursday

Thursday: summary

In her six lessons today, Josie has had a student for maths, a different teacher from her last lesson in English, missed the second of her English lessons to go to German, and then missed half her German to go to a violin lesson, had a French lesson from which half the class was missing because they had gone to an extra maths activity, and gone to a geography lesson supervised by the headteacher and led by an English teacher giving instructions in information technology.

Today Josie had ten activities in her six lessons (three in Maths, three in English and one in each of her other lessons). Ninety-eight minutes (from a timetabled 300 minutes) were spent in room changes and lesson register-taking (33 per cent), 45 minutes (15 per cent) in entering information on to a database – which I have not included under groupwork as only one pupil typed at a time, to the precise instructions of the teacher and with no group collaboration – 44 minutes (15 per cent) were spent in teacher-led talk, 30 minutes in reading in French (10 per cent), 26 minutes in sums (9 per cent), 25 minutes were spent in dance (8 per cent), 22 minutes in groupwork (7 per cent) and ten minutes in note-taking (3 per cent).

Friday: lesson one – maths (0850 – 0940)

The first lesson of the day was the last maths lesson of the week. The pupils sat in their usual places. This lesson was not related to the other three, which were about different kinds of triangles, but consisted of the first of the term's three 'assessment assignments' – a timed test. Ms Studleigh spent four minutes explaining the test (boys spoke five times, girls not once) using the test sheet itself (Figure 2.26). She also referred pupils to notes she had written on the board beforehand (Figure 2.27). Then she dictated an introduction before the pupils began the test (Figure 2.28). For the rest of the lesson the pupils worked individually, with Ms Studleigh explaining but not correcting or giving answers (Figure 2.29).

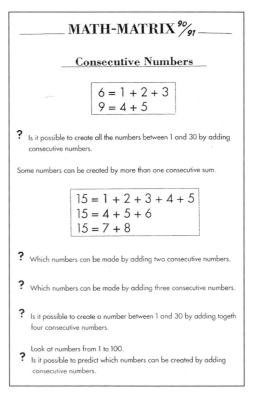

Figure 2.26 Assignment sheet used in maths, Friday

Maths Assignment: CONSECUTIVE NUMBERS

- Begin this lesson and finish for homework.
- Do all the work in rough FIRST.
- Compare answers - there may be more than one way of expressing answer using consecutive numbers

WRITE UP

Introduction - explain what you are doing
1-30 answers
Comments: what do you notice?

For the write-up: include as much information as possible - the more you put into it the more credits you could get.
Are there any numbers that cannot be done?
Can you see any patterns? Explain this
Do we include 0?

In Your Comments / Conclusion

State which nos between 1-30 cannot be done - do you notice anything about this?
Is there a pattern for predicting which nos can be done? -
Investigate some numbers between 30 & 100

Explain CLEARLY any patterns

Figure 2.27 Notes written on the blackboard in maths, Friday

1	−	Intro Explain	1
2	-	what u did.	2
3	1+2		4
4	-	1 - 30 answers	8
5	2+3		16
6	1+2+3		
7	3+4	Conclusion	
8	-	state which nos can't be done	
9	4+5	pattern	
10	1+2+3+4	pattern which nos can be	
11	5+6	done.	
12	3+4+5	Investigate nos between 30	
13	6+7	Explain clearly any	
14	2+3+4+5	patterns clearly.	
15	1+2+3+4+5 / 4+5+6 / 7+8 .		
16	-		
17	8+9		
18	5+6+7 / 3+4+5+6		
19	9+10		
20	2+3+4+5+6		
21	1+2+3+4+5+6 / 6+7+8 / 10+11		
22	4+5+6+7		
23	11+12		
24	7+8+9		
25	12+13		
26	5+6+7+8		
27	2+3+4+5+6+7 / 8+9+10		
28	1+2+3+4+5+6+7		
29	14+15		
30	4+5+6+7 / 9+10+11, 6+7+8.		

Figure 2.28 Josie's notes, written in maths, Friday

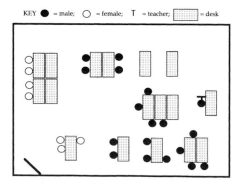

Consecutive Numbers   5/2/9

We have to find out which
numbers between 1 and 30 have
the sum of consecutive numbers.

eg 15 = 1+2+3+4+5
    15 = 4+5+6
    15 = 7+8.

1 Can not be done
2 Can not be done
3 1+2
4 Can not be done
5 2+3
6 1+2+3
7 3+4
8 Can not be done
9 4+5
10 1+2+3+4
11 5+6
12 3+4+5
13 6+7
14 2+3+4+5
15 1+2+3+4+5/4+5+6 /7+8
16 Can not be done
17 8+9
18 5+6+7/3+4+5+6
19 9+10
20 2+3+4+5+6
21 1+2+3+4+5 +6/ 6+7+8/10+11
22 4+5+6+7
23 11+12
24 7+8+9
25 12+13
26 5+6+7+8.

Figure 2.29 Josie's responses to the assessment assignment, maths, Friday

KEY ● = male; ○ = female; T = teacher; ▦ = desk

Figure 2.30 Plan of the science room showing seating arrangements, Friday

Friday: lesson two – design and technology (0940 – 1030)

This was a seamless continuation of the previous DT lesson earlier in the week, with the ten boys and ten girls working on their wooden boxes and chatting to each other and the teacher.

Friday: lessons three and four – science (1045 – 1225)

After break, the class had a double lesson (100 minutes) of science. There were 17 boys and 7 girls in this top set (Figure 2.30).

Mr Carter introduced a new topic (the second of the week), Respiration, which the class had some knowledge of, having studied the topic the previous year. In the three-minute introduction to the first activity, Mr Carter chose eight boys to speak and three girls, and seven boys and two girls called answers out. Given the gender ratio, this was a fair distribution, although these figures don't take into account repeat utterances – it could have been the same girl speaking five times. For four minutes, the pupils labelled a diagram and Mr Carter read out the answers (Figure 2.31).

For the next 26 minutes pupils made their own notes explaining the breathing process. There was a fair amount of societal chat during this activity: Josie's group worked quickly, efficiently and individually and completed the task in just over half the time allowed. They then talked to me as the teacher went round the groups, checking their notes (Figure 2.32).

For ten minutes, Mr Carter summarized the process of respiration so that pupils could amend or add to their notes and then, with the help of a boy, he spent seven minutes demonstrating a simple experiment the class would conduct in their table groups. The experiment (blowing through lime water to prove that people exhale carbon dioxide) took five minutes and for a further 18 minutes pupils wrote up the experiment, to these instructions written on the blackboard (Figures 2.33 and 2.34).

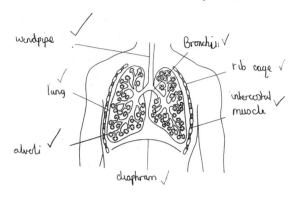

Figure 2.31 Josie's labelling of the diagram, science, Friday

Breathing in and out 5/2/9

Air moves in and out of the lungs because when the diaphragm moves down the lungs full up and when the diaphragms moves up the lungs empty the ribs move up and down as well, when you breathe in the air pressure changes from when you breathe out. when you breathe out the air pressure is greater when you breathe in the air pressure is less.

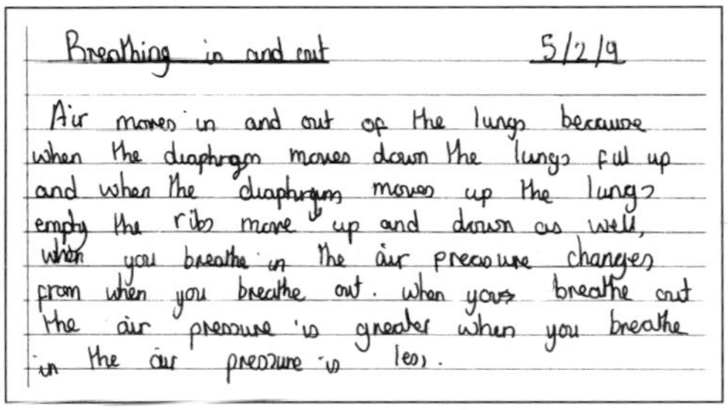

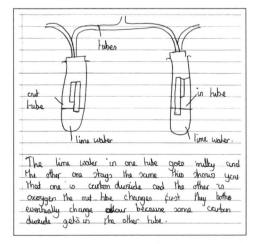

Figure 2.32 Notes Josie made from her textbook in science, Friday

The Huff and Puff Apparatus

1 Draw equipment (Label "in" tube and "out" tube)

2 What does the lime water do?

3 What does this show you?

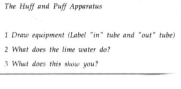

Figure 2.33 Notes written on the blackboard in science, Friday

The lime water in one tube goes milky and the other one stays the same this shows you that one is carbon dioxide and the other is oxygen the out tube changes first they boths eventually change colour because some carbon dioxide gets in the other tube.

Figure 2.34 Josie's account of the experiment in science, Friday

Respiration.

Respiration goes on in every cell in the body. Respiration means burning up food to release energy from it. Burning is an oxidation process. so oxygen is needed for respiration, carbon dioxide is produced by burning, so is a waste product of respiration.

Equation

glucose + oxygen → carbon dioxide + water + Energy.

$C_6 H_{12} O_6 + 6O_2 \rightarrow 6CO_2 + 6H_2O$

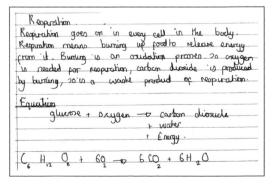

Figure 2.35 Notes that Josie copied from the blackboard in science, Friday

KEY ● = male; ○ = female; T = teacher; ▭ = desk

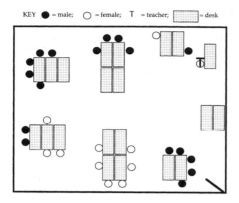

Figure 2.36 Plan of history room showing seating arrangements, Friday

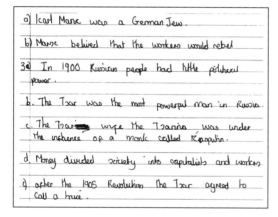

Figure 2.37 Classwork done by Josie in history, Friday

For the final 14 minutes Mr Carter wrote notes on the board which pupils copied into their books (Figure 2.35). During this activity, boys asked five questions, girls none. I noted other categories I would include on a form designed to gather data about whole-class discussion: when are pupils answering and when are they asking and when are they speculating or expressing an opinion and what is the gender difference if any?

Friday: lesson five – physical education (1350 – 1440)

After lunch, the girls had netball and improved on their changing time so that 23 minutes of the 50-minute lesson were spent on the game.

Friday: lesson six – history (1440 – 1530)

The final lesson of the week was history and Mrs Burton introduced the lesson with a whole-class question and answer activity, drawing on what the class had done in the previous history lesson. Boys spoke nine times, girls not once. Is there an unwritten code that says that girls don't (won't?) contribute to whole-class discussion? Or is it that the teacher concentrates on the boys as a form of control? Certainly the boys were particularly restless – as they had been in science (Figure 2.36).

After four minutes, Mrs Burton asked the class to continue with their worksheets. It really was noisy now and I could see that the teacher was going to face a grim slog to the bell and having me as an observer wasn't going to help. I asked her if she minded if I left the lesson to do some photo-copying and returned at the end of the lesson to take Josie's latest answers for photo-copying. When I returned there was such a noise I didn't go in, but waited for the bell. Mrs Burton had collected the work in, but when I asked if I could photocopy Josie's and return it she said: 'Oh, you needn't bother, they don't really need it. It was just some classwork' (Figure 2.37). It was on this note that the week ended.

Friday: summary

Today, Josie's 300 minutes of lesson time were divided like this: 70 minutes (24 per cent) in room changes and lesson register-taking, 52 minutes spent note-taking (17 per cent), 37 minutes doing sums (12 per cent), 34 doing comprehension (11 per cent), 32 in whole-class discussion (11 per cent), 5 in groupwork (2 per cent) and 68 minutes (23 per cent) in

Table 2.1 The distribution of the 1500 minutes of Josie's timetabled week

Activity	Monday	Tuesday	Wednesday	Thursday	Friday	Totals	%
Room changes & register	45	76	41	98	66	326	21.5
Teacher-led talk	86	43	73	81	28	311	20.5
Note taking & comp. exs.	94	38	9	10	96	247	16.5
Art & design	0	97	90	0	45	232	15.5
Maths	18	20	0	26	37	101	7
Groupwork	0	0	47	15	5	67	4.5
P.E.	0	18	0	25	23	66	4.5
Vid-watching	57	0	9	0	0	66	4.5
Reading	0	0	0	45	0	45	3
PSE show	0	0	25	0	0	25	1.5
Singing	0	8	0	0	0	8	0.5
Redrafting	0	0	6	0	0	6	0.5
Totals	300	300	300	300	300	1500	100

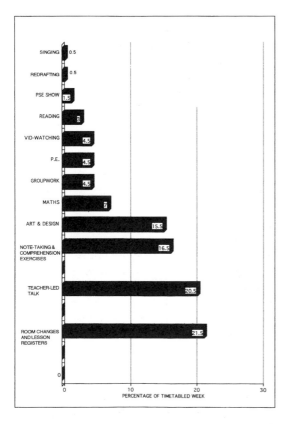

Figure 2.38 Bar graph showing the distribution of the 1500 minutes of Josie's timetabled week

other non-academic activities (DT and PE). There were 14 activities in the day's five lessons, nine of these in the double science lesson, eight of which involved some form of note-making. Josie was in a different pupil group for each lesson.

Josie gets taught a lesson: summary of the week

Distribution of the 1500 minutes of Josie's timetabled week

Table 2.1 shows Josie's learning activities, generically, throughout the curriculum. Figure 2.38 illustrates Table 2.1 in graphic form. Art, design and PE stand apart, but in all the other subjects there is a common approach to teaching and learning styles and a common notion of a knowledge-based curriculum, so that pupil activities tend to be much the same in different lessons: note-taking, comprehension exercises, watching videos and a great deal of whole-class, teacher-led 'discussion'. This was a typical week. I asked Josie every day if this or that lesson was normal, ordinary, 'the kind of thing you usually do', and she said that it was.

The greatest block of curricular time is not actually spent in lessons, but in moving between them. Room changes and lesson registers take 21.5 per cent of the time – the equivalent of about a day each week, or one year of secondary education between the ages of eleven and sixteen. Teacher-led talk consumes the greatest amount of lesson-time (20.5 per cent), followed by pupils working individually on note-making and comprehension exercises from textbooks or duplicated worksheets (16.5 per cent). Art and design lessons take up 15.5 per cent of the week. The remaining 26 per cent of the week consists of maths (7 per cent), groupwork, PE and video-watching (4.5 per cent each), silent reading (3 per cent), the PSE presentation (1.5 per cent) and singing and redrafting (0.5 per cent each).

Lesson content

An examination of Josie's talking, reading and writing during the week demonstrates the low level of cognitive and affective engagement required in her schooling, the piecemeal nature of the knowledge-based curriculum and the essentially passive and limited nature of the learning process. Chapter 1 identified general practices likely to promote or suppress educational citizenship. The general practices regarded as likely to develop educational citizenship were those designed to promote a critical disposition, moral awareness and an equal social interaction of adult–pupil and pupil–pupil relationships (symmetrical reciprocity). There was little evidence of such practices in Josie's lessons. General practices likely to suppress such development had been identified in the theory as: indoctrination (by suppressing the development of a critical disposition), the isolation of the curriculum from social relevance, the promotion of the cognitive at the expense of the affective, hierarchical systems of authority/responsibility, and complementary reciprocity in adult–pupil and pupil–pupil relationships. Such practices were typical of the lessons observed during the tracking of Josie through her timetabled week.

In whole-class discussion, or teacher-led question and answer sessions, Josie barely contributed and in the small-groupwork most of the talk was societal rather than task-related. These talk activities (367 minutes), to which can be added the societal chat of art, and design and technology formed the largest group of 'learning' activities.

Josie's personal, silent reading was very limited: 49 minutes for the week; and on three days she did no reading at all. The 49 minutes spent on reading covered three activities in two lessons, and each time were used as a time-filler. The first reading activity was to read from a geography textbook for seven minutes at the end of a lesson; an activity mirrored in a French lesson (for 12 minutes) later in the day. The only other reading of the week was a 'make-do' lesson in French when half the class had gone to a sponsored maths activity, and the remaining pupils read French stories.

There were other forms of reading: the 81 minutes during the week devoted to comprehension (in geography and history) required the reading of worksheets. In English there was a shared reading of *Romeo and Juliet*, in small groups and as a whole-class. The 122 minutes of note-taking required the reading from textbooks or from the blackboard. The 66 minutes of video-watching can be regarded as the reading of media texts. Other than the French stories, Josie had no opportunity to choose any text for herself; and the texts selected by the teachers were dull, undemanding, irrelevant. The learning context made it easy for pupils to abdicate from most of the reading if they wished: mindlessly copying from the board, cribbing a partner's comprehension answers, daydreaming during the videos, not following the text in a class reading, not bothering to seek any meaning of the text when reading in small groups.

Similar criticisms can be made of the writing: dull and undemanding and repetitive in lesson after lesson: recording someone else's data, either by copying, summarizing or short comprehension answers. There was virtually no opportunity to make a personal statement, for imaginative writing, for discursive writing, for extended writing. Little value seemed to be given to the writing: only 6 minutes in 1500 (0.4 per cent) were given to any further shaping of a first draft and a teacher gave away a pupil's text which she had spent a lesson creating, explaining, 'It's only classwork'.

Other learning activities also seemed purposeless and profligate in the consumption of curricular time. Are production-line decorative carpentry and painting Dolly Vardens (250 minutes) the kind of practices suited to a design and technology curriculum for the twenty-first century? Was 101 minutes of sums, which seemed to have no application to real life needs, useful?

The way in which the collection of lessons that constitutes Josie's timetable is compiled lacks cohesion: one subject follows another without any connection or appropriacy, lessons in a particular subject can occur at any time of the day, pupil grouping systems vary, she misses some lessons to go to others because the timetable is overcrowded, she has more than one teacher for the same subject. From a timetabled 1500 minutes, 21.5 per cent was lost in the room changes that are required to sustain a curriculum that, for Josie, is divided into thirteen discrete areas and a timetable that, for Josie, is divided into 27 blocks, 24 of 50 minutes' length and three of 100 minutes. During the week, Josie changed rooms 30 times.

Looking at the work produced by Josie, does she benefit from the subject specialism that the National Curriculum imposes? It is the insistence on subject specialism that necessitates the compartmentalization of knowledge, of disruptive room changes and, because of the short time span of lessons, the expediency of short activities that do not allow the development of personal engagement with the subject being studied.

Talk

It seemed that silence had a talismanic property and its imposition was the first criterion of the successful teacher. ('I'll teach you not to talk in my lessons' said Ms Studleigh, the student.) It was as if teachers had chosen the criterion that was the most difficult to impose – and maybe this was how it was viewed, that the best teacher was the one who could bend the class to her will, the most potent representation of which would be to make pupils act against their powerful natural desire to communicate with each other. This provokes the image of teacher as controller not facilitator, and there was much evidence of this, both in the daily life of the school and within lessons. However, all the teachers fought a losing battle to impose silence upon their classes. There were examples of societal chat in every lesson. Yet few thought to use pupil-to-pupil talk as a positive part of the learning process. What talk there was, was directed by, and through the teacher, who decided the subject and direction of the talk and who should speak (Table 2.2).

In this process, boys appeared to gain a much greater share of the teacher's attention than girls. Table 2.2 shows the 12 occasions upon which teacher-led talk was recorded systematically. It shows the number of boys and girls in each class and differentiates between unrequested and requested responses to the teacher. An unrequested response refers to when a pupil talked without being specifically selected by the teacher, but the teacher accepted his response. For instance, in geography Bill asked, 'What's the answer to that one, then, anyone?'

Table 2.2 Pupils' contributions to whole-class discussion, Key Stage 3

Activity number	Subject	No. of boys	No. of girls	Boys' unrequested responses	Girls' unrequested responses	Boys' requested responses	Girls' requested responses
28	Music	16	10	67	5	4	0
30	English	10	13	4	2	0	0
31	English	10	13	4	5	0	0
33	English	10	13	7	0	0	0
37	R.E.	17	10	21	1	1	3
39	R.E.	17	10	4	0	0	0
41	German	17	16	6	2	0	1
43	Maths	20	11	5	5	14	4
53	Maths	20	11	5	0	0	0
55	Science	17	7	7	2	8	3
63	Science	17	7	5	0	0	0
65	History	17	10	8	0	1	0
Totals		188	131	143	22	28	11

and Simon called out his response, which Bill acknowledged. A requested response refers to when a teacher chooses a particular pupil (who may or may not have signalled a desire to speak) to respond. For instance, in science, despite the frantic urgings of 'Sir! Sir!' from boys with arms stretched high, and ignoring called-out answers, Mr Carter asked Samantha.

Table 2.2 clearly shows that there is a higher incidence of boys than girls talking voluntarily (unrequested responses) and being asked, by the teacher, to talk (requested responses). From a total of 165 unrequested responses, boys make 143 and girls 22. Of the 39 times on which teachers chose a particular pupil to speak, teachers chose boys 28 times and girls 11 times. There is only one occasion when girls speak more often than boys (Activity 31, four minutes of teacher-led talk in English, when boys speak four times, girls, five times). However, in nine of the lesson activities from which data were gathered, there were more boys than girls in the class so the raw scores of Table 2.2 need to be analysed in a way that takes the gender ratio of pupils within a class into consideration when comparing the talk responses of boys and girls. Table 2.3 seeks to do this (Table 2.3).

Table 2.3 converts the raw figures of Table 2.2 to percentages. If there is a more or less equal involvement in teacher-led talk by boys and girls, then the response percentage, by gender, should be close to the class percentage by gender. For instance, if a class consisted of 60 per cent boys and 40 per cent girls, then these percentages should be reflected in the response percentages (about 60 per cent for the boys and 40 per cent for the girls) if the teacher has sought to ensure a fair and balanced contribution from both boys and girls to 'whole-class discussion'. However, this is not the case. In music, for instance, boys comprise 61.5 per cent of the class number but account for 93 per cent of the unrequested responses and 100 per cent of the requested responses. Only on one occasion (Activity 43, maths) is the boys' response percentage less than their number percentage; in crude terms, boys get more than their fair share of teacher-time and attention in teacher-led talk that is purportedly open to the whole class. Figure 2.39 illustrates the Table 2.3 data concerning the boys in graphic form. The bar-chart clearly shows that, after allowing for the gender ratio of the classes, boys are three or four times more likely to make unrequested responses in all subjects; and that in four of the six subjects in which data were collected, boys were three or four times more likely than girls to be asked by teachers for their responses.

Table 2.3 Contributors to whole-class discussion by % of the class population

Activity number	Subject	% of boys in the lesson	% of girls in the lesson	Boys', % of unrequested responses	Girls', % of unrequested responses	Boys' %, of requested responses	Girls', % of requested responses
28	Music	61.5	38.5	93	7	100	0
30	English	43.5	56.5	66.5	33.5	0	0
31	English	43.5	56.5	44.5	55.5	0	0
33	English	43.5	56.5	100	0	0	0
37	R.E.	63	37	95.5	4.5	25	75
39	R.E.	63	37	100	0	0	0
41	German	55	45	75	25	0	100
43	Maths	64.5	35.5	50	50	78	22
53	Maths	64.5	35.5	100	0	0	0
55	Science	71	29	78	22	73	27
63	Science	71	29	100	0	0	0
65	History	63	37	100	0	100	0

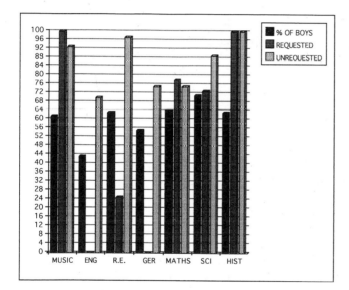

Figure 2.39 Bar chart showing the proportion of boys' responses to teacher-led talk, in comparison with the gender ratio of the classes

Over the 12 activities for which responses were recorded, boys consisted of 59 per cent of the number of pupils, yet had 77.5 per cent of the number of unrequested responses and 64.5 per cent of the requested responses. Girls, 41 per cent of the population, had only 22.5 per cent of the unrequested answers and 35.5 per cent of the requested answers. The closer correlation between number and requested answers suggests that teachers do attempt to balance boys and girls (although they still tend to favour the boys) when choosing particular pupils to respond. The disproportionately high percentage of boys' unrequested responses suggests that boys make a greater per capita contribution to teacher-led talk than girls. Whatever the reasons, the type of lessons that are typical of classroom practice at Tiverdale appear to encourage the participation of boys more than girls.

Seating

A perusal of the plans depicting seating arrangements reveals the existence of two separate classroom communities: boys and girls. The analysis of teacher-led talk suggests that significant parts of lessons are biased towards one of these communities: the boys. That boys consistently register more of the teachers' time, whether they sit at the front (science), back (English) or sides (maths) of classrooms, implies that seating arrangements alone do not explain the greater involvement of boys in teacher-led talk. There are some tentative indications that boys sit to the front in the sciences (science and maths), girls to the front in the arts (English and German). The role of the teachers in stipulating seating arrangements is not known.

Independent learning

The normal working pattern of silent individuality meant that it was hardly possible to record any examples of independent learning, which is based upon the interaction of individual, collaborative and cooperative working (Factors 1, 2 and 3 are collaborative groupwork, cooperative groupwork and individual responsibility). The lack of opportunity for independent learning was reinforced by the teacher-control of the tasks undertaken during lessons, their assessment, the time which would be spent upon them and the manner in which they would be executed. Thus there were no opportunities for Factors 4, 5, 6 and 7 (pupil-designed tasks, pupil-designed assessment, pupil-negotiated deadlines and pupil-initiated research). Pupils made no use of a range of language technology (Factor 8). The use of technology was limited to a brief instructional session in the computer room, the use of calculators in maths and the watching of video programmes. There was no involvement with the community or use of the environment (Factor 9). There was no sense of audience for the work of pupils (other than the PSE presentation) and the presentation of work was exclusively by hand-written manuscript (Factors 10 and 11, a sense of audience and the presentation of work in various forms). There was no evidence of reflexivity (Factor 12).

Further conclusions about Josie's week are made at the end of Chapter 3 where the various strands of the tracking of pupils at Key Stages 3 and 4 are brought together. To end this chapter, I would like to stress that the criticisms I make concern the system of education that a knowledge-based National Curriculum imposes and are not aimed at specific teachers, who seem to me to be as much victims of the system as are their pupils. Whether one or another teacher could have paid more attention to gender equality, or exercised a greater degree of Gradgrindian discipline is neither here nor there, and makes no real difference to the quality of the educational opportunity that was being offered. The very best teachers at Tiverdale, those most adept in their lesson presentation, achieved no more than making something pointless slightly more entertaining; but not any more *educational* in any sense that is relevant to contemporary citizenship and the workplace. I also want to emphasize that this case study should not be dismissed as a one-off. Josie's week is typical of the school experience of the majority of Key Stage 3 pupils throughout the United Kingdom. Ask your own son or daughter.

3 See Emily Play

A National Curriculum case study at Key Stage 4

INTRODUCTION

Forestmead, like Tiverdale, was a comprehensive school with a broad and balanced intake that organized the timetable into 30 weekly lessons, each of 50 minutes length, with six lessons each day, four in the morning session, two in the afternoon. Forestmead had about 750 eleven to sixteen-year-old pupils on roll. I phoned and spoke to Brenda Whittacker, the senior deputy head, whom I had met on a cross-curricular course. She was interested and enthusiastic about the idea of a Learning Across the Curriculum survey and promised a response as soon as she had consulted Eric Bentley, the headteacher. Brenda quickly phoned back to confirm that the tracking could go ahead, dependent on the permission of teachers whose classes would be visited, and invited me to attend a staff briefing the following day to answer any queries the staff might have. With the teachers' consent, and that of the tracked pupil, the tracking could take place the week after half-term, the first week of March.

At 0815 the next morning I drove into the school car park. The school buildings, nearly 30 years old, looked dated in a way that older buildings in the vicinity did not. The frenetic 1960s architectural chic that typified schools built in that period – lots of glass in aluminium frames with accompanying brightly coloured panels, flat roofs, a central tower block – looked very temporary in the enduring context of the surrounding Greenshire granite. Eric Bentley, the head, was one of the youngest and most recently appointed headteachers in Greenshire, having succeeded one of Greenshire's longest-serving headteachers two years earlier.

In the short time that Eric had been headteacher, he had raised the image of the school in a number of ways that promoted the notion of a successful institution. How cosmetic these changes were remained to be seen during the week's tracking. But immediate impressions were – as they were intended to be – powerful: the foyer area had been redecorated and refurbished and the receptionist's original booth had been expanded into an attractive open-plan work area. Flourishing potted plants and soft-furnished contemporary chairs in the waiting area suggested a new dynamic of school management. Whilst waiting to see Eric, I was offered coffee from a state of the art percolator and browsed an exhibition of pupils' work attractively presented on hi-tech, free-standing display boards (I later learnt that the exhibitions were changed fortnightly and always featured school and community activities).

I was ushered into Eric's office – an office at least four times the size of his predecessor's. Eric rose from behind his desk, smiled, shook hands and invited me to sit in an armchair around a coffee table. I began to explain the purpose of the week, how a similar study at Tiverdale had suggested that language performance in English in many lessons was way below the demands of the Profile Components for English in the National Curriculum.

Eric listened for a few minutes and then said: 'Look, I wouldn't bother with all that stuff just now, Rhys, just keep it simple, ay? We can always go into a bit more detail later. The thing is to get in there and get it done, isn't it? Just say you're looking at language across the curriculum and leave it at that. Come on, we better go.'

He stood up, put on his suit jacket and held the door open for me. Along the corridor were more well-designed displays illustrating the annual French exchange trip made by Forestmead pupils. We walked up the corridor to the staff room. The staff were standing or sitting, drinking coffee, waiting for the morning briefing. Brenda smiled hello.

'All right then,' said Eric, 'today's briefing. As you know, Brenda, as part of her brief as deputy head, has been looking into learning across the curriculum and she and Linda were going to go on a course run by Rhys here, which has had to be cancelled, but now Rhys has offered to work here, with us, to look at the same thing but specific to our school. Brenda, do you want to take it from there?'

Brenda spoke: 'What Rhys is offering is a curriculum audit of what links, principally language links, we have across the curriculum, and he wants to do that by tracking a Year 10 pupil through all her lessons for a week. Which means, if you have this pupil, he'd be coming into your lessons.'

Eric: 'Right then, does anyone object to Rhys coming into their lessons?'

There was a murmuring in the science corner, but no-one voiced a public objection.

Eric: 'Thank you very much, ladies and gentlemen. This tracking will be the week after half-term and Brenda will sort out a pupil before then.'

For the Key Stage 4 tracking, in the light of experience gained at Tiverdale School, I amended the form that I used to record the details of learning activities. The top section of the form was expanded to include details that had been collected during the tracking at Key Stages 1 and 2 (Meganporth) and Key Stage 3 (Tiverdale), but which had not been planned into the original form: the duration of a learning activity, whether classroom support was available (e.g.: ancillary, technician, other teacher), the class grouping system (mixed ability, setted, banded, individual needs), the total number of pupils in the class, and the numbers of boys and girls. The second section was adjusted to distinguish between teacher-led talk and pupils' collaborative groupwork talk in the Speaking and Listening English attainment target. A new section concerning teacher-led talk was added to allow the recording of pupils' voluntary and requested utterances, by gender. To see if I could discern some pattern that unified a Key Stage 4 curriculum that was organized into discrete subject lessons, two more sections were added to the form: one to record evidence of cross-curricular skills, themes and dimensions as defined by the National Curriculum Council publication, *The Whole Curriculum* (1990a); and the other to record explicit evidence within lessons of the aims of the school.

Monday: registration (0845 – 0855)

On the Monday morning, I arrived at Forestmead School just after half-past eight and made my way to Andy Crayton's tutor group room on the second floor of what used to be the 'ROSLA block'. These buildings are a feature of comprehensive schools that had originally been secondary modern schools. With the raising of the school leaving age (hence the acronym ROSLA) to 16 in 1974, secondary modern schools often needed more class space to accommodate the extra intake. Like the ROSLA block I had originally taught in when I started teaching at Saltair School, the Forestmead block was separate from the rest of the school.

This separation from the main school buildings sometimes led to incidents of vandalism, partly because the blocks weren't as easy to supervise outside lesson times, partly because they were the province of the older pupils of the school who were more likely to cause damage to property, and partly, in the early years, out of a sense of frustration: pupils who had looked forward to their school release date at the age of 15 had seen it recede a year into the future. On earlier visits to Forestmead (my first, as a visiting CSE Drama Assessor, had been 12 years before) the block had seemed dingy: old lockers had been kicked in, the toilets were vandalized, there were graffiti on doors and desks, the walls were dirty. Now, the corridors were carpeted, there were posters and paintings on the walls, broken lockers had been removed. The block had been renamed the Drama and Design Annex and also contained three English and humanities classrooms. The classroom floors were carpeted and the furniture was in good repair.

I chatted to Andy as the class assembled for registration. The pupil I was to track, Tamsin, was in this tutor group. I had met her on the day of the staff briefing after she had been recommended as a 'good all-rounder' by Mrs Bramcote, head of Year 10. She had seemed interested in the project and I had shown her the forms I would be using, and stressed that she should not feel pressured into 'volunteering'. On the contrary, Tamsin had said, it sounded like fun and she looked forward to the tracking. Andy took the register but when he called Tamsin's name there was no reply. She was absent. I asked Andy whom he felt would make a good replacement for Tamsin and he mentioned three or four pupils and discreetly pointed them out to me. I explained to the class what I was there for and moved among the various groups, chatting, answering questions. I could see that there was an interest in the tracking, but that it was unlikely that anyone was going to volunteer: the sense of the power of the peer group and the difficulty of standing apart from it (being seen as a creep for volunteering to do something) was very strong. I worked my way round to Emily and chatted with her group.

'We'll do it if we can do it together,' said Sharon, linking her arm in Emily's and laughing.

That would have been all right, but I doubted that it would be possible.

'Are you both in the same classes for all your lessons?'

'Oh, no. We are for some.'

'Then it won't work. When you go to different lessons, I could only go with one of you.'

'Yeh.'

'What about if I go with you both to all the lessons you're together and stay with Emily for the ones you're apart?'

Emily laughed and grimaced. 'I don't know.'

'I don't need to sit with you or anything. I just need to be in the same classroom and be able to record what you do and say, and afterwards photocopy what you've read or written.'

'Go on,' said Sharon, nudging Emily.

The bell went and pupils started to leave, going their various ways to different lessons. Sharon and Emily gathered up their bags.

'All right then,' said Emily.

'Thank you. What lesson have you got first?'

'English with Mrs. Jones.'

'I'll follow you.'

(That evening, Emily took home a letter explaining the tracking, and brought back to school the next day a consent form signed by her mother.)

Monday: lesson one – English (0855 – 0945)

Timetable for Emily Jay			Registration Group (10) 54 Teacher: Mr Crayton Baseroom: Room 54		
DAY 1	2	3	4	5	6
Mon E 51 MH	H 52 MO	S 72 TG	S 74 KO'D	BS 53 SS	M 32 BL
Tue TP 54 AC	E 51 MH	BS 53 SS	DR 59 FD	GM 3 MC	PE 32 AT
Wed H 51 MH	M 32 BL	E 51 MH	PE 32 AT	S 74 TG	SE 69 BH
Thu S 74 KO'D	S 72 TG	GM 3 MC	M 32 BL	DR 59 FD	DR 59 FD
Fri S 74 KO'D	H 52 MO	BS 53 SS	GM 3 MC	M 32 BL	E 51 MH

Forestmead Community School session times: a.m. 08:45 to 12:30
p.m. 13:30 to 15:15

Code	Subject	Set	Level	Teacher (s)
E	English Language	01	2	Mrs Harvey
S	General Science	01		Mrs Graham & Mr O' Dowd
PE	Physical Education	07		Ms Tregear
H	History	01		Mr Oldman
GM	German			Mrs Chawietz
M	Mathematics	01		Miss Layton
DR	Drama			Mrs Duncan
BS	Business Studies			Mrs Sears
SE	Social Education	02		Mr Holden
TP	Tutor Period	02		Mr Crayton

Figure 3.1 Emily's timetable

It wasn't far to follow: the next but one classroom on the same floor of the block (see Figure 3.1 for Emily's timetable). Despite the fact that the move from registration to the first lesson (English) was only along a short corridor, eight minutes (0855–0903) of putative lesson-time was used up before the first activity took place, time mostly spent in awaiting the arrival of the teacher from the main school site. The teacher, Mo, the second deputy head, unlocked the door and the pupils moved in. Mo saw me, laughed and gave a mock frown:

'Oh no, Rhys, what a way to start my week. You're not going to be in here are you?'

'Yeah. You knew didn't you?'

'Oh yes, I'd just forgotten. Do you want to talk to the class?'

'No, I'd just rather sit invisibly at the back. I'll get out of your way.'

I sat at the back of the class as Mo introduced the lesson: 'O.K., folks. Some of you have got your work out, if you haven't the filing-cabinet's open – let's go!'

Mo was right, some of the pupils had taken their work from the filing-cabinet, now others did the same. Within one minute, the class had settled down to work. This was a change from the usual preamble that had typified lessons at Tiverdale and also clearly suggested a continuity from one lesson to another. The pupils were working individually, continuing an assignment on the William Golding text *Lord of the Flies.* – 'What do we learn about the character of Ralph in the opening pages of the novel? How and why does he change during the course of the novel?'

The class was grouped by ability (the second of five sets) and comprised 28 pupils, 15 boys and 13 girls. The novel's characters are exclusively boys. There is nothing intrinsically wrong with studying books by dead, middle-class, white, male authors but as we approach the millennium I feel that for fifteen-year old comprehensive pupils, nearly a combined decade of study (28 pupil-terms – one for each member of the class) of the work of a 1950s public school teacher, about 1950s public school boys, is disproportionate. Here again are the questions that were never addressed during the range of lessons observed at Tiverdale: why? Why study this particular text? What is its relevance to us, now, in Forestmead?

The arrangement of desks was a variation on the standard Forestmead layout of four columns of four tables facing the front of the classroom, each table accommodating two pupils

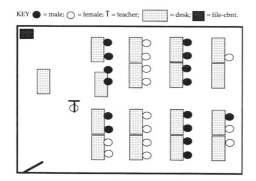

KEY ● = male; ○ = female; T = teacher; ▦ = desk; ▨ = file-cbnt.

Figure 3.2 Plan of the English room showing the seating arrangements

(Figure 3.2). Here, there was a central aisle and two side aisles. This arrangement – all the pupils were facing the same way, towards the teacher's desk and the blackboard – suggested a didactic presentation by the teacher or solitary work by the pupil. The isolation of the tables into islands of four pupils made eye-contact and conversation within each group difficult. The serried rows also prevented easy communication between these islands, for to make contact pupils either had to twist uncomfortably around in their seats, or whomever they were talking to had to.

Another factor that inhibited communication between the islands was the gender grouping: roughly alternate rows of boys (rows one and three) and girls (rows two and four). In almost all cases, turning to speak to someone on another island would have meant engaging a member of the other gender in conversation. Previous lesson observation in schools throughout Greenshire had suggested that most boys and girls do not easily and naturally converse in lessons. A clear indication of this was that it was rare for a boy or girl to choose to sit with a member of the other gender. In this lesson, one boy sat at the back with his girlfriend and her friend. I had not yet seen (either at Tiverdale or Forestmead) a mixed group of friends sitting together. Friendship groups appeared to be exclusively single gender; although occasionally a pair of pupils, consisting of boyfriend and girlfriend, sat together, as distinct from a boy sitting with a friend who, coincidentally, was a girl, or vice versa.

I was becoming increasingly aware of a complex system of classroom territorialization, that was not simply a matter of gender grouping (although this was its most obvious manifestation). Other factors were: the positioning of gender groups towards the back, front or sides of the classroom in different subjects; the way that different classes formed into different sub-groups for most lessons and that pupils put themselves, seemingly unconsciously into these groups; the permanence of seating arrangements and locations within the classroom, once established; and the way that seating arrangements imposed or disrupted teaching and learning styles.

For the next 14 minutes (0904–0918) pupils worked individually on the Ralph assignment whilst Mo walked around giving individual support. This averaged 30 seconds' 'support' for each pupil, although some pupils got longer, and some had no interaction with Mo at all. Mo's method was to start with the front island to her right, work her way along it, then up the other right hand islands and down the left hand side.

Next Mo drew the class together to give some tips on literary criticism: use of quotes, how to make notes, non-chronological writing, how to interrogate the text by posing questions. She summarized: 'Make your own notes, sort them into an order and then add your special bits'. During this seven-minute activity (0918–0925) boys spoke nine times and girls three times. Although the class was in a gender ratio close to 1:1, Mo asked for boy/girl responses in the ratio of 3:1, that is she asked six boys to speak but only two girls.

For the final 20 minutes of the lesson (0925–0945) the pupils returned to silent, individual work with Mo offering individual support as she walked around the class. This activity began with Mo's admonition: 'I would like you to concentrate, so don't natter, please'. This comment was obviously intended as a low-key and sensitive way of reiterating to pupils that they were not to talk. In another light, it was a prohibition on any opportunity for pupils to share, to question each other's opinions, to pursue a line of enquiry together. It reduced the teacher to the rule of silence supervisor rather than climate creator and denigrated collaboration, cooperation and discussion with the dismissive pejorative, 'natter'. A collaborative approach could have reduced the massive content load on each pupil. The three questions embedded in the assignment

1   What do we learn about the character of Ralph in the opening pages of the novel?
2   How does he change during the course of the novel?
3   Why does he change?

required a close, silent and individual reading of the whole text (250+ pages in the Faber edition the class was using), page-referenced note-making and gathering of quotations, an analysis of Ralph's character, comparison with other characters, organization of the data for presentation in essay form, drafting and redrafting. All of this was to be done alone, in silence, even though 28 people in the same room were engaged on exactly the same task. Why couldn't pupils have worked in pairs or collaborative groups? Why couldn't some of the pupils have studied some of the other main protagonists of the novel: Piggy, Simon, Jack? They could still have have learned the same literary skills, but the pool of research for discussion and sharing would have been much greater. If one wanted to study a book about teenagers in the aftermath of the holocaust, there are more contemporary texts, texts with girls as main protagonists in powerful roles (*Z for Zachariah* or *Brother In The Land*). Why not a thematic approach, with some groups studying *Lord of the Flies*, others other texts and then comparing findings? Why did the whole structure and ethos of the lesson emphasize isolation, silence and secretiveness: not discussing work with others, keeping findings to oneself?

The answer to these questions is that this class were studying for their National Curriculum Tests at the age of sixteen, in this case, the GCSE English Literature examination. One of the factors of independent learning is pupil-designed assessment, on the basis that assessment can control the curriculum and its presentation, and that pupils might be inhibited from learning independently if there was an external assessment system that was alien to the natural processes of independent learning. Recent government legislation had abolished the option (popular with teachers and pupils) of 100 per cent coursework examination and, for Mo's class, the course would end with a timed examination under controlled conditions on this text, with a high probability of a question similar to the one the pupils in this class were working on. Any collaboration under those circumstances would be regarded as cheating. In that sense, Mo was doing her professional best to prepare the class for their terminal exam – the form of assessment having a heavy influence upon the curriculum (the set text of *Lord of the Flies*) and its presentation in this lesson.

Within its own self-justified context, the lesson was efficient in achieving its aims. The pupil workforce endeavoured silently on the respectful study of a cultural icon. The teacher–supervisor ensured that silence and output was maintained by regular inspections on the factory floor. Halfway through the work shift, the supervisor exhorted the workers to greater levels of production by reminding them of efficient techniques. When the hooter sounded for the end of the shift, the workforce left the factory after tidying their workplaces.

Emily had worked industriously, her head bent close over the novel, left hand curled around the book, right hand making notes in her English exercise book. By the end of the lesson, she was on her fifth page of notes, which concerned only the first six pages of Chapter 1 (Figure 3.3).

continued overleaf

Character of Ralph   unsure

fair hair
school sweater
grey shirt
sweaty hair (forehead)
Quite tall
teachers at school telling
them to dress
still got school sweater on
because he might be scared
of someone saying that
his school uniform might
not be correct.

Piggy-fat boy-spectacles, fat,
short

Ralph was sure that he
knew that there wasn't
any group ~~[crossed out]~~

Ralph takes responsabilities
for the island, he know what
he has to do, but I think
he is a little unsure about
it at the moment.

We could tell that Ralph
was happy because it said
"but then the delight of
a realised ambition
overcame him." In the Middle
of the scene he stood on
his head."

When Piggy said about the
Pilot Ralph allowed him-
self to clam down. Ralph
was sure that the pilot
had dropped them off
on the island due to
the war, so that they
would be safe and that
the Pilot would back to
take them home again.

Ralph for a short time
became interested about
how they got to the island.

Ralph discovered that piggy
"had ASS-mar"

Figure 3.3 Notes
made by Emily during
English, Monday

Ralph was wearing black shoes, he became curious of the weight of his clothes. He then fiercely kicked his shoes off and ripped his stockings with its elastic garter in a single movement. Then leapt on to the terrace and pulled off his shirt.

All ralph has on at the moment is his shorts

later he stands there in the terrace and takes off his shorts and pants (Naked)

Ralph discovered that the fat boy was called piggy and that he didn't want anybody making fun of him. Ralph shrieked with laughter

He jumped up "piggy piggy!" Ralph pleasbly piggy clapped his hands in apprehension. "I said I didn't want—" "piggy piggy" then then jumped up into the air and played into airoplanes.

Piggy seemed a little upset that ralph was making fun of him but he will get over it.

"piggy" piggy grinned reluctantly piggy pleased despite himself at even this much recognition "So long as you don't tell the others"

Piggy looks a bit happier now knely that Ralph was fat or might not tell the others.

Ralph spoke to himself sanding the bass things of delight "whizz oh !!" Ralph said this because he looked into the coral reef and saw A school of tiny glittering fish flicked hither and thither

Monday: lesson two – history (0945 – 1035)

The move from English to history was from one classroom to the one next to it, but it was eight minutes (0945–0953) before the class were seated, the register taken by Mr Oldman, the head of the history department, textbooks handed out and the first activity begun. Because history was an option open to all pupils to choose for GCSE study, the class was, in effect, a mixed-ability group. However, some mixed-ability option groups are more mixed in ability than others. During the morning break, Mr Oldman gave me the following analysis of mixed-ability options groups in relation to his own subject.

'Assume history as in the same option group as computer studies, French, rural science and child care. The bright girls go for the language, the highest-achieving boys for computer studies, the lowest-achieving boys for rural science and the lowest-achieving girls for child care. The bunch in the middle are funnelled into the humanities option. Those at the top are generally self-motivated and often have greater home support, the lowest-achievers are generally amiable and malleable; so the humanities subjects end up with the most difficult pupils, pupils who are there because there's nowhere else to be. They get easily bored but haven't got the commitment of the bright kids or the placidity of the less able. On top of that, humanities groups are always large. The other subjects have some element that limits class size: French – academic ability, child care – lack of academic ability, only girls will do it anyway, computer studies – facilities and resources, rural science – only farmers' sons want to do it. Whereas all history requires is chairs, desks and textbooks, doesn't it? And that's the truth of it, my boy.'

This was a (typically?) large and boisterous history option group of 30 pupils, equally divided between boys and girls. Figure 3.4 shows another variation on the four columns, each of four tables. In the history classroom, the tables were divided into four rows of four with no central aisle. It was an arrangement that suggested the college or university lecture theatre. Access to pupils within the body of the class was difficult: there was little room behind the chairs to move along the rows, particularly with pupils' bags either on the floor behind chairs or hanging from their backs. In addition, the side aisle on the teacher's left was narrow and blocked by bags. The teacher could effectively offer little more than a front-of-house presentation and a patrol along two sides of the pupil square. When Mr Oldman moved into the rows to talk to individuals, they were caught in an awkward and submissive position: as he had to stand behind pupils to read their work over their shoulders, to address him, they had to twist around and look up at the authority figure who was leaning over them. There was no need to cram the desks in this way, for this was a corner room (one of the perks of being head of department, Mr Oldman told me) and was half as big again as the regular classrooms. However, the extra room-space remained unused.

The alternating rows seen with a different class in the English lesson, with boys in the first and third rows, was roughly adhered to, but with more of a flank of girls to the teacher's left. It was in this area, and between the boys on the right in the back two rows, that I expected to observe societal chat

KEY ● = male; ○ = female; T = teacher; ▨ = desk

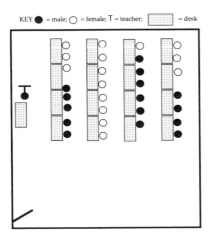

Figure 3.4 Plan of history room showing seating arrangements, Monday

because here pupils could make eye-contact with members of the same gender. This proved to be the case during the lesson. As in the last lesson there was only one girl/boy pair sitting at the same desk (in fact, it was the couple from the English lesson). There appeared to be another pair in the first row, but this was actually a row of three girls and five boys. The boy at the same desk as the girl had one leg under the table to his left and had twisted his body to present his back to the girl, who was sitting as far up her end of the table as she could.

The first activity was a 12-minute teacher-led 'whole-class discussion' (0953–1005) of pages 28 and 29 of *The Rise of Communist China*, a Schools' Council History Project 13–16, published in 1977. The copies used during this lesson had been bought at that time and nearly 20 years of use had taken its toll on their condition. Pupils were not required to put their hands up or to wait to be chosen by the teacher, but were free to contribute when they wanted. There were 14 contributions by boys and five by girls. For the following 26 minutes (1005–1031) the pupils were asked to read and make notes of pages 30–41. Mr Oldman walked round the class offering encouragement to individuals and making general appeals for silence. These were not heeded but the class worked in an amiable if superficial way. He referred to girls and boys as 'my loves' and 'my 'andsomes'. Emily worked quietly and diligently, making notes on pages 30–32 (Figure 3.5). For the final four minutes (1031–1035), Mr Oldman neatly drew the lesson to a conclusion. Boys made four voluntary contributions, girls none.

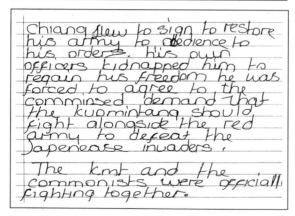

Figure 3.5 Notes made by Emily from her history textbook, Monday

Monday: morning break (1035 – 1050)

After the class had left for the morning break, Mr Oldman offered to show me some work on the Bosnian civil war done by a Year 9 top set, and pointed to the display which that class updated every day with newspaper cuttings and their own written comments and observations. The folders he showed me were superb examples of the kind of work pupils can produce when they are interested and feel a pride in the production of their work. Totally absorbed, I read one of the folders. It was a lucid analysis of the history of the area from pre-Roman times, and clearly composed in the pupils' own words, rather than copied from text-books or newspaper articles.

'Of course, you can't get much out of this lot,' bemoaned the head of history, nodding his head to the empty tables to indicate the class I had observed.

'Couldn't they do something like this, investigate a topical issue, have their own display . . . make their own books and folders like these did . . .?'

'Not on the syllabus, my dear,' said Mr Oldman.

Monday: lesson three – Science 1 (1050 – 1140)

I had chatted to Mr Oldman through most of breaktime and now made my way across to the main school and walked to the science wing. On Emily's individual computer-printed timetable (Figure 3.1), the lesson was designated as a double period of general science with

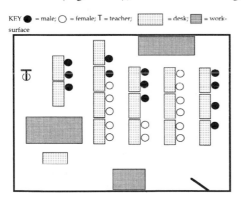

Figure 3.6 Plan of Science 1 room showing seating arrangements, Monday

Mrs Graham. In fact, the class had a single period of biology with Mrs Graham and then a single period of physics with Mr O' Dowd. Mrs Graham's lesson was known as Science 1, Mr O' Dowd's as Science 2. Mrs Graham's lab was light and cheerful. There were 25 pupils in this setted group (the second set of six), 13 girls and 12 boys (Figure 3.6).

The table arrangement was similar to the last lesson, in that the rows had no central aisle and all faced the front of the class. This time, however, there were 5 rows and 15 tables. The general pattern of alternating boy/girl rows still applied, although the second row had two boys and the third row, two girls. Again, there was only one girl/boy pair sitting at the same table. The first activity was teacher-led talk, introducing a new topic on Sound. The class had a background in this topic from work undertaken in Year 9. This activity lasted for 15 minutes (1056–1111). Boys made 12 voluntary contributions, girls none. Boys were asked to speak six times, girls three times. The subject under discussion was *What constitutes noise rather than sound?* During the discussion Mrs Graham addressed the pupils as 'ladies and gentlemen' and asked them to signal if they wished to speak by 'putting your paws in the air'.

Maybe I'm oversensitive, but the divisive gender nomenclature of 'loves' and 'handsomes', 'ladies' and 'gentlemen' seems to me to enforce the impression of two quite separate groups within each class, an impression reinforced by the seating arrangements and the dominance by boys of teacher-led talk. The practice of 'paws in the air' (let alone the implications of the phrase) strengthens the power of the teacher as the controller of all that

Figure 3.7 Notes made by Emily in Science 1, Monday

The ear has two functions. firstly, It is sensitive to sound. It also contains receptor cells which are sensitive to the position and movement of your head. These cells help with balance.

The outer ear and middle contain air. The inner ear though is filled with two sorts of fluid perilymph and encolymph. The cells which are sensitive to sound waves are inside the cochlea. Sound waves need to be made stronger or amplified before these cells will respond to them. firstly the sound waves make the air in the outer ear vibrate. This makes the eardrum vibrate. touching the eardrum is a tiny bone or ossicle called a hammer. As the eardrum vibrates the malleus vibrates too. The vibrations

pass along the chain of ossicles. The malleus vibration on the anul or incus. and the incus vibrations on the stirr up or stapes. The stapes lies against a membrane over the oval window. The oval window transmits the vibrations to the parilymph.

The chain of events help to amplify the size of the vibrations. The vibration in the perilymph are then passed into the the conchlea. As the perilymph vibrates it makes the membrane in the cochlea move up and down on the membrane in the are hair cells. The hairs are embedded in a plate of Jelly as they move up and down, the hairs are pulled and pushed against the Jelly plate. This makes the hair cells send messages along the auditory nerve to the

Figure 3.7 continued

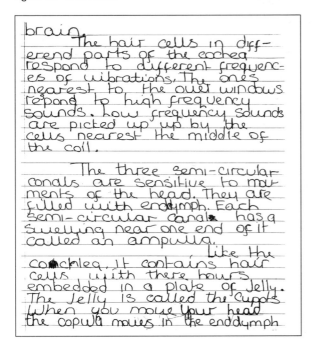

brain.
The hair cells in diff-
erend parts of the cochea
respond to different frequenc-
ies of vibrations. The ones
nearest to the ouet windows
repond to high freq uency
sounds. Low frequency sounds
are picked up up by the
cells nearest the middle of
the coil.

The three semi-circular
conals are sensitive to mov-
ments of the head. They are
filled wuith endymph. Each
semi-circular canals has a
swelling near one end of it
called an ampulla.
Like the
cochlea, It contains hair
cells with there hours
embedded in a plate of jelly.
The Jelly is called the Cupola.
When you moue your head
the copula moues in the enddymph

happens, a power made obvious by: the positioning of the classroom furniture to face the teacher and the blackboard, the notion of a teacher's space as separate from the pupils' space as stage is from audience, teachers' reference to pupils by their first names, but pupils' reference to teachers by the titles of 'Sir' or 'Miss', the unlocking of the classroom doors by the teachers, and a register taken at the start of every lesson to ensure that no pupil has absconded.

For the remaining 29 minutes of the lesson (1111–1140) pupils made notes from their textbook. They were told that they may refer to the worksheets they had completed last year if they wished. Emily's notes were copied verbatim, apart from her excision of a few phrases, from the textbook (see Figure 3.7 opposite and above).

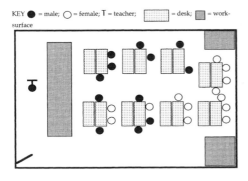

KEY ● = male; ○ = female; T = teacher; ▢ = desk; ▨ = work-surface

Figure 3.8 Plan of Science 2 room showing seating arrangements, Monday

Monday: lesson four – Science 2 (1140 – 1230)

At 1140, the class moved to another lab for the second part of their double lesson. However, it was not the second part, but a completely different lesson, albeit still under the broad aegis of general science. This was a lesson about energy conservation. This lab was quite different from the biology lab. It was cluttered and untidy. The room seemed smaller and more crowded (Figure 3.8).

There was a different seating pattern from the last lesson, even though it was exactly the same group of 25 pupils – 13 girls and twelve boys. What remained common was that boys tended to dominate the front of the class, with girls behind them; in the first half of the room there were 10 boys and 3 girls; in the second half there were 10 girls and 2 boys. For only the second time during the Key Stage 3 and 4 tracking, there were two tables with boys and girls seated together (the first time was the history lesson at Tiverdale).

The first activity (1145–1153) was an eight-minute introduction accompanied by a diagram Mr O' Dowd drew on the board to illustrate the points made. Boys made 11 voluntary contributions and were asked to respond twice. One girl made a voluntary response – significantly or not it was one of the girls in the mixed group closest to the teacher. No girls were asked to respond. For the next four minutes (1153–1157) the class copied the diagram from the board (Figure 3.9).

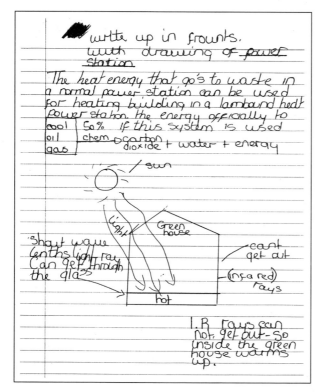

Figure 3.9 Diagram copied from the blackboard by Emily in Science 2, Monday

For the next six minutes (1158–1204) there was teacher-led talk on how the system of energy conservation depicted by the diagram could be improved. Boys made four voluntary contributions and the same girl who responded before spoke once. Mr O' Dowd amended the board diagram. For the next seven minutes (1204–1211) the class copied an addition to the board diagram (Figure 3.10). Talking was discouraged: 'I'd appreciate your attention not your conversation, folks.'

This pattern of micro-activities, common in lessons at Tiverdale, continued until the end of the lesson. A further eight minutes (1211–1219) were spent in teacher-led talk about the greenhouse effect, with the teacher drawing annotated diagrams on the board. Boys and girls both made four voluntary responses and Mr O' Dowd asked both a boy and a girl for a comment. The class then copied this diagram into their books for nine minutes

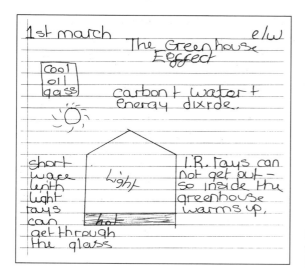

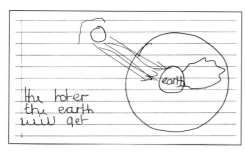

Figure 3.10 Second diagram copied from the blackboard by Emily in Science 2, Monday

Figure 3.11 Third diagram copied from the blackboard by Emily in Science 2, Monday

(1220–1229) leaving Mr O' Dowd one minute to sum up the lesson before the bell to end the morning session rang at 1230 (Figure 3.11).

Monday: dinner break (1230 – 1330)

Mr O' Dowd showed an interest in the forms I had been completing and asked to see what I had written. I explained about independent learning. To my surprise (because this had been a very didactic lesson) he agreed that a more independent approach would be of greater interest and benefit to teachers and pupils alike. However, he reached the same conclusions his colleague Mr Oldman had: 'But it can't be done: lessons too short and too much to cover in the damn syllabus.'

During the morning's observation I had been struck by the various trappings of institutional power and control: pupils' uniform, a register of attendance taken every 50 minutes throughout the day, the ceremony of the keys to open the design and drama block, pupils locked out of classrooms apart from lessontime, the computer-printed timetables, the didactic character of the teaching style, the arrangement of classroom furniture, the emphasis on silent, individual work, the use of authoritative texts. The invested power structure embraced adult workers as well: the insistence on ties for male teachers, teachers not being allowed to use the photocopying room, the better classroom facilities for HoDs, the head's use of first names but staff referring to him by title. The external pressures upon teachers of a hierarchical power structure beyond the school were evident: the imposition of the National Curriculum, prescribed examination board texts and restrictive syllabuses, changes in the assessment procedures for public examinations made by the Department for Education, with their consequent effect upon teaching styles. Despite the reservations of teachers (Mr Oldman, Mr O' Dowd) about the structure within which they worked, steps had been taken by the school management to suggest the power and success of the system to the public: the glamorous foyer, the executive suite of secretarial and Head's office, the power-dressed head, the displays.

Monday: afternoon registration (1330 – 1335)

I did not attend the registration periods as these were not included in the 1500 minutes of curricular time that was the subject of the study. As well as a ten-minute tutor group registration at the beginning of the morning session and the five-minute tutor group registration at the beginning of the afternoon session, each class was also registered at the beginning of each of their six daily lessons.

Monday: lesson five – business studies (1335 – 1425)

The first class of the afternoon was another option group, and therefore mixed-ability. Within the unstated hierarchy of choices within an option group, business studies is regarded, I was told by Mrs Sears, the subject teacher, as not particularly academically demanding and more likely to appeal to boys than girls, a point reflected in the class numbers: 16 boys and four girls (although there were three other girls absent).

Figure 3.12 shows an unusual table arrangement: five rows of two tables and then a rhomboid of six desks divided by a central aisle. The teacher's desk was positioned in an offset position to one side of the class and the usual teaching space was reduced by the first of the five rows. The teacher, Mrs Sears, tended to address the class from the hatched

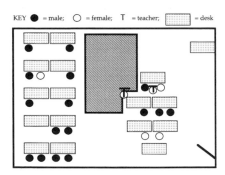

area, which, rather than the stage/audience presentation of earlier lessons, had more of an in-the-round feel to it. Although Mrs Sears's presentation was didactic and the pattern of the lesson was to the usual alternation of teacher-led talk then short written task, her physical presence within the class lent a sense of intimacy, heightened by her habit of sitting or leaning against the table in the rhomboid with the single boy at it – more or less the centre of the room, and therefore in a position as close as possible to all the pupils. The four girls did not form their own enclave, even though there was plenty of room to the right at the back of the class. There

Figure 3.12 Plan of business studies room showing seating arrangements, Monday

were two girl/boy pairs, but one pair had been asked to sit together as they received support from the ancillary, Sharon.

The first 15 minutes of the lesson (1343–1358) were given to a teacher-led introduction to the subject of indirect and direct taxation, part of a topic on taxation that had begun before half-term. Boys spoke voluntarily 13 times, girls 3 times; Mrs Sears asked five boys and two girls for a response. Bearing in mind the 4:1 ratio of boys, this was a much more equitable distribution than in other lessons today which had had a virtually equal boy/girl split in terms of numbers, but in which boys had been disproportionately favoured during teacher-led talk.

Table 3.1 shows the percentage of the number of boys and girls in a lesson and then shows the percentage of times boys and girls voluntarily responded during teacher-led talk (volunt. respons., %) and the percentage of times the teacher asked boys and girls to contribute (asked respons., %).

Table 3.1 Teacher-led talk opportunities by gender ratio

Subject	Boys, %	Girls, %	Boys' volunt. respons., %	Girls volunt. respons., %	Boys' asked respons., %	Girls' asked respons., %
English	54	46	75	25	75	25
History	50	50	78	22	0	0
Science 1	48	52	100	0	66	33
Science 2	48	52	75	25	75	25
Business studies	80	20	83	17	75	25

These figures seem to suggest that whether there is a majority of boys or a more equal distribution, then boys are three times more likely to contribute, or to be asked to contribute to class discussions. I had wondered at Tiverdale if girls responded more willingly to women teachers in teacher-led talk, or if women teachers tended to request more contributions from girls than men teachers did. Table 3.1 suggests otherwise: English and Science 1 were both taken by women teachers and show a similar favouring of boys as the two lessons (history and Science 2) taken by men.

Mrs Sears then dictated notes to the class on 'The Advantages of Indirect Taxation', writing the correct spelling of various words on the board at pupils' requests: government, commodity, individual, cigarettes . . . Emily's notes show confusion in her third paragraph, a confusion illustrated by the deterioration in her handwriting (Figure 3.13). Then Mrs

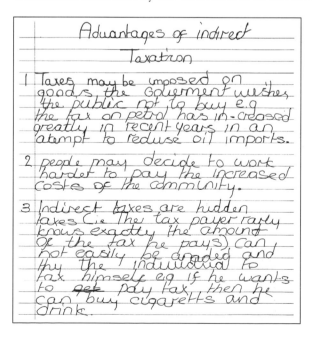

Figure 3.13 Emily's record of dictated notes on indirect taxation, Monday

Advantages of direct taxation.

1) Allowence can be made so that those with extra respon-sibility made ag incometax allowence for wife dependent reletives etc.

2) There is a graded Scale so that tax rates get progressi-vly higher the more income a person recieves therefore the greatest burden falls on the well off.

3) They help to cheack inflation because they take money from would-be consumers and dampen daw dmand.

How much TAX is payrd on the following these prises are what the consummers pay.

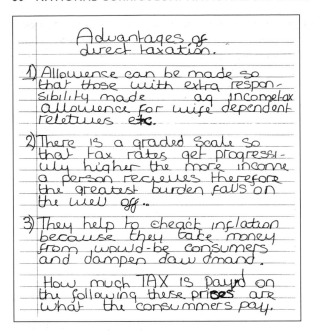

Figure 3.14 Emily's record of dictated notes on direct taxation, Monday

Sears dictated notes on direct taxation (Figure 3.14). What Mrs Sears actually said, what the class were listening to, went as follows: 'New subheading . . . advantages of direct taxation . . . one allowance can be made so that those with extra responsibility . . . so that those with extra responsibility . . . may secure concessions . . . may secure concessions one cee two esses . . . one allowance can be made so that those with extra responsibility so that those with extra responsibility may secure concessions for example ee gee income tax allowances . . . allowances for wife . . . yes dependent relatives . . . one allowance can be made so that those with extra responsibility may secure concessions for example income tax allowances for dependent relatives . . . ' and so on in this vein.

The dictation took 17 minutes (1358–1415). For five minutes (1415–1420) Mrs Sears led a discussion into how pupils could calculate the VAT they had paid on items they had recently bought – a simple exercise that captured everyone's interest; and not surprisingly, for this was a discussion about something real that directly affected them. Mrs Sears asked one boy to speak, but no girls and there were 16 voluntary responses from boys and three from girls. One of the girls was Emily, who spoke in teacher-led talk for the first time that day. She said, 'No, they haven't', to a general query to the class from Mrs Sears as to whether the government had imposed VAT on daily newspapers. Thus, in 83 minutes of teacher-led talk so far today, Emily's oral contribution has been of two seconds' duration (0.04 per cent).

For the last five minutes (1420–1425) pupils copied from the board the data that had emerged from the VAT discussion and began to work out the VAT paid on the listed items (Figure 3.15).

Computer games	£9.99 £34
Moter Bike piston	£18
sweets	10 P
Choc Bisc	54 P
Gameboy	£ 10P
Shoes	£ 110
moter car	£ 11,500

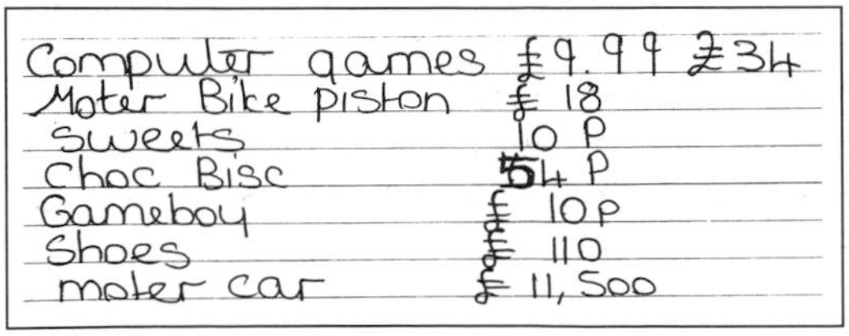

Figure 3.15 Notes Emily copied from the blackboard in business studies, Monday

Mrs Sears discouraged the pupils from talking or working together: 'It actually makes it harder if you sit next to someone who has the same ideas as you because it's harder to find things out for yourself,' she explained. Once again, the attitude promulgated by teachers that conversation and collaboration are not educational. By the time most of the pupils had written the list out, the bell rang, but there was a real buzz as pupils tried to work out how much VAT Wayne had paid for his new trainers which had cost £110.

Monday: lesson six – maths (1425 – 1515)

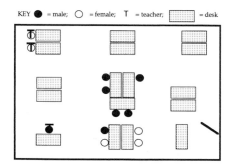

KEY ● = male; ○ = female; T = teacher; ▨ = desk

The last lesson of the day was maths. Emily was in the lowest set, a small group of three girls and six boys. There were four adults in the room: myself, Miss Layton, the head of maths, David, a support teacher, and Carol, a student (Figure 3.16).

There was no whole-class introduction. Emily's group opened their exercise books and got on with work from their textbook while Miss Layton started off the boys' group on a new topic: *Investigating Corners, Edges and Faces of Shapes.* This was a pretty grand title for indolently playing with stickle-bricks for the rest of the lesson. Miss

Figure 3.16 Plan of maths room showing seating arrangements, Monday

Layton then moved to the two joined tables at the top of the row that contained the teacher's desk and she and Carol spread out their timetables and diaries to plan Carol's teaching for that half-term. David, the support teacher, moved across to Emily's group which was quietly working and then came and talked to me about sailing.

Monday: summary

During the day, Emily has had five different lessons and been in a different pupil group for each of them. Although the lessons included English, maths, science, history and business studies there was little difference in teaching and learning style. In fact, Emily spent her day's lesson time in only three ways: making or copying notes (131 minutes or 44 per cent of lesson time), sitting passively during teacher-led talk (83 minutes or 28 per cent) or doing sums (41 minutes or 14 per cent). Forty-five minutes (or 15 per cent of lesson time) were spent in movement between classes. In all lessons, apart from maths (where they chatted comfortably throughout the lesson), pupils were discouraged from talking to each other, although Communication is a National Curriculum cross-curricular skill. This embargo included an English lesson, one of the National Curriculum Profile Components of which is Speaking and Listening. In 100 minutes spent in two science labs, pupils used no equipment and neither performed nor watched any experiments. There was no evidence of any of the factors of independent learning. On the contrary, the didactic teaching styles, the passive learning experiences, the emphasis on individual work (duplicated by every other member of the class), the prejudice against pupil communication, all legislated powerfully against independent learning.

Tuesday: lesson one – tutor period (0855 – 0945)

The first period on Tuesday was tutor period with Andy Crayton. I asked Andy what the class would be doing.

'Having a bit of a chat.'

We looked at the pupils. They were sitting in gendered friendship groups talking quite quietly, unselfconsciously (Figure 3.17). Andy was sitting at his desk. He began marking exercise books.

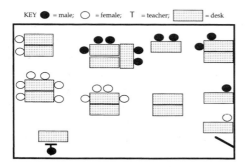

Figure 3.17 Plan of tutor group room showing seating arrangements, Tuesday

'What's the difference,' I asked, 'between a registration period and a tutor period?'

Andy grinned. 'A tutor period is just like a registration period only longer.'

Andy settled to his marking and I looked through yesterday's forms. The class continued to chat. The sound level didn't rise or fall. It was the conversational level of a group of around 30 people, about the same as for 30 teachers in a staffroom. Tutor period, then, was another part of the dynamic facade, ostensibly the period in which the tutor gets to know pupils on a one-to-one basis, the friendly figure, the adviser, the confidante when needed. Andy was probably right to do his marking and leave the class to their conversation, for there are obvious implemental difficulties in a system that asks a teacher to be one kind of authority figure for 29 lessons a week and another for one lesson a week. It would be unrealistic to expect pupils to speak openly, frankly, confidentially to a teacher in 50 minutes, when for the other 1450 timetabled minutes they operate under a regime in which conversation is discouraged, the affective domain is absent from lessons, there is a complementary reciprocity in the relationship between the authoritarian teacher and the obedient pupil, and gender differences within the tutor group suggest that about half the class (the girls) would be less likely to speak.

A weakness of the tracking research was that I had not gone to the daily 20-minute tutor periods held before the start of the afternoon session at Tiverdale. (I had not done this as my agreed brief was to observe the 1500 timetabled minutes of lesson time. At Forestmead, the tutor group period was allocated within that lesson time-span. At Tiverdale, the PSE lesson was, but tutor group periods weren't.) It may have been that Tiverdale offered an effective counselling programme, or an extension of the PSE lessons, within the tutor group sessions; or it may have been that the tutor group sessions were similar to the extended registration of the Forestmead tutor group lesson. However, the quality of tutor group, PSE (Tiverdale) or Social Education (Forestmead) lessons is a secondary consideration.

The central issue is that personal and social development, affective development, is seen in both schools as quite separate from the cognitive development, or academic training, that informs the curriculum. The most significant effect this has upon teaching and learning styles is that teachers seem to feel no responsibility for stimulating the development of a critical and ethical disposition in their pupils. In both schools, education is seen in the Peters, Hurst and Dearden tradition as knowledge-based; and knowledge is seen from a positivist viewpoint as existing independently of a peopled environment. The teacher's job is to transmit neutral knowledge to unquestioning pupils. The most effective way of doing this is to divide the curriculum into clearly defined and prescribed subject areas and to divide the timetable into short sessions for the transmission of the knowledge selected within that subject, as appropriate to different age and ability groups. As knowledge is seen to consist of unquestionable fact, then the complementary reciprocity of a didactic teaching style and a subservient learning style becomes the inevitable and expedient method of transmission.

Tuesday: lesson two – English (0945 – 1035)

The second lesson of the day was English. The class teacher's attitude to conversation was underlined by Mo's comment whilst taking the register: 'I prefer not to talk over the racket, please.' Racket was not an accurate description of the sound level. This business of registers at the start of every lesson! The constant roll-calls put me in mind of films like *Escape From Alcatraz* or *The Great Escape*. No wonder it's hard to foster an atmosphere of mutual trust during a tutor period that is preceded and succeeded by the unlocking and locking of classroom doors and the taking of a register to make sure no inmate has gone AWOL. Dynamic institutional talk about empowerment, emancipation and participation seemed pretty hollow in this prisonlike regime of suspicion.

This was the same setted group as yesterday (Set 2) with the same teacher, and the lesson was a facsimile of yesterday's lesson. There were 14 girls and 15 boys and they sat more-or-less in the same four alternating boy/girl rows of yesterday (Figure 3.18).

There were two pupils absent yesterday who were now present: a boy making up the two-boy/two-girl quartet at the back, and another girl making up the pair of girls in the back row. One boy from the third row was absent. All the pupils who were present on both days were sitting in the same seats; and the absent pupil's seat was left vacant to await his return, as had been the seats of the two absent pupils yesterday. Classroom territoriality.

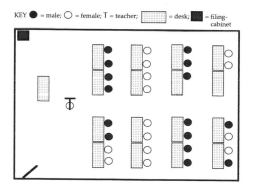

KEY ● = male; ○ = female; T = teacher; ▭ = desk; ■ = filing-cabinet

Figure 3.18 Plan of English room showing seating arrangements, Tuesday

For seven minutes (0955–1002) Mo reviewed the note-making techniques mentioned yesterday and set a target: that pupils should complete their notes on the first section of the essay, dealing with the first 20 pages of the novel. Three girls spoke voluntarily and five boys. Mo asked three girls to speak and two boys. For the next 27 minutes (1003–1030) the pupils worked individually in near silence and Mo moved around the class offering support. At 1030, Mo spent two minutes (1030–1032) drawing the lesson to a close and set homework: to carry on with the notes. The class packed away and waited for the bell for break. Once again, Emily had worked assiduously and had added to her notes.

Tuesday: lesson three – business studies (1050 – 1140)

The lesson after break was business studies. Three girls who were absent yesterday, plus the girl who was seated at the front for ancillary support, now took up the tables at the rear of the rhomboid (Figure 3.19).

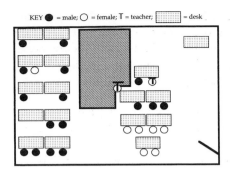

KEY ● = male; ○ = female; T = teacher; ▢ = desk

Figure 3.19 Plan of business studies room showing seating arrangements, Tuesday

Yesterday, I had sat at the last table on the right, by the door, but when I arrived the places were taken by two girls. I moved across the central aisle to take a vacant seat in the last row on the left. No sooner had I sat than a boy came in:

'That's my seat.'

'Do you mind if I sit here today? I need to sit at the back so I can see everyone.'

'Yeh, but I always sit there, sir.'

'He always sits there, sir,' confirmed the boy on my left.

The dispossessed boy looked plaintive, uncomfortable.

'Hey, Thommo, he's nicked your seat,' teased one of the girls opposite.

'Come on then,' I said, 'here you go.'

I moved out to the spare place in the next row down. Thommo didn't thank me; why should he, it was his seat. He sat with a sigh. Territorial possession.

The lesson conformed to the familiar pattern: teacher-controlled didactic introduction followed by pupils working silently and individually on the same written task. For 18 minutes (1058–1116) Mrs Sears demonstrated again the calculations for computing VAT and then amplified notes she had written on the board about different kinds of direct taxation. Boys made three voluntary contributions; girls none. For ten minutes (1116–1126) the class copied notes from the blackboard into their exercise books (Figure 3.20).

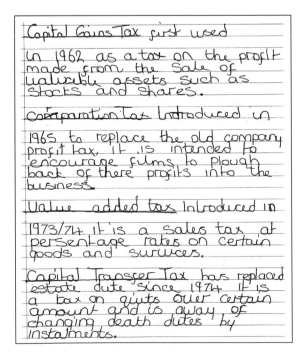

Figure 3.20 Notes copied from the blackboard by Emily in business studies, Tuesday

For the last 11 minutes of the lesson (1127–1138) Mrs Sears explained about inflation. As yesterday, in the closing minutes of the lesson, a topic – barter – that the pupils could identify with sparked interest and real discussion, with the pupils asking questions rather than answering them (a boy bluntly asked Mrs Sears, 'What could you barter? You haven't got anything.'). Boys made five voluntary contributions, girls three. Emily was one of the contributors:

'If people . . . like, if people exchange what they're wearing for food, they'll have nothing more to exchange because they'll have eaten all the food and they won't have any clothes left.'

Emily's point was treated seriously (no-one sought to make facetious capital out of the nudity aspect) and as Mrs Sears and the girls pursued the notion of skills barter, the boys began to discuss the subject among themselves. The rigidly-controlled, teacher-led lesson was changing to a self-motivated small group discussion. However, it appeared that Mrs Sears only has a didactic model for lessons, and that her perception was not that learning was breaking out but that control was breaking down. She called the lesson 'to order' (her phrase), cutting the group discussion short.

As I watched this process, two points occurred to me. First, it is easier for the teacher to maintain control of the class during teacher-led talk if the pupils are not interested, for once they are, they will seek to break out of the teacher-led discussion to express themselves more directly and quickly to each other. Second, Mrs Sears interpreted the boys' spontaneous discussion as an erosion of her control; there was no recognition that she had done a better job when she found something that the class wanted to talk about amongst themselves. Mrs Sears's conception of good teaching seems to mean the teacher dominating a biddably silent class, with any talk directed to and through her.

Tuesday: lesson four – drama (1140 – 1230)

The last lesson of the morning was drama. I had assumed that this lesson would allow more group activities, more chance for pupils to talk, discuss, reflect on what they were doing, but in fact the lesson was fairly passive and, again, teacher-dominated. The drama suite was a converted classroom that had had the windows painted black. The room was shabby and cave-like and smelt sweaty. The strong tendency to gender segregation remained: no pupil sat between two members of the other gender – nor had done in any lesson either this week or during the Key Stage 3 tracking at Tiverdale (Figure 3.21).

Mrs Duncan, the teacher, arbitrarily divided the class into four groups (three of which comprised five pupils and one of three pupils) by counting heads anti-clockwise from where she was seated. Group A, the first five pupils to her right consisted of two boys and three girls, Group B, four girls and one boy, Group C, three boys and two girls and Group D, the three boys on Mrs Duncan's immediate left. Group A then left the room whilst the rest of the class decided a mime for Pupil One in Group A to perform. Pupils One

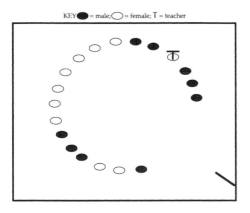

KEY ● = male; ○ = female; T = teacher

Figure 3.21 Plan of drama room showing seating arrangements, Tuesday

and Two were then invited into the room and Pupil Two watched Pupil One perform a mime which Mrs Duncan had whispered to Pupil One when he re-entered the room. The 'game' (Mrs Duncan's definition) was a mime version of Chinese Whispers. This took until 1155 (15 minutes). Then Pupil Three was invited in and Pupil Two performed his understanding of Pupil One's mime. At 1158, Pupil Three performed her understanding of Pupil Two's version of Pupil One's mime for Pupil Four, who had now been asked into the room, and at 1202 Pupil Four performed for Pupil Five (who had so far spent 22 minutes of the 50-minute lesson in the corridor). This took until 1207. From the time that the sequence of mimes had started, all pupils had had to remain silent, for otherwise they might have given clues away (another example of the prevalent lesson atmosphere of secrecy, of not telling others, of not sharing work). At 1207, Pupil Five (a girl) revealed that she had been miming the changing of a nappy. Pupil One (a boy) revealed that the original mime had been the gutting and skinning of an animal.

This first group of five pupils had taken 27 minutes to go through the mime sequence, leaving only 23 minutes of the lesson for the 13 pupils in the other three groups to perform. Necessarily, there was a rather rushed feel to the rest of the lesson, which there need not have been other than for the teacher's insistence that every mime be performed under her scrutiny. Had she allowed each group to perform their mimes to themselves, then there would have been ample time, and a more positive use of that time in involving more pupils actively. Between 1223 and 1225 Emily got to watch a boy's mime and then perform her version of it. As she watched she talked to herself: 'Do it again! (Laughs). I know what that one is! No . . . I got an idea, I got it!' When the boy revealed his mime, Emily said: 'The first time I saw him do it, I thought he was like peeping in on people taking photographs.'

In a 50-minute drama lesson, Emily had had two minutes of primary involvement, watching and performing a mime. Her only speaking is recorded above. This lesson was similar to the business studies lesson that preceded it and the English lesson before that: teacher-controlled throughout, talk disallowed without the teacher's permission, and talk seen as giving something away, of letting others in on what you know, of revealing a secret and therefore diminishing yourself: all part of the ethos that learning is a lonely business and any hard-won information you have gathered, whether it is about Ralph or VAT or what mime someone is doing, should not be given away.

Tuesday: lesson five – German (1335 – 1425)

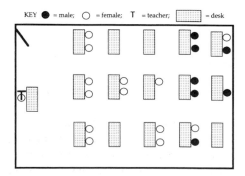

KEY ● = male; ○ = female; T = teacher; ▭ = desk

Figure 3.22 Plan of German room showing seating arrangements, Tuesday

The first lesson of the afternoon was German. The class was setted (Set One) and comprised 20 pupils (13 girls, 7 boys), evidence to support Mr Oldman's observations on the gender-loading of language studies option groups (Figure 3.22).

For the first time, girls dominate the front of the class. Do the most confident, adept pupils in a particular lesson take the front, possibly because they will be more able to attract the teacher's eye? There was no evidence really in this lesson, because it was taken by a supply teacher and there was very little teacher–pupil

> *Describe where you live, say what you have in your bedroom. Say what you like to eat, what you like to do and what you dislike. Add anything else you can remember. Finish it off with von Dienem - boy; von Deiner girl; Lieber Brieffreund - boy; Lieber Brieffreundin - girl.*

Figure 3.23 Notes written on blackboard by teacher, German, Tuesday

discussion. For seven minutes (1341–1348) the supply teacher wrote on the board the instructions the German teacher had left, which concerned the writing of a letter to a (fictitious?) penfriend (Figure 3.23).

Pupils were helpful to the supply teacher, girls responding voluntarily three times, boys twice ('She's got our books, Miss, look, they're there . . . there's paper in her desk drawer, Miss.') Four pupils were withdrawn for conversational German with the Assistante. The class settled down to write their penfriend letters (Figure 3.24). This took the remaining 36 minutes of the lesson (1349–1425). The scope for extended autobiography was plentiful: 'Add anything else you can remember . . .'

Witte about family and
friends what pets I have
what
Write about brother (sister) not
Write about pets if got any

Dear friend
I am called Emily
I am 10 years old and I
live in [redacted]

Liebe Briefreondin
Ich heiße
Emily ich bin funfzehn 15 Jahre alt
Ich wohne ins ins. Ich habe
ein bruder und kein
Schwester Sein name ist
Shayne er ist neunzehn und
ich haben ein hund, zwei
katze ein kaninchen und
ein vogel da.

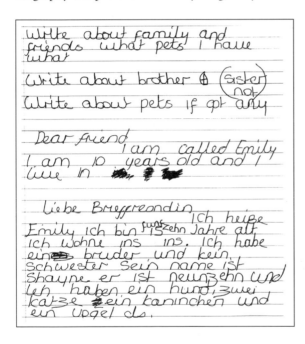

Figure 3.24 Draft of letter to her penfriend, written by Emily in German lesson, Tuesday

Tuesday: lesson six – physical education (1425 – 1515)

The last lesson of the day was PE, with pupils segregated, not just for the changing, but for the activities that followed. The girls played volleyball for 30 minutes (1440–1510).

Tuesday: summary

The day had seen the same hotchpotch of short, unrelated lessons that characterized the timetable at Tiverdale: a tutor period that didn't really exist, a lesson of silent note-making in English, more listening and note-making in business studies, followed by an extraordinary drama lesson of sitting in silence, letter-writing with a supply teacher in German, rounded off with half-an-hour's PE. Emily had been in a different group for every lesson and four different grouping systems had been used: tutor group, set, mixed-ability option and gender. The type of lesson activities were much the same as yesterday, with teacher-led talk dominating (89 minutes or 30 per cent of lesson time), followed by note-making (37 minutes or 12 per cent of lesson time). During the teacher-led talk, Emily spoke for 24 seconds or 0.5 per cent of the time. The rest of the lesson time consisted of 36 minutes (12 per cent) of letter-writing, a fill-in activity due to the absence of the teacher, and 30 minutes (10 per cent) of volleyball. A hundred and eight minutes of possible lesson time (36 per cent) was lost today in room-changing, register-taking and tutor period.

Wednesday: lesson one – history (0855 – 0945)

The first lesson of Wednesday morning was history, which, for the second session of the week, was taken by a different teacher from Mr Oldman. The pupils also studied a different topic, in a different classroom. With Mr Oldman, they were studying the rise of Communism in China, with Mo (who is also their English teacher) they were doing a course on Health Through the Ages. To compound the lack of continuity, Mo was away on a course and the lesson was taken by a colleague covering the lesson. Mo had left instructions that a video should be set up by the AVA technician and shown to the pupils. However, there was a problem in getting the machinery to work which delayed things; not that it really mattered for the video was only 23 minutes long and Mo had left no further instructions. The video (*Sanitation and Sewage in Victorian Britain*) was watched from 0910–0933 and then the pupils chatted quietly until the lesson ended at 0945.

Wednesday: lesson two – maths (0945 – 1035)

The second lesson was maths and the class, sitting in the same places, worked quietly on the tasks they had been working on yesterday (0949–1035; 46 minutes) while the teacher and the support teacher chatted with each other.

Wednesday: lesson three – English (1050 – 1140)

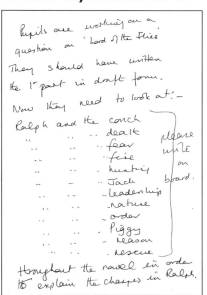

The third lesson was English, but with Mo away on her course, the class continued making notes on Ralph in *Lord of The Flies* (1052–1140; 48 minutes). Mo had left instructions for the cover teacher that were intended to ensure that there was more than enough work to occupy the pupils throughout the lesson (Figure 3.25). However, pupils seemed to do little work, but chatted quietly. Occasionally, the cover teacher, would make a general comment ('Come on now', 'Watch the noise now'), but throughout the lesson he sat at the teacher's desk and marked a pile of exercise books he had brought with him. I have drawn attention to the micro-activities within lessons as a form of teacher control, but another tactic is to

Figure 3.25 English lesson notes left by the subject teacher for the cover teacher, Wednesday

over-burden pupils with tasks that cannot possibly be completed within the given time. Neither Mo, in this lesson, nor Mr Oldman with the note-making in history on Monday, can have had any expectation that the pupils would finish either task – but their imposition guaranteed that no pupil could claim that they had no work to do.

Wednesday: lesson four – physical education (1140 – 1230)

The morning ended, for Emily, with volleyball in the hall. (1155–1220; 25 minutes).

Wednesday: lesson five – Science 1 (1335 – 1425)

The first lesson of the afternoon was Science 1 but the teacher was absent although there was supply cover. The class did exercises on light from a worksheet that was distributed at the beginning of the lesson (1340–1425; 45 minutes). Both the execution of the exercise by the pupils and the supervision by the teacher were as desultory as in every other classroom lesson today (Figure 3.26).

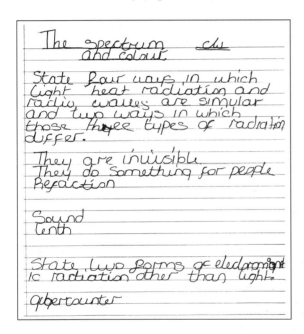

Figure 3.26 Emily's answers to the Science 1 worksheet, Wednesday

Wednesday: lesson six – social education (1425 – 1515)

The final lesson of the day was social education. The teacher spent two minutes introducing the guest speaker (1433–1435). The speaker gave a 30-minute presentation on drink-driving (1435–1505) which was followed by a ten-minute video on the same subject (1505–1515).

Wednesday: summary

Of the six lessons today, two were taken by 'cover' teachers (members of the Forestmead staff who were timetabled as having a marking period that coincided with the lesson they supervised) and one lesson was taken by a supply teacher (a teacher employed on a daily basis to take the lessons of a member of staff, either when it is known beforehand that the member will be absent, or after the member has been absent for three consecutive days). The supply teacher who took German yesterday took science today (so much for the need for subject specialism). Internal cover was provided for English and history lessons, which meant the cover teachers losing their marking periods unless, as they both did, they marked during the cover periods. Both supply teachers and cover teachers are obviously not expected to do any more than babysit a class which is working to instructions left either by the absent teacher or her head of department. Of the three other lessons, one was given over to a presentation by a visiting speaker, one consisted of a game of volleyball and the other was maths in which Emily and her group worked quietly and largely unsupervised, even though there were only nine pupils in the class and two teachers. In fact, Emily has not been taught by a subject specialist in any of her lessons today; rather she has been supervised by an assortment of substitutes as she undertook a series of written tasks, which she was expected to complete individually and silently.

Once again, Emily was in a different pupil grouping for each lesson, although these were not different from previous lessons, i.e. she was in the same group as she had been earlier in the week for the same subject lessons: history, maths, English, PE and science (although for only two of these did she have the teacher she had had the day before). As four of the lessons were taken by Forestmead teachers providing internal cover, supply teachers or guests, and the other two lessons were maths (groupwork) and PE, there was none of the teacher-led talk that characterized lessons earlier in the week. Predictably enough, when that element was removed from lessons it was replaced by its usual partner in most lessons: note-taking. Today 93 minutes (31 per cent of lessontime) was spent on note-taking and comprehension exercises, and 46 minutes on sums (15 per cent). The other three activities were video-watching (11 per cent), listening to a guest speaker's talk (11 per cent) and volleyball (8 per cent). Seventy-one minutes (24 per cent) were spent in room changes and lesson registration.

Thursday: lesson one – Science 2 (0855 – 0945)

The first lesson of the day was Science 2 and Mr O' Dowd introduced a new topic on forces and energy and distributed printed notes for pupils to put in their folders (Figure 3.27). He explained the experiment that he wanted the pupils, in the groups at their tables (same as previous lesson) to conduct (0905–0910; five minutes). For the next quarter of an hour, pupils conducted the experiment: heating a test-tube containing water with a Bunsen burner (0910–0925; 15 minutes). This was the first example of collaborative work for the week. It was not to last long. Next the pupils wrote up the experiment individually (0925–0940; 15 minutes) before spending five minutes packing away (Figure 3.28).

Thursday: lesson two – Science 1 (0945 – 1035)

In the next part of this 'double' lesson, the class moved to Lab One. Mrs Graham was back today and the class was told that today's lesson was to be an assessment assignment on pendulums. She explained where the equipment was (0945–0950; five minutes). The pupils were to work in collaborative groups which they chose for themselves (Figure 3.29).

All but one of the groups were single sex; there was one group of four with one boy in it – this in a class that is almost equally divided: 13 girls and 12 boys. The pupils worked

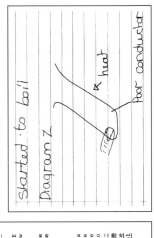

Heat energy on the move

Diagram A

heat — cold water

Method: We filled a test tube with cold water and held it of the bunsen burner and heated it at the bottom, we held the test tube at the top.

Results: the water started to heat at the bottom and then started to rise to the top of the test tube if the water

Started to boil

Diagram Z

← heat

Poor conductor

Figure 3.28 Emily's writing-up of the classroom experiment in Science 2, Thursday

FORCES AND ENERGY

Forces can change the shape and size of an object - measured in NEWTONS. Forces have size and direction (vector quantities) - Measuring forces in context - RESULTANT FORCE of two or more forces acting on a body. Forces cause extension or compression of springs - proportional to force applied. Forces act in pairs (every action has an equal and opposite reaction) they change the speed or direction of an object -centripetal force and circular motion. Newtons first (object remains at rest unless an unbalanced force acts on it) & third laws (every action has an equal and opposite reaction).
Turning forces - moment of a force - balanced moments and equilibrium - calculate the moment of a force.

Forces in buildings and structures - shape and strength - triangles in steelwork and bonding in brickwork. Centre of gravity (mass) and be able to find it for an irregular lamina.

All objects have MASS (kg) and attracted to centre of the earth by a force called GRAVITY - force of attraction is known as WEIGHT. Know that under the influence of this force objects accelerate in free fall as speed increases so does air resistance - when air resistance = weight object falls at constant speed (terminal velocity) - If no air present all objects fall at the same speed - speed = distance/time. The acceleration depends on the mass of the body and the force applied. Know the equation WEIGHT = m * g Know about Newtons second law of motion (change in speed depends on applied force)- be able to use the equation force = mass * acceleration

POTENTIAL & KINETIC energy - know that one form of energy can be converted to another - using kinetic energy in windmills and waterwheels. energy is conserved (changes form but not destroyed) Food and fuels are chemical potential energy sources- electricity generation from coal, oil and natural gas - using these substances produces carbon dioxide -build up of carbon dioxide in the earth's atmosphere and the Greenhouse effect - the decisions we have to make over future energy uses.
Heat energy can be transferred by CONDUCTION, CONVECTION and RADIATION. Saving energy by use of loft insulation, water tank insulation, cavity wall insulation, double glazing, thick curtains and draught excludes. Saving energy by making use of solar energy, using low energy light bulbs, using microelectronics and fibre optics wherever possible.
Use of alternative energy source - wind, waves ,hydroelectric and tidal generators as renewable energy sources.

Energy transfer is needed to make things work. FRICTION and the important part it plays in making things work - drive systems e.g.gears , chains, belts and pulleys - state of car tyre & road surface - speed - kinetic energy) of the affects its stopping distance. Kinetic energy = $\frac{1}{2} mv^2$.

High friction and low friction in sport - how do we achieve it - thrust and drag and their importance.
Forces in liquids - car brakes - piston area and force. PRESSURE is measured in Pascals - pressure =force/area - relate to snow shoes, house foundations, elephant and girl in stiletto heels.

Know that the unit of energy is the JOULE, and that the work done is found from ENERGY = FORCE * DISTANCE MOVED. Compare the efficiency of a device = input / output energy.
POWER is the rate of doing work and is measured in WATTS.

MOMENTUM and collisions - momentum is always conserved in a collision - when momentum changes a force is exerted, the more rapid the change of momentum the greater the force used - crumple zones and safety helmets used to increase the impact time and to reduce the force. Explain how motion is produced in rockets - relate this to the conservation of momentum - know that momentum is calculated from mass * velocity and use this to calculate momentum or velocity. Calculate rocket thrust from rate of fuel consumption and exhaust velocity.

Figure 3.27 Notes distributed to pupils in Science 2, Thursday

KEY ● = male; ○ = female; T = teacher; ▨ = desk; ▨ = work-surface

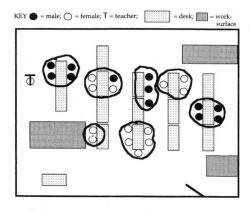

Figure 3.29 Plan of Science I room showing collaborative groups, Thursday

enthusiastically and methodically for the next 31 minutes (0950–1021) and then spent nine minutes making notes for their assessment of the experiment which would be written individually later. The pupils obviously enjoyed the lesson: there was a good atmosphere. This double lesson of science was the first time in the week (excluding PE which is collaborative and competitive, rather than collaborative and cooperative), that pupils have worked in groups, a total of 46 minutes out of 708 minutes of lessontime, or only 6 per cent of the time.

Thursday: lesson three – German (1050 – 1140)

The next lesson was German, and was conducted in German throughout by Miss Chawietz who had returned from illness. The first part of the lesson (1058–1125; 27 minutes) was led by the teacher and was based on a conversation exercise in the pupil's textbooks. As the pupils responded, so Miss Chawietz used the blackboard to build up a vocabulary list of verbs, nouns, adverbs and adjectives which pupils could pick and choose to make up sentences about leisure pursuits.

For the first time in the Key Stage 3 and 4 tracking, girls appeared to dominate the verbal exchanges with the teacher. Girls responded voluntarily 48 times, boys 12 times; the teacher asked girls to respond 12 times, boys five times. Emily did not speak during this 27-minute session. There were nearly twice as many girls in the group – 15 : 8. Transferred to the kind of table used for Monday's lessons the statistics look like this (Table 3.2).

Compared with the earlier figures, there seems to be the suggestion that a class has to consist of nearly two thirds girls before they make a similar contribution to discussion as boys will make when they only represent about half the pupils, i.e that a class *is not representative of equal opportunity by pupil-numbers alone*: an approximately 1:1 ratio of boys (English, history, science) gives around a 1:3 ratio of voluntary responses (Table 3.3).

Also, in the German lesson, a class of 35 per cent boys is still getting 31 per cent of asked responses, whereas asked responses for girls in 1:1 ratio classes is somewhere around half their numerical percentage (see Table 3.2). Business studies is the only lesson in which the

Table 3.2 Teacher-led talk opportunities by gender ratio German, Thursday

Subject	Boys, %	Girls, %	Boys' volunt. respons., %	Girls volunt. respons., %	Boys' asked respons., %	Girls' asked respons., %
German	35	65	20	80	31	69

Table 3.3 Teacher-led talk opportunities by gender ratio (all Forestmead lessons)

Subject	Boys, %	Girls, %	Boys' volunt. respons., %	Girls volunt. respons., %	Boys' asked respons., %	Girls' asked respons., %
English	54	46	75	25	75	25
History	50	50	78	22	0	0
Science 1	48	52	100	0	66	33
Science 2	48	52	75	25	75	25
Business studies	80	20	83	17	75	25
German	35	65	20	80	31	69

percentage of boys and girls in the class closely correlates with the percentage of voluntary and requested responses during teacher-led talk.

Next, pupils worked in pairs (more collaborative work), using the support of the vocabulary on the board to converse about what they do during their leisure time (1125–1133; eight minutes). To end the lesson (1133–1140; seven minutes) the teacher dictated sentences in English and pupils wrote them in German, referring to the board when necessary: 'I have visited the museum . . . I have played golf . . . I got to know some nice people . . .' Just before this activity started, a boy queried the instructions, which the teacher had given in German. Emily turned and, with class and teacher listening, confidently, clearly and accurately explained what was about to happen. She spoke for nearly a minute – longer than she had in all the rest of the week's lessons put together.

Thursday: lesson four – maths (1140 – 1230)

The last lesson before lunch was maths, and the class did what they had done in the previous maths lessons, got on with their arcane tasks whilst chatting quietly. The class was taken by a supply teacher, with David the support teacher also present. (1146–1230; 44 minutes). These are really weird lessons: ten pupils in two groups with two teachers, just sitting quietly doing interminable sums or making shapes with stickle bricks; presumably there's an infinite number of shapes one can make with stickle bricks.

'I like Maths,' Emily had told me as we walked over to the lesson. 'I don't have to do anything.'

Thursday: lessons five and six – drama (1335 – 1515)

The afternoon session comprised a double lesson of drama. From 1340–1515 (95 minutes) the pupils worked in groups, following the instructions on a worksheet. The instructions were for a piece of improvisation involving an argument between a middle-aged couple and their son and pregnant daughter-in-law who had left university and come to live with them. The worksheet promulgated the secrecy ethos that pervades lessons: 'Now read your separate instructions. Do not tell the others what you have read.' The worksheet also expressed some unsympathetic and stereotypical views about women: 'she had a baby' – not *they* had a baby; 'Jim had to leave college' – not he left college; 'to earn enough money to support Betty and the baby' – not to earn enough money to support himself, Betty and the baby.

At the teacher's insistence, and because it would be patently silly otherwise, the pupils worked in mixed groups of four – two boys, two girls, as required by the characters in the sketch. The worksheet required pupils to improvise out of their age-range and experience of life, which may have reinforced stereotyping, because the improvisations descended into an angry stand-off between the characters: 'Why are you late? You've been down the pub again!' 'Shut up, I'm the one who earns the money, aren't I?' and so on. The groups disintegrated into antagonistic or giggling boy versus girl pairs. The lesson ended with a self-conscious and half-hearted showing of the improvisations accompanied by embarrassed guffaws and 'shuttups'.

Thursday: summary

Today, Emily had been engaged in four different learning activities: pupil groupwork (149 minutes or 50 per cent of lessontime), sums (44 minutes or 15 per cent), teacher-led talk (37 minutes or 12 per cent) and note-making (31 minutes or 10 per cent). Thirty-nine minutes (13 per cent) were spent in movement between rooms and lesson registration.

The surprise activity, in the light of the common pattern of lessons throughout the week, was the groupwork which occupied 50 per cent of lessontime. This should be seen in the context of the week's learning styles and the conditions of the groupwork. The 149 minutes of groupwork today represented the total groupwork time for the week – 10 per cent of lessontime. Nearly two-thirds of this time (95 minutes) comprised the drama lesson, which on analysis proved to be less than successful and was only taken by 18 pupils in a year group of 128. The science groupwork was based upon expediency rather than pedagogy: there was not enough equipment for pupils to work individually. This leaves eight minutes of pair work in German, when pupils tried out newly learnt phrases on each other. Again, this may have been expediency: if pupils don't talk to each other in a language lesson, when do they? Groupwork is rarely encouraged of itself, and pupil-to-pupil talk is not valued – not even recognized – as a powerful aid to learning. But this is not surprising if learning is seen to mean note-taking, the predominant activity of the week. If learning means note-taking, then the best classroom condition for learning is individuals working in silence. The image is of an old-fashioned library rather than a contemporary learning centre.

Although Emily had no subject lesson that she had not had earlier in the week, in most of the lessons there seemed no direct link with the previous lesson: from the Greenhouse Effect to a new topic on Forces and Energy in Science 2, from light to pendulums in Science 1, a groupwork improvisation in drama having no connection with the whole-class mime of the last lesson in content or style.

Friday: lesson one – Science 2 (0855 – 0945)

The first lesson was Science 2, and Mr O' Dowd began with a four-minute recap of the experiment conducted the previous day (0900–0904). He asked three boys and three girls to make comments. For the next 12 minutes (0904–0916) pupils silently, and individually, read from their text-books the section relevant to the experiment, having been told by Mr O' Dowd to use the index to find the required pages. The remainder of the lesson (0916–0946; 30 minutes) consisted of copying notes from the board (Figure 3.30). As individuals finished, they made notes from their textbooks to help with their homework (Figure 3.31). Every other lesson today followed this format of teacher talk followed by note-making.

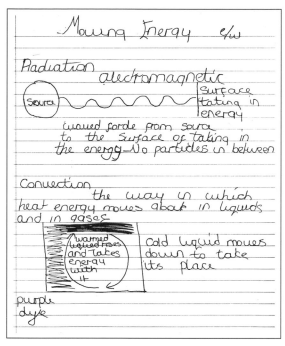

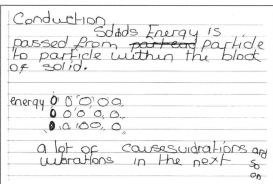

Figure 3.30 Notes copied by Emily from the blackboard in Science 2, Friday

Figure 3.31 Notes Emily copied from her textbook in Science 2, Friday

Friday: lesson two – history (0945 – 1035)

In history, the subject was Communist China. Mr Oldman delivered an entertaining and erudite 26-minute lecture on Communist China, looking at bias, propaganda and interpretation of facts (0955–1021). Until the end of the lesson (1022–1035; 13 minutes) pupils made notes on the lecture, also referring to their textbooks.

Friday: lesson three – business studies (1050 – 1140)

In business studies, Mrs Sears addressed the class on ways of curbing inflation (1056–1112; 16 minutes). Until the end of the lesson (1112–1140; 28 minutes) pupils read the chapter on inflation in their textbooks and made notes on it. Emily's notes are a direct copy from the textbook (Figure 3.32 opposite).

Friday: lesson four – German (1140 – 1230)

In German, the pupils copied a chart from the board (Figure 3.33) and filled it in in German (1145–1230: 45 minutes).

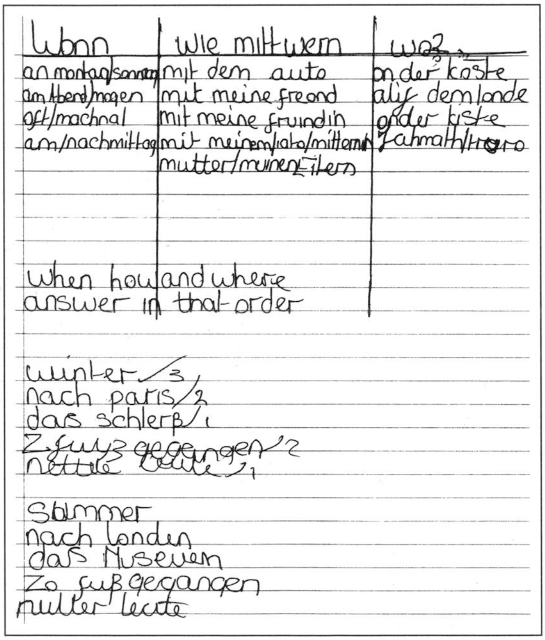

Figure 3.33 Notes copied from the blackboard by Emily in German, Friday

Friday: lesson five – maths (1335 – 1425)

In maths, the pupils carried on where they had left off the previous lesson: chatting quietly as they automatically made stickle-brick shapes or did simple sums (1335–1415: 40 minutes). Once as a student I had a holiday job in a factory, picking broken biscuits from the conveyor belt. It was a mindless job that required no application. The boredom was relieved by chatting to the other work mates on the production line. The pupils seemed to conduct their maths lessons in exactly the same spirit.

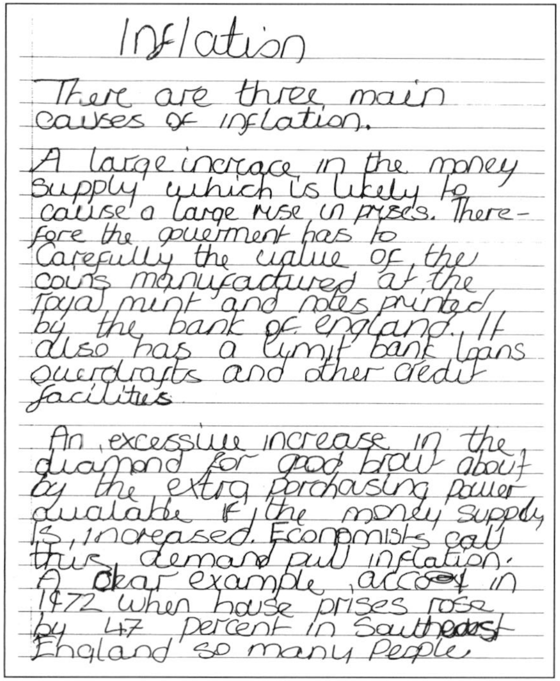

Inflation

There are three main causes of inflation.

A large increase in the money supply which is likely to cause a large rise in prices. Therefore the government has to carefully the value of the coins manufactured at the mint and notes printed by the Bank of England. It also has a limit bank loans overdrafts and other credit facilities

An excessive increase in the demand for good food about by the extra prchasing power available if the money supply is increased. Economists call this demand pull inflation. A clear example, occured in 1972 when house prices rose by 47 percent in Southeast England so many people

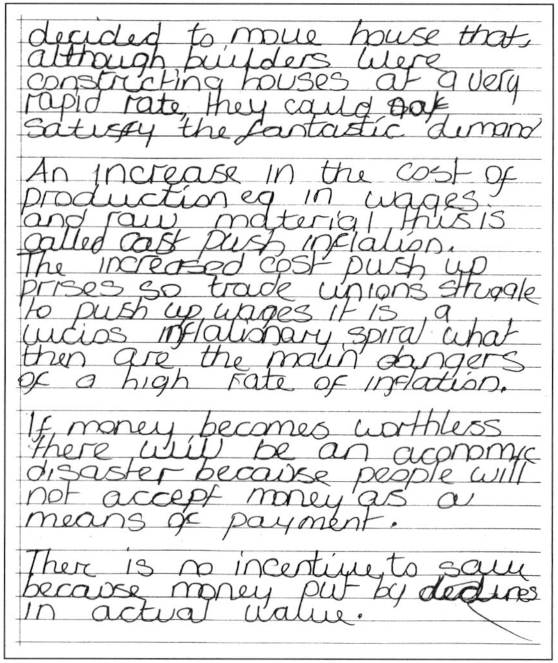

decided to move house that although builders were constructing houses at a very rapid rate they could not satisfy the fantastic demand

An increase in the cost of production eg in wages and raw material. This is called cost push inflation. The increased cost push up prices so trade unions struck to push up wages it is a vicious inflationary spiral what then are the main dangers of a high rate of inflation.

If money becomes worthless there will be an economic disaster because people will not accept money as a means of payment.

There is no incentive to save because money put by declines in actual value.

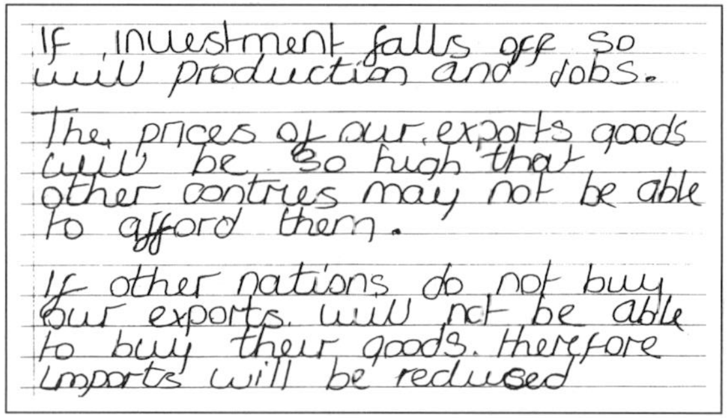

If investment falls off so will production and jobs.

The prices of our exports goods will be so high that other contries may not be able to afford them.

If other nations do not buy our exports will not be able to buy their goods, therefore imports will be reduced

Figure 3.32 Notes copied from her textbook by Emily in business studies, Friday

Friday: lesson six – English (1425 – 1515)

The pupils spent the lesson carrying on individually with notes on *Lord Of The Flies* (1435–1515: 40 minutes). Mo was still absent so the lesson was taken by the head of maths, Miss Layton. Emily had spent most of Tuesday's lesson reading Chapter 1, but the relatively few notes made on Wednesday and today, when the lessons were taken by cover teachers, compared with the copious notes made on Monday, when the lesson was taken by the subject teacher, illustrates the indolence that pervades lessons taken by cover and supply teachers (Figure 3.34).

Friday: summary

Today's lessons comprised only three activities: lectures (46 minutes or 15 per cent of lesson time), note-taking (168 minutes or 56 per cent) and sums (40 minutes or 13 per cent). I commented to Emily on the difference between the level of difficulty in German and English, the two lessons that sandwiched maths, and asked Emily why she was in the bottom set for maths when she obviously found the work easy. Her answer exposed the inefficiencies of a seemingly effective bureaucratic system and also showed how an opportunistic individual could exploit the system to her advantage:

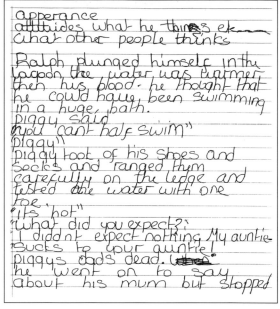

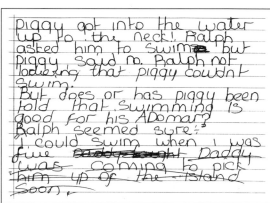

Figure 3.34 Notes made by Emily on Chapter 1 of *Lord Of The Flies* during English on Tuesday, Wednesday and Friday

'Oh, I shouldn't be there, I've always been in Set 2 for maths. It must have been a mistake when the computer printed out my timetable. But no one ever said anything so I just stayed there. It's my time off.'

See Emily play. So ended the week.

See Emily play: summary of the week

Distribution of the 1500 minutes of Emily's timetabled week

Table 3.4 shows Emily's learning activities, generically, throughout the curriculum. Figure 3.35 illustrates Table 3.4 in graphic form.

Table 3.4 The distribution of the 1500 minutes of Emily's timetabled week

Activity	Monday	Tuesday	Wednesday	Thursday	Friday	Totals	%
Note-taking & comp. exs.	131	37	93	31	168	460	30.7
Room changes & register	45	108	71	39	46	309	20.6
Teacher-led talk	83	89	32	37	46	287	19.1
Maths	41	0	46	44	40	171	11.4
Groupwork	0	0	0	149	0	149	9.9
P.E.	0	30	25	0	0	55	3.7
Letter	0	36	0	0	0	36	2.4
Vid-watching	0	0	33	0	0	33	2.2
Totals	300	300	300	300	300	1500	100

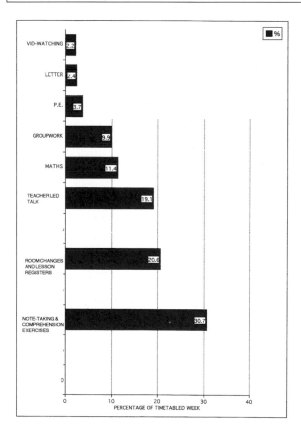

Figure 3.35 Bar graph showing the distribution of the 1500 minutes of Emily's timetabled week

Lesson content

Figure 3.35 shows the predominant lesson style of the week to be didactic teacher-led presentations followed by individual note-taking: 63 per cent of the actual lessontime was spent in this way, 14.5 per cent of the time was spent on maths and the rest of the time was made up of odd bits and pieces: two short volleyball sessions (4.5 per cent), the writing of a letter in German – the closest all week a pupil got to making an individual statement (3 per cent), watching two videos (3 per cent). Twelve-point-five per cent of time appears to have been spent on groupwork, but reservations about the validity of this figure have been made earlier: the groupwork was a matter of expediency rather than pedagogy and was, in the main, of poor quality. The groupwork occurred in only four of the week's 30 lessons: drama (95 minutes), Science 2 (15 minutes), Science 1 (31 minutes) and German (8 minutes.) All the groupwork occurred on one day. Eighty-seven per cent of lessons contained no groupwork; 20.5 per cent of lessontime was taken up by room changes and register-taking.

The limited and repetitive experiences offered to pupils is powerfully demonstrated in Figure 3.35: over 80 per cent of the pupils' time is spent either in, or moving between, lesson after lesson of the same format: lecture followed by silent individual note-making or sums. Based on the percentages in Figure 3.35, here is another way of envisaging Emily's week: a day and a half of making notes, a day of lectures, a day of registration and room changes, half a day of groupwork, half a day of sums, and the remaining half a day spent on writing a letter, watching a video and playing volleyball.

Talk

The Forestmead tracking confirmed the trends suggested at Tiverdale:

- that most talk was teacher-led rather than pupil-to-pupil;
- that most talk was of a factual, not a discursive nature;
- pupils' contributions were generally limited to short phrases lasting only a few seconds that were offered as answers to the teacher's question;
- boys were three times more likely to contribute voluntarily to teacher-led talk;
- boys were three times more likely to be asked to contribute by teachers;
- teacher-led talk was the common form of introduction to a lesson;
- teacher-led talk as an introduction was invariably succeeded by pupils working, individually, in silence;
- pupil-to-pupil talk was discouraged and sometimes pupils were punished for talking;
- boys and girls rarely talked to each other.

Seating

The Forestmead tracking confirmed the trends suggested at Tiverdale:

- boys and girls chose to sit apart;
- boys were asked by the teacher to contribute to teacher-led talk more than girls, wherever they sat in the classroom;
- classroom furniture was arranged to signify discrete areas between the teacher and the pupils.

In addition, the Forestmead tracking illuminated the territorial possession signified by classroom seating. Other pupils would not sit in an absent peer's usual place. Pupils had 'their' seats in every different classroom.

Independent learning

Apart from the few instances of collaborative groupwork (Factor 1), there was virtually no evidence of any of the factors of independent learning. There was no sense of cooperative groupwork (Factor 2) or of individual responsibility (Factor 3) in the independent learning definition of the term, in which the responsibility of the individual is defined in relation to the collaborative groups that an individual is a member of, within the embrace of concentric cooperative groups. Independent learning promotes the responsibility of the individual to others. The Forestmead ethos championed the responsibility of the individual to herself at the expense of others and actively discouraged collaboration and cooperation. Pupils did not design their own tasks, had no stake in the assessment of their tasks, and no control over the timing of tasks (Factors 4, 5 and 6). Although pupils did a great deal of individual reading and concomitant note-making, not once did they initiate their own research (Factor 7). Pupils did not use a range of language technology (Factor 8), in fact pupils did not use any technology. Apart from the guest speaker for social education, there was no interaction with the community and no use of the environment (Factor 9). There was no sense of audience for the pupils' work other than teacher as marker (Factor 10). There was no range of presentation of pupils' work (Factor 11). The sole medium of presentation was hand-written manuscript. There was no evidence of reflexivity, of personal engagement, of self-critical and critical reflection (Factor 12).

Cross-curricular elements

It proved problematical to gather data on the National Curriculum cross-curricular elements of dimensions, skills and themes and the institutional cross-curricular elements of the school's aims. The difficulty stemmed from the vagueness of their wording and therefore the subjectivity required in deciding whether they were:

- present within lessons;
- intended to be present;
- effective if they were present.

For instance, one of the National Curricular cross-curricular dimensions 'which should permeate every aspect of the curriculum' (NCC, 1990a) is Preparation for Life in a Multicultural Society. In many lessons (science, maths, PE) there was clearly no evidence of this dimension: it was not present in lessons. However, although in no lessons was there any explicit reference to Preparation for Life in a Multicultural Society, it was possible to argue that the content of some lessons might be implicitly useful in promoting this dimension. For instance, some knowledge of Communist China might offer pupils a perspective from which to view indigenous Sino-British communities (history). A broader view of multiculturalism, to encompass class and gender, might allow that *Lord Of The Flies* could be maintained to have a contributory effect to an understanding of different cultures (English). In that global economies certainly affect local cultures, business studies may be said to play a part in promoting the dimension of Preparation for Life in a Multicultural Society.

This led to the second consideration: if such undercurrents were detectable, were they intentional? Was Preparation for Life in a Multicultural Society one of Mo's criteria (or one of the Southern Examining Group's criteria, or one of the School Examination and Assessment Council's criteria) for selecting *Lord of the Flies* as a public examination text? Was Preparation for Life in a Multicultural Society one of the recognized aims of the history and business studies lessons on Communist China and taxation? There was no evidence, in discussion with these subject teachers, that they had given consideration to this issue: that the presence of cross-curricular elements should be deliberately implicit – although this was more-or-less the claim of the deputy head i/c Curriculum Development when I asked for a copy of the Forestmead cross-curricular policy: 'It's happening all over the place. We just haven't got round to documenting it yet.'

The third question concerned the effectiveness of lessons to promote cross-curricular elements whether they were intentionally or unintentionally, explicitly or implicitly, present in lessons. It can be argued – as I do in Chapter 7 – that it may not be necessary for either teachers or pupils to be aware of that which is being learnt beneath the surface of a subject lesson. I suggest that teachers can unintentionally indoctrinate pupils, in the sense of suppressing the development of a critical disposition. Might there be evidence of a 'benign' form of indoctrination, so that, although Preparation for Life in a Multicultural Society was not acknowledged by teacher or pupil as an explicit aim of a lesson, the general atmosphere and pedagogy was actively promoting this dimension? There was no evidence, in the lessons that I observed, of any link between lesson content and contemporary society. Moreover, life in a multicultural society involves attitudes and beliefs that constantly need to be re-examined and possibly redefined. In the lessons that I observed, there was no evidence of this kind of personal reflexivity, or of the social and intellectual dialectic that might stimulate it. Knowledge consisted of immutable facts and learning concerned the cognitive and not the affective domain.

These three considerations made it impossible to collect quantitative data about National Curriculum cross-curricular elements or school aims. The qualitative data of observation and the collation of texts studied and created during the week by Emily strongly suggested that there was little or no evidence of cross-curricular dimensions or school aims within lessons, either at an implicit or explicit level, or as a conscious or subconscious aim of the teacher, and therefore no evidence of their effective or ineffective application. Indeed, for one of the dimensions, Equal Opportunities (Gender) there was evidence to suggest that the school system actively promoted the unequal and superior opportunities of boys. On the other side of the coin, the cross-curricular skill of Communication was actively suppressed by constant injunctions for silence.

The above considerations also applied to the cross-curricular skills of numeracy, study, problem-solving, personal and social education, information technology, flexibility and adaptability, of which the NCC considers 'it absolutely essential that these skills are fostered across the whole curriculum in a measured and planned way . . . what is beyond dispute is that in the next century these skills will be at a premium' (NCC, p. 3, 1990a). There was evidence of communication and numeracy, but at a very low level: the understanding of simple instructions and the offering of short-phrase factual answers by pupils during teacher-led talk; and the mindless doing of sums whilst chatting societally. The NCC publication *The Whole Curriculum* does not define any of these cross-curricular skills. 'Study' is defined in the English Orders (1990) as the ability of pupils to 'Select reference books and other information materials and use organisational devices to find answers to their own questions' (*Cox 5–16*, Reading, Level 5 iv, 1989). No pupil selected a reference book; there were no other information materials available than reference books distributed by the teachers, and no pupils found answers to their own questions. There was no evidence of problem solving, personal and social education or information technology. What evidence there was of flexibility and adaptability was not promoted by the school management but was detectable within the pupil body as a subversive defence against the invasions of the system, for example, pupils' interpretation of the command 'Silence' was adjusted to different teachers; or Emily's exploitation of the timetabling error that allowed her to use maths as 'my time off'.

The same is also true of the National Curriculum themes of Economic and Industrial Understanding, Careers Education and Guidance, Health Education, Education for Citizenship and Environmental Education. It is possible to find a few scattered examples that might be used to illustrate some implicit policy (business studies for Economic and Industrial Understanding, the drink-driving lecture for Health Education) but no suggestion that these themes are 'essential parts of the whole curriculum' (NCC, p. 4, 1990a).

Thus, it was not possible to find positive evidence to suggest that cross-curricular elements or the school aims were intended to contribute not just to separate dimensions, skills and themes, but through them to a holistic learning experience for pupils. The opposite was more likely to pertain, with negative evidence of certain cross-curricular elements and a disorientating organization of the curriculum.

Curricular disorientation

There were several practices that contributed to a disorientation of the separate subjects that constituted the school curriculum.

- Lessons in the same subject could occur at any time of the day or week. On Monday, English was the first lesson in the morning, on Friday it was the last of the afternoon. All the afternoon lessons (apart from the single period of social education) were also timetabled during morning sessions at some point in the week. There seemed to be no pattern; apparently any lesson could happen at any time.
- This lack of pattern was also shown in the lack of connections between lessons. There was no attempt to block disciplines together so that links could be explored as in projects like *Minorities* and *Centennial* (see Chapter 6): what flow is there to, say, Tuesday: English to business studies to drama to German to PE?
- There was also a lack of connections between lessons in the same subject: history and science were both taught by two different people in two different classrooms, studying two different topics so that pupils never had two consecutive lessons on the same topic: Communist China in Room 43 with Mr Oldman, followed by health and sanitation in Victorian Britain in Room 42 with Mo, then back to Communist China with Mr Oldman and so on. Or in science: a lesson on sound with Mrs Graham in Lab One was followed by a lesson on the greenhouse effect with Mr O' Dowd in Lab Two, then a return to Lab One for a lesson on light, back to Lab Two for a new topic on Forces and Energy, then to Lab One for the fifth new science topic of the week 'Pendulums'.
- Teacher absence also disrupted continuity. During this week, Emily had cover teachers or supply teachers for lessons in English, German, history and science.

The various elements of room change within a subject, teacher change within a subject, teacher absence, change of topic within a subject, left only business studies and PE undisrupted during this week, i.e.: following the same topic in the same room with the same teacher throughout the week. Mrs Sears spent the three lessons of business studies dealing with taxation and in the two PE lessons the same teacher took the same group for volleyball.

Lesson times

There seems to be a uniformity here, but at the expense of any recognition that some lessons may benefit from being longer than others. One example would be to have a double PE lesson, for in the 100 minutes devoted to single periods, 45 per cent of the time was lost in changing. The eight science periods may be better blocked as four doubles, so that experiments could be given more time – 50 minutes was not really long enough to arrive, be registered, get the gear out, make a few mistakes, get the experiment done, and pack away and write it up.

Grouping systems

A further disorientation was caused by the different grouping systems used, so that Emily did not have two consecutive lessons with the same group of pupils (a very effective means of institutional control, for these constantly forming and disbanding groups are unlikely to develop a dynamic strong enough for them to achieve a corporate identity and purpose). Emily did not work with the same class-grouping of pupils in any of her different GCSE subjects. She had four of her subjects taught in different ability sets (English, science, maths and German) and three of her subjects were taught in different option groups (history, business studies and drama). Of her three non-examination subjects, PE was grouped by gender, and non-examination tutor group and social education were the only lessons she shared with a common class, her tutor group.

This system casts the individual into a void where making cross-curricular connections with other pupils, or with unifying aspects of the curriculum, is almost impossible. It may be that Emily is the only pupil in the school following her particular pattern of lessons. She spends her lesson time in alienated classes, within which groups and individuals are discouraged from relating to each other, studying subjects that are isolated from each other in terms of either a holistic concept of knowledge or of transferable skills, and in which no attempt is made to relate their content to the relevance of her own personal and social life.

Option choices

Emily's timetable is limited in learning styles and in content: no RE, no geography, no music, no computer studies, no art, no design, no technology, no outdoor education. As a profile of a well-educated GCSE student, Emily's list of subjects appears eclectic: English, science and maths, history, German, drama and business studies. What educational philosophy (rather than institutional logic) justifies the personal, social and vocational legitimacy of these arbitrary subject choices, their disparate grouping systems, and their attendant repressive pedagogy?

Pupil-tracking at Key Stages 3 and 4: conclusions

There are many similarities between Tiverdale and Forestmead schools in their philosophy, their organization and their rhetoric. Both appear to share a philosophy of education located firmly within the Peters, Hirst and Dearden tradition that underpins the National Curriculum: that educational attainment is best measured, and therefore served, by the accumulation of knowledge (see Chapter 7). In organizational terms, this philosophy leads to the division of knowledge into prescribed subjects, with prescribed syllabuses for pupils of different ages and abilities. This curriculum is administered via a timetable which requires the individual pupil to join a series of different teaching groups, established by different criteria, for short, discrete lessons in different rooms with different teachers.

One of the effects of this policy is to isolate the individual within the system. This isolation leads to disempowerment and the silencing of the oppressed. Neither Josie nor Emily had any officially recognized decision-making role to play within their school structures. Both school handbooks laid out expected codes of behaviour and sanctions for deviations from the code. Neither handbook suggested that pupils were consulted or played any part in the formulation of these rules. The audience for the handbooks was not the pupil, but the parent (made obvious by the many textual references to 'your child'). Within lessons, pupils had no say in their education. The content, style and pace of all lessons were dictated exclusively by the teachers. Thus, the system disempowered the majority; and then the disempowered were effectively silenced: by their disempowerment itself, which suggested that their voice was not important, not even necessary for the running of the institution; by the absence of any official route for voicing, such as a pupils' council or representation on school committees or the board of governors; but most powerfully, by the ethos of lessons which discouraged collaboration and the development of a critical disposition, the two most critical conditions for effective voicing.

The inevitability of this system seems to unfurl from its basic philosophy of education:

- the notion of learning based on subject knowledge rather than (independent) learning skills **leads to**
- the division of the curriculum into discrete subjects, each seen to require a different specialist teacher **which leads to**
- the division of the school day into short, uniform periods of time for the dissemination of neutralized subject knowledge, which is regarded as having a hierarchy of difficulty **which leads to**
- the division of the pupil body into myriad subject groupings, each using different evaluative criteria **which leads to the disempowerment of the majority.**

The combination of a liberal philosophy of education, a positivist attitude to knowledge and a public examination system that imposes timed tests upon individuals of their memory of knowledge-based syllabuses, has the following practical effects upon lessons:

- a didactic transmission of 'factual' information unrelated to the real world, its communities and environments **and**
- a view of talk as time-wasting and collaboration as cheating and therefore a concentration on silent, secretive, individual work **and**
- a reliance on teacher disseminated texts as the source of authority of knowledge rather than pupil research **and**
- no sense of negotiation with the teacher about lesson content or structure, or the assessment of pupils' efforts **which leads to the silencing of the disempowered.**

Furthermore, the observable attendant effects, in policy and practice, of the philosophy of education espoused by both schools, were inconsistent with the aims of the National

Curriculum, and those school aims that claimed that Tiverdale and Forestmead were committed to develop pupils' interests and intellectual capacities in stimulating lessons. There was a gulf between the rhetoric and the reality of Institution. Both schools were claiming to offer the benefits of educational citizenship; but it was difficult to collect any evidence of a pedagogy, such as independent learning, that was explicitly and commonly intended to promote educational citizenship within lessons.

The function of the National Curriculum is to realize the aims of the Education Reform Act 'to promote the spiritual, moral, cultural, mental and physical development of pupils at school and of society, and to prepare pupils for the opportunities, responsibilities and experiences of adult life' (ERA, 1988). A conclusion can be drawn, that the ends that are claimed for National Curriculum education are not consistent with the means advocated for their development. The findings of the Key Stage 3 and 4 tracking clearly depict practices within schools that are likely to suppress attributes of citizenship appropriate to the third millennium.

I suggest that the aims of the National Curriculum are not translated into practice and that they *cannot* be, because the aims are dissonant with the content of the National Curriculum; that is, that the aims imply a skills-based education typified by experiential learning, whereas the National Curriculum, in operation, enforces a limited academic course restricted to the rote-learning of subject-specific knowledge.

4 All are efforts in vain

A case study of an unstructured independent learning project

Chapters 2 and 3 comprised case studies of the typical presentation of the National Curriculum at Key Stages 3 and 4. As a direct contrast, in the first section of this chapter I present a case study of an early (1988) and ill-defined independent learning project, *Breaking Down The Barriers*, as seen through the eyes of one collaborative group – The Outfit – and told in their own words. The principal findings concern the independent learning that went on in an unstructured and unsupervised five-week course but was not given recognition, the gender divide within the group, the feelings of failure rather than success of the group and teachers' feelings that the project was of limited value. In short, in a book that promulgates cooperative and collaborative groupwork as the key to educational development, I present an example of the kind of groupwork that gives groupwork a bad name, and for which I was responsible.

I am aware that this case study, if not contextualized by the chapters preceding and succeeding it, is likely to have proselytizers of the 'Back to Basics' ideology (such as Chris Woodhead, Melanie Phillips, John Marenbohm, Sheila Lawlor, Nicholas Tate, John Marks, *et al.*) rubbing their hands in glee at what appears to be strong evidence that attempts at democratizing the classroom are highly irresponsible, non-educative and doomed to failure. It would have been easy to have skipped this chapter and leapt in a single bound from my critique of a didactic pedagogy (the National Curriculum as represented in Chapters 2 and 3) to examples of successful independent learning projects that are consolidated by the positive testimony of enthusiastic pupils, teachers, parents and professional observers. But I believe that the self-perceived failure of The Outfit informs as much, if not more, than the clear success described in Chapters 5 and 6. Change is a process, not an event and this chapter links Chapters 2 and 3 with Chapters 5 and 6 to give a more honest and full account of the process of developing from a knowledge-based to a critically reflective curriculum, from a didactic to a democratic pedagogy (from rote-learning to independent learning) and from a liberal education philosophy to a philosophy of educational citizenship. The case study of The Outfit reveals the trauma that moving from one system to another can cause, and what can happen if the transition is not completed and pupils are suspended in the anarchic limbo that does indeed characterize poor libertarian education.

In the second section of this chapter, I offer an analysis of the The Outfit project diaries, once again drawing on the twelve factors of independent learning, as I did in my analysis of the case studies at Key Stages 3 and 4. With Josie and Emily, I believe that my research convincingly illustrates that beneath the institutional veneer of shining efficiency and polished organization, the learning experience was essentially dull and lacklustre. With The Outfit, using the same research procedure (a well-documented case study) and the same tools of analysis (the twelve factors of independent learning), I intend to reveal the opposite:

that whilst the immediate impression is of disorganization and dissent, beneath the surface a meaningful educational experience was taking place.

BREAKING DOWN THE BARRIERS

Two Year 9 English classes at Carnmore, an 11–16 comprehensive school in Greenshire, were combined to form one cooperative group of 32 pupils, whose ability ranged from above average to special needs. The project took place during English lessons over the five school weeks leading up to half-term (from Wednesday 21 September to Thursday 20 October 1988). After the autumn half-term break, two more lessons (Tuesday 1 November and Wednesday 2 November) were devoted to the various collaborative groups' end-of-project presentations. In each week of the project there were three 70 minute English lessons, so the total lesson-time spent upon the project was around 19 hours, or four full school days, a close approximation to the amount of classroom time that was the subject of the Key Stage 3 and 4 trackings (although the curricular time was five days, movement between lessons reduced the *classroom* time to four days for both Josie and Emily).

The project teachers were myself and Sandy Bell, an English teacher with a responsibility for the school library, who had an interest in resource-based learning. No instructions other than the sheet below (Figure 4.1) were given to the pupils, apart from the proviso that the collaborative groups should be mixed in gender and contain members from both the original teaching groups. This ensured a spread of ability within each collaborative group and reduced the possibility of friendship groups forming.

Neither Sandy nor I addressed the whole class during the next five weeks, nor did we formally check work in progress, unless invited to do so by a collaborative group. Pupils were encouraged to find their own work areas (either of the two available English classrooms, library, corridors, foyer, hall, public library, within the local environment and community). Sandy and I toured around the groups, observing but not intervening, and only offering advice at a group's request. During the course of the project, pupils were asked to keep their own diaries, private documents which nobody else (including Sandy and I) should see without the diarist's permission. At the end of the project, I asked each group if I could collect their diaries to see what common themes might have emerged and they all agreed. A reading of the 32 diaries suggested two common themes: first, the difficulties of group dynamics, in particular the clash between boys and girls, with girls feeling boys were lazy and boys thinking girls were bossy; and second, the identification of pupils with the product, not the process, of the project as the sole criterion of success.

BREAKING DOWN THE BARRIERS

This project is designed to break down some of the barriers that exist between and within groups of people.

THE TASKS:

1) Working in a mixed group of 3 - 5 members, research a topic for presentation to an audience of your choice. The presentation must include a literary and an oral component.

2) Working in pairs - although you may take the group's advice - make a liaison within the community.

3) Working individually, undertake an activity that is new to you.

4) Keep a written record of your group, pair and individual work.

ALL TASKS MUST BE PRESENTED IN WRITING TO YOUR TEACHER FOR APPROVAL BEFORE YOU BEGIN WORK.

DEADLINES:

COMPLETION: THURSDAY, OCTOBER 20TH, 1988.
PRESENTATION: TUESDAY, WEDNESDAY AND THURSDAY, NOVEMBER 1ST - 3RD, 1988.

Figure 4.1 Stimulus sheet given to pupils involved in the *Breaking Down The Barriers* independent learning project

I decided to make a closer textual analysis of the diaries of one collaborative group, a group that had named themselves The Outfit. This I did and the conclusions that I reached helped in the planning of later independent learning projects and in the development of the twelve factors of independent learning. But I felt that the full story of The Outfit was still to be learnt. In August, 1991, nearly three years after the project, I contacted the members of The Outfit (who were by this time either in work or further and higher education) to arrange an interview. Transcriptions of the interview, which was audio and video recorded, provided further reflective and corroborative data of the analysis of the diaries. This intensive study revealed to me the pupils' opinions about the development of certain aspects of independent learning, particularly the dynamics within a collaborative group between boys and girls, with a detail that complemented and illuminated the participant observation of myself and Sandy.

The following section recounts the project experience of The Outfit. For reasons of space and balance it is not possible, in this text, to print the full analysis of the diaries and tapes which runs to 30,000 words. The edited account in this book concentrates on the collaborative groupwork of The Outfit and refers only briefly to the individual and pair work that is described in the diaries. The account is chronological and draws on the observations of all five members of the group as recorded in their project diaries. This seems to me to be the clearest way of illustrating the building frustration within the group, a frustration that explodes in violence. In an attempt to convey my role as a participant observer as the project unfolded, I have written my commentary in the present voice.

The Outfit consisted of five members, two girls and three boys. Peter (thirteen years and five months old) was a special needs pupil, although not statemented. He had an affable nature. When he left school he wanted to work on a farm, like his father. Gideon (the oldest member of the group at thirteen years and nine months) was not a good mixer, generally keeping himself to himself. He had not chosen to be in this group originally, but due to illness, his preferred group had dwindled to three pupils who were absorbed into other groups. Sally (thirteen years and seven months) had joined the school at the beginning of term when her parents had moved into the area to take over the local post-office. Sally had an impish side to her personality and a mischievous sense of humour. Anne (thirteen years and four months) was the most obvious initial leader of the group, confident, outspoken, a natural organizer, bossy in a kindly, elder sister kind of way. James (the youngest member of the group at thirteen years and two months old) had a similar background to Peter, although James' father owned his own farm. James was more confident and had a sharper sense of humour than the other two boys.

Lesson one: Thursday, 22 September, 1988

In this first lesson, the pupils from the two classes were invited to form their own collaborative groups, to give themselves a name, to decide on a topic that the group would investigate and to formulate a code of conduct. If time allowed, groups could also give some consideration to their pair and individual work. (In retrospect, this seems – on my part – to have been hopelessly rushed and naive, but more of that later.) The Outfit formed quickly and chose a topic on crime in the community . . .

Peter has allied himself with James, both for his initial contribution to the groupwork and for the pair work. There is some confusion: the project on crime is 'a good idea' but the project itself is 'a bit boring at times' (Peter). Peter has a concrete idea for his first contribution, that involves the local community:

> Next lesson James + I will try to get our police report in for the rest of the group to look at. (Peter)

Is there a subconscious voice at work, perhaps hinting to Peter that this could be a very demanding project? Is that why he qualifies any plans:

> I will try to get our police report in . . . Our pair project is to try and . . . James and I are going to try and . . . (Peter)

Gideon is to work on his own: 'I will be writing up ways of stopping crime in general'. There is a poignancy about Gideon's last two sentences:

> I will be writing up ways of stopping crime in general. Breaking down Barriers is a good project because it makes people more confident – [*but not confident enough to work with anyone else in his collaborative group; RG*] – I'm should be working with Malcolm Bennett But he's been away. (Gideon)

A pairing of Malcolm Bennett and Gideon would have been the reverse of the Peter and James partnership, in which James is the natural leader. In the Malcolm/Gideon pair, Gideon would have been the dominant personality. Malcolm, an easy-going special needs pupil, would have happily gone along with any decisions or ideas of Gideon. There would have been no need for the diffident Gideon to have had to argue his corner as there may be now. Also, with the pairings of James and Peter, and Sally and Anne, Gideon is immediately cast as the loner, within this newly-formed group (and once again within the general peer-groupings of his day-to-day school life).

Gideon's entry suggests that the group are organizing themselves well at this stage: different people allocated to different short-term tasks that will push the project forward by the next lesson, an agenda for which has been decided:

> Next lesson we will be starting on our play and writing up information. (Gideon)

This idea is corroborated by Sally:

> me and Anne are going to St Jude Library and the rest to the police station . . . Next lesson we will write up from the books about crime and violence . . . (Sally)

Anne's brisk summary of the lesson confirms the idea that the group is generally on task:

> Sally and I are going to the library to do some research on crime. Peter and James are going round to a police station . . .

Sally is the first to mention the perceived problem of working with boys:

> It's harder to work with the other sex for they always talk and don't listen to what we have to say. (Sally)

This comment presages the girls' later feelings that it is the girls who should do the organizing and the boys who should do as they are bid by the organizers. At this early stage, Sally mentions that the group has a clear sense of a real audience, 'the top class in primary school' and ideas for the format of the presentation: 'a play involing bulling and the boys will do that and we us girls will do the talk.' However, the seeds of fragmentation are sown. Tasks will not be shared, they will be allocated: 'the boys will do that and we us girls . . .' (Sally)

Lesson two: Tuesday, 27 September, 1988

Despite Sally's comments yesterday about working with boys, in Anne's absence through illness, Gideon and Sally collaborate, both as contributors and as the organizers of the collaborative group's activities:

> Me and Sally started writing up information and organised are group out.   (Gideon)

However, they are not writing together, as becomes evident from Sally's comment:

> Today I acheived finishing my talk on crime and the others in the group have done their own pieces   (Sally)

Sally's phrasing is interesting. She doesn't just write that she has finished a piece of work, but regards it as an achievement.

Peter starts his entry with the statement 'i think that i should do more than i have done'. Why does Peter think he should have done more? He knows that there are no sanctions to be imposed by the teachers. If ever there was an opportunity to do less and get away with it (and this is true of all the pupils involved) *Breaking Down The Barriers* is it. So what pressures are upon him, in the absence of teacher disapprobation: peer influence, self-criticism? The diaries (an opportunity for peer-pressure to express its disapproval) don't – as yet – reveal any animosity towards Peter, although Sally notices without further comment: 'the others in the group have done their own pieces except for Peter' (Sally).

I think that it's a lack of self-esteem based on Peter's own assessment of his contribution that makes him write and feel as he does. The group is a team, and by not pulling his weight, as he sees it, Peter, with his sense of fair play, would feel that he is letting the team down. What does Peter feel he has not done enough of: writing, organizing, decision making? As with Peter's last entry, there are elements of confusion:

> James and I have made up our minds . . . but we have not realy disided on what we are going to do.   (Peter)

Peter does not mention the police interview, although all the others do. This may suggest that he feels no partnership of this particular initiative, perhaps because James has done all the organization, and may be an explanation for the self-criticism in the opening sentence. Or it might be that Peter feels that he should have done more written work – for this is the simple identification with product that all of the pupils use as the main criterion for success. This nobly Stakhanovite but misplaced notion that 'success' and 'hard work' are best measured in the number of hand-written pages (often copied directly from library or text books) that a pupil produces per lesson occurs later in the day's diary entries. Sally has read the police officer's response to James' and Peter's questionnaire and has found it 'very interesting' (Sally). Piecing together comments from Gideon and James, it can be seen how the 'police report' (Peter) or 'interview' (Anne) of Thursday's lesson has changed. James (and Peter?) have written out some questions which they delivered to the police station earlier in the day and collected during this lesson. In terms of conventional lessons, this seems to James to be an indolent way of spending their time: 'We didn't get time afterterwards to do any work' (James).

Maybe it is this use of lesson time (particularly when Gideon and Sally have been assiduously writing) that contributes to Peter's feeling that he should have done more. I think James and Peter are being overly harsh on themselves. Their initiative was very time-effective: they didn't even have to make notes of the police officer's answer. It was an original piece of research, unlike the facts that Sally will have culled from the library books. It has a relevance to the local community: the answers are about the local community by a representative of that community. By giving the policeman a good length of time and privacy, the answers to the questions are likely to be more considered. The written responses are likely to be fuller and more accurate than if the boys had taken notes during an interview. There is physical evidence of the interview (the policeman's handwriting) that means that the boys could not be accused of misinterpretation. The letter will be an attractive artifact in a folder or as part of a display. By their initiative (even if that initiative was primarily a way of wriggling out of having to do some written work – notes of interview and write-up) the two boys have accomplished a great deal, arguably more than Sally and Gideon. Yet they do not recognize this, they don't value what they have done, because they are assessing their contribution against the conventional standards of 'schoolwork'. To James and Peter, and possibly the majority of observers, the two boys have worked a fast one, sloping off to town on a trumped-up errand whilst others were doing the real work: 'writing up information' (Gideon). This is not meant to denigrate or demote the work that Gideon and Sally have done, but to promote James' and Peter's efforts as worthy of praise and as a valuable contribution to the work of the group. Pupils need to be collators and disseminators of information ('writing up information' (Gideon) 'finishing my talk' (Sally)) but they also need to be gatherers of data, creators of research programmes.

Lesson three: Wednesday, 28 September, 1988

During this lesson, Naomi Roberts, formerly a teacher and currently a singer, actress and director of a professional repertory company, talked, one at a time, with all the collaborative groups about their end-of-project presentations. For the first time, The Outfit appear to have had some problems:

> We dissagreed more and more and more and more, owing to this we got nowhere.
> (Gideon)

> We have dicided on a play for a Drunk driver case and we have not agraed on much more.
> (Peter)

In contrast to Peter and Gideon's views, Sally, Anne and James write positively. Anne's entry rebuts Peter's contention that little has been agreed upon:

> Drawn up a play. Tonight Gideon will write up about history of police force. James is doing the modern policemen. Sally a I are doing the play about drink driving, and what happens at a magestrates court.
> (Anne)

Significantly, Anne mentions every member of the group as having a clear task, other than Peter. James' entry is an interesting contrast with Gideon's:

> We spent this lesson working out a play and discussing the homework   (James)

James has spent his time productively 'working out' and 'discussing' various issues (subject of the play) and plans (for homework). Sally writes that 'We have decided on a play', Anne, that the group has 'Drawn up a play'. Yet Peter and Gideon regard the lesson as dissenting and negative.

There is obviously a difference here, perhaps based upon different perceptions of the nature of talk. One pupil's discussion is another pupil's argument. Peter and Gideon, more reticent characters than the other three, may well feel unsettled and uncomfortable in an atmosphere of vigorous discussion, in which opinions are challenged, perhaps robustly dismissed if not articulately substantiated. James, Sally and Anne are more likely to have enjoyed the cut and thrust, the muscularity of this kind of talk. Perhaps Gideon and Peter come from a background in which voices are only raised in anger and not enthusiasm, where the forthright exchange of opinions happens only as argument. If so, they are likely to retreat from involvement and not to value the talk for what it is. Are there different perceptions of talk as a worthwhile classroom activity? Talk isn't proper work . . . Gideon volunteers for writing tasks – and, so far, individual writing tasks. This could be for two reasons: that he sees writing as more valuable than talk; that he chooses writing as a preferred language activity because it is a form in which he feels more confident. Peter finds both written and oral work difficult and demanding. Gideon and Peter have different perceptions of what the lesson has achieved, compared to the other group members. Gideon and Peter don't think that much has been achieved. But it can be argued that a lot has been accomplished: a decision has been reached by the whole group about the form for the live presentation (a play), the subject of the play (drink-driving) and the setting of the action (a magistrate's court). Anne and Sally are to work collaboratively on the script, whilst James and Gideon, working individually, will write about the development of the police force to the present day. The group has had the opportunity to talk their ideas for the play over with a professional actress and director. The script will be based on ideas outlined by the group during the lesson. James' work will be based on his interview with Constable Rowell and Gideon will draw on his earlier research for his piece.

Lesson four: Thursday, 29 September, 1988

Peter's entry is more positive than yesterday. He mentions that the group has now decided on two plays that will involve all five members of the group. One play will be about drunk-driving, as previously agreed, and the second will be about shop-lifting. The plan to present the play to a real audience, pupils from the primary school, is reaffirmed. There is no mention of argument. Is it fanciful to sense relief in Peter's opening phrase? 'We have definitly decided . . .' The play also gives Peter the chance to make an equal contribution: 'with all five of us in it' (Peter).

Anne mentions that Peter is also collaborating on a piece of writing with James: 'Peter was doing a written report with James'. Only Gideon and Sally refer to 'disagreement' (Gideon) and 'arguing' (Sally); and their comments are qualified:

> Still a lot of disagreement but some work was done.   (Gideon)

> the arguing has not been so bad today and we have a lot done . . .   (Sally)

If Peter has begun to find a more secure and purposeful role via his involvement with the play and the written report, then Gideon's isolation seems reinforced. It is not clear what happened, but it seems that Gideon showed his piece on the history of the police to some members of the group, there was some disagreement and the work was destroyed. James and Peter make no mention of this incident. Anne only reports that 'Gideon didn't do anything'. The main information comes from Sally and Gideon. Did they argue? Gideon isn't saying: 'Most of mine got ripped up . . .' Sally states that Gideon himself destroyed the work:

> we have a lot done, except for Gideon who ripped up his piece of work so he is doing it for homework! (Sally)

Is there a suggestion of triumph, a frisson of excitement in the use of that exclamation mark? During the lesson, did Sally become aware of the power of her own language to precipitate action? I wonder what happened, what led up to the ripping of Gideon's work. Was this an act of spiteful bullying, deliberately designed to provoke the most isolated member of the group? Was this another example of the lack of interface between 'argument' and 'discussion' that led to a spontaneous act of self-immolation? Was there a reasoned discussion during which Gideon was persuaded that his piece needed to be reworked to fit the intentions of the group, so that, as a symbol of his agreement with the others, he ruefully tore the draft in half? Whatever happened, the conflict was contained and resolved within the group: neither Sandy nor I was asked to intervene, and, somehow, it was decided that Gideon would rework the piece out of school time:

> I did it again for homework.   (Gideon)

> he is doing it for homework!   (Sally)

> he will do the police force work tonight.   (Anne)

Perhaps the group has been strengthened by the blood-letting, with Gideon accepting the need for a rewrite which he will do, voluntarily, in his own time.

There seems a sense of purpose and energy about today's entries. Is this because the group has found a common, shared task upon which they can all work together; something, as Peter perceptively remarks, 'with all five of us in it'? There are certainly references to a whole range of activities to do with the play:

> Today we made some props for the play . . .   (Sally)

> Drew up some cards for the play.   (Anne)

> We have got the plays . . . started out.   (James)

> we also started another play . . .   (Sally)

> We also did a play.   (Anne)

> In the dinner time we are making the car for our play and props   (James)

In addition, other written work is ongoing: Peter and James are collaborating on a written report, Gideon will redraft his report on the police force, and James mentions that a start has been made on an introduction (this may be the collaborative work with Peter or something different). Work is taking place during lessons, at lunchtimes and in the evenings and the group has now been together for eight days and has not yet sought the advice of a teacher. What would later be recognized as clear markers of a collaborative group in trouble are also emerging: the increasing gender divide, the isolation of one member of the group, a focus on written product, the idea that writing is synonymous with 'work' and that talk is a wasteful activity, the mishandling of talk so that discussion degenerates into personal attack.

Lesson five: Tuesday, 4 October, 1988

Only Peter and Sally make entries today. Peter's entry is not in chronological order:

> We have had an argument on the play and Anne has written out a play scrip for James, Gideon and I to lern for homework   (Peter)

The chronology was: after the previous lesson, Sally and Anne had, over the weekend, handwritten five copies of their playscript; they had presented the scripts to the boys (each of whom had a part) and the first rehearsals during the lesson had been unsatisfactory. The boys were asked to learn their scripts by tomorrow's lesson. Sally claims that Gideon was the main problem:

> Today we tryed to go through the play, But Gideon particulry just laughed and mucked around   (Sally)

Is this Gideon's revenge for the criticism his work had received in the last lesson? It seems to me that it is quite possible that the girls received a taste of the same medicine they were dishing out to Gideon.

At this point, Sally records, without realizing it, the major difficulty of collaborative groupwork – one cannot force people to collaborate. The girls deliver an ultimatum:

> they've got to learn the play by next lesson and if they don't they will be chucked out of the play cause they are just mucking around.   (Sally)

It's an unworkable ultimatum. Sally cannot expel the boys and still stage the play. Either they find a way to work together on the play, or it is the play that is jettisoned. Sally and Anne are learning a fundamental lesson about minority rule: it only works as long as the majority are complaisant. One can sympathize with the girls' frustration: they have spent the weekend writing a play and made copies of it for the rest of the group. The boys are the first audience for their work and they react irresponsibly, 'Gideon particulry' (Sally). Nevertheless, Sally is optimistic that the group will resolve its problems: 'Peter and James aren't so bad but we will manage somehow'. Her last comment, aimed at the boys, is relevant to all the members of the group (and indeed to all collaborative groups): 'their problem is that they won't listen to other people's ideas.'

Lesson six: Wednesday, 6 October, 1988

Today the play was rehearsed, successfully it seems:

> We have now written up and learnt the play (Anne)

> Today we rehearsed are play and timed it. (James)

> Today we learnt most of the plays. (Gideon)

As before, one of Peter's comments is illuminating: 'we have had to sort our acting of the play lots of times due to stupidity'. There were problems then, not so much of argument and disagreement, but because of levity and irresponsibility: 'stupidity' (Peter) and 'mucking about' (Anne). As yesterday, criticism is aimed by a girl against the boys, and once again, it is Gideon who bears the main brunt of the criticism:

> The boys aren't doing much they just keep on mucking about . . . We have only one particular problem – Gideon he is continually mucking about (Anne)

Criticism is not just across the gender divide. Peter records that 'we are having a few problems with Gideon gigiling'. However, when stock is taken, a considerable amount of work has been completed in a fortnight:

> So far we have written two plays, two talks and doing the History of our police.
> (Gideon)

> We are know halfway through the project and have got the written work, play, and the spoken part nearly sorted out. (James)

Anne looks to the future:

> all we now need to do is sort out which order we need to do the whole talk [*sic; refers to end-of-project presentation, RG*] in to the infants. (Anne)

Lesson seven: Thursday, 6 October, 1988

Today the group presented their plays to English teacher, Sandy Bell. It is not clear from the comments whether the group invited Sandy to watch, whether she asked to watch, or whether, on a tour around the groups she happened upon a rehearsal and was invited to stay:

> We have had miss S Bell to watch are plays (Peter)

> Mrs Bell watched the play (Sally)

> We did and performed the plays to Miss Bell (Anne)

> Miss Bell came around and listened to both plays (James)

There is no suggestion that Sandy was not welcome, or that she intervened unnecessarily. The group seems to have found her comments reassuring and helpful:

> She thought that they were quite good . . .   (Peter)

> one is almost perfect the other need some improvement.   (Gideon)

> she said that it had a good base but needs polishing up.   (Anne)

> she thinks we have done quite well so far.   (James)

Peter, Sally and Anne all mention Gideon's lack of commitment. Peter redrafted his entry. Originally he wrote:

> Gideon has done nothing apart from acting in the plays and then he was laughing and what you could call being a bit silly and written a side of A4 writting.   (Peter)

His amended version is much kinder to Gideon (for there seems little doubt that Gideon has been messing around):

> Gideon has done acting in the plays and written a side of A4 writting.   (Peter)

Interestingly, Sally also makes two excisions to the final phrase of her entry, which refers to Gideon: 'he doesn't like working with us MATURE WOMEN' becomes: 'he doesn't like working with us girls' which becomes: 'he doesn't like working with us teenagers' (Sally). These changes in Peter's and Sally's entries suggest that they are using their diaries to reflect upon and analyse the progress of lessons and the relationships within the group, rather than just to record events. Peter considers and then retracts his mild criticism of Gideon. Sally retreats from what might have been regarded as a sexist interpretation of Gideon's behaviour, so that her final comment (although illogical as they are all teenagers) emphasizes Gideon's alleged immaturity in relation to age rather than gender.

The Gideon problem is one that Sally and Anne obviously feel is beyond solution within the group, and needs some external resolution:

> Today the boys weren't so bad for Mrs Bell watched the play and they did not muck around . . . It made a change that Gideon was quite whilst Mrs Bell was watching but no doubt he will be back to normal next lesson.   (Sally)

> It made a change Gideon didn't muck about so much – but he was quiet as Mr Griffis is going to sort him out.   (Anne)

What is Gideon doing wrong? He does not seem to be rude or belligerent. He is certainly not refusing to be involved. In fact, he is cooperating: he has learnt his lines for the play. The problem seems to be that he doesn't take things, particularly the plays, as seriously as the others, certainly Sally and Anne:

> Gideon didn't do anything . . .   (Anne 29.09)

> Today we tryed to go through the play, But Gideon particulry just laughed and mucked around . . .   (Sally 04.10)

we are having a few problems with Gideon gigiling . . . (Peter 05.10)

We have only one particular problem – Gideon he is continually mucking about . . .
(Anne 05.10)

Gideon has done nothing apart from acting in the play and then he was laughing and
what you could call being a bit silly . . . (Peter 06.10)

For his part, Gideon feels that Sally is overbearing and singles him out for blame whatever
goes wrong:

Sally is still too bossy and blames me for everything

The use of 'still' in the phrase 'Sally is still too bossy' (Gideon) is interesting. What period
of time does the adverb qualify: from the ultimatum about play rehearsals or perhaps further
back; as far back as the incident that led to Gideon tearing up his work? There is some
gender clash, for Peter and James are muted in their criticisms compared to Sally and Anne.
Perhaps Gideon genuinely finds it difficult, even embarrassing to work with girls. Perhaps
his sabotage of the girls' play is a revenge for the incident in which his own work was
criticized and destroyed.

As well as the rehearsal of the two plays and Sandy's comments to the group, other work
has taken place during the lesson:

James and I have started to rehurse our talk   (Peter)

I did my history of the police.   (Gideon)

Today me and Anne learnt our talk and we each say a couple of paragraphs each at a
time.   (Sally)

We also practised mine and Sally's talk.   (Anne)

Me and Peter have done our talk . . .   (James)

In addition, the group has begun to prepare some wall displays:

Miss Bell . . . helped us sort out our wall displays . . .   (James)

Lesson eight: Tuesday, 11 October, 1988

[*Visit by author, Nicholas Walker. No diary entries.*]

Lesson nine: Wednesday, 12 October, 1988

Apart from Anne (who was absent) the group use today's diary entry to comment on
the previous day's visit by local (although internationally published) author, Nicholas
Walker. Like Sally Roberts, Nicholas had been invited to talk to each of the collaborative
groups.

Peter and James report, without comment, that Nicholas had visited. Gideon gives more specific information:

> He talked about the presentation of our work and writing to the newspapers. (Gideon)

Gideon, with more of a penchant for written work (he is still working on his history of the police force), is perhaps more likely than James or Peter to have been interested in what Nicholas, as an author, had to say. Maybe Peter and James have no further comment as Nicholas, it appears, had some criticism to offer the pair, as Sally acidly comments:

> The author was quite a help to us because he pointed out to Peter and James that there talk did not make much sense.   (Sally)

In the event, Peter and James did shorten their talk, although not enough for Sally and Anne's approval:

> Anne and Sally moaned that our talk was too long, we had already shortened it by 2 sides of A4.   (James)

As well as discussion with Nicholas, other work continued. This impresses me: the group didn't just sit and idly wait for Nicholas to get round to them ('we had an author Nicholas Walker to speak to us as a group and as individul groups' (Peter)), but carried on with other work in progress:

> Gideon finished the history of the police force Peter did the crime in general and I wrote more for the wall display.   (James)

In today's lesson, as before, quite a lot of work is accomplished but not without disagreement. In Sally's telling comment, 'it has been painful'.

> Today we have done our talks and plays . . .   (Peter)

> Today we practiced our plays . . . I've almost finished my history of the police and will do in my homework.   (Gideon)

> . . . we did go right through it [*the final presentation; RG*] . . . Our talk [*Anne and Sally's; RG*] went well . . .   (Sally)

> Sally and I have finished the talk and the other play.   (Anne)

> Today we rehearsed our project all the way through . . . we have done a lot of work.   (James)

Some of the 'interrupting' and 'shouting' (Peter), the 'critasizing' and 'shouts' (Gideon), the 'inturuptions' and 'moans and groans' (Sally), the 'disagreement' and 'arguing' (Anne) was productive, in that it led to changes designed to improve the overall quality and impact of the final presentation:

> . . . as James and I done our talk Anne and Sally kept interrupting us shouting 'it's Boring and to long' so after we done that we decided not to have the seien with the accident . . .   (Peter)

Sally's version is similar:

> . . . the boys talk seemed to drag on so they have taken our advice and shortened it after a few arguments . . .   (Sally)

Peter and James must have produced quite a lot of work if they had to excise sections on two occasions – they had already edited at Nicholas Walker's suggestion. Revisions were also made to the format of the play that includes the magistrates' court:

> We have now changed the play in parts so the audience (primary school) can join in the play and decide what they would do if they were the judge in the court. (Anne)

It has taken a large part of the lesson to reach this decision:

> Today we tried to do the play. There was a lot of disagreement . . . We spent forty minutes trying to get it right . . . The boys don't like the idea much . . .   (Anne)

There are also niggling personal clashes, one concerning Peter yawning:

> . . . i was yowning because i was late to bed last night and they [*Anne and Sally; RG*] kept shouting at me . . .   (Peter)

> They even shouted at Peter for yowning.   (Gideon)

> They even told Peter off for yawning.   (James)

The boys all refer to Sally's habit of chewing gum:

> . . . all through the lesson Sally kept Eating bubblegum.   (Peter)

> She eats bubblegum constantly . . .   (Gideon)

> Sally ate bubblegum all lesson.   (James)

Everyone is feeling fractious. In the cumulative account of the day's diary entries, nobody escapes criticism from someone else in the group. The conflict lines, if drawn on a flow-diagram, would be more complex than before, in that there are more interactions, but also simpler, in that all the conflicts are cross-gender. There is no male/male criticism and no female/female criticism:

> Anne and Sally kept interrupting us shouting 'it's Boring and to long' . . .   (Peter)

> . . . they kept shouting at me and kept starting agin . . .   (Peter)

> . . . as normal Sally was changing or critasizing every other word. She eats bubblegum constantly and shout at us (me James and Peter) for everything . . .   (Gideon)

Anne and Sally moaned that our talk was too long . . .   (James)

. . . we still had inturuptions by James and Gideon not so much by Peter.   (Sally)

I don't think Gideon is enjoying this project very much for he always looks bored . . .
                                                                          (Sally)

. . . unlike me and Anne they always muck around or either don't listen to what we say
and just ignore us.   (Sally)

Gideon and James giggled and made stupid comments all the way through. Now it is
getting to the point if the play is worth doing with the boys.   (Anne)

Peter has already made up his mind to not bother working. He is just not pulling his
weight.   (Anne)

The focus of the problem seems to be Sally's powerful effect upon the group, which is
expressed in multiple ways: she disregards the code of the cooperative group (gum-
chewing); she is personal in her criticisms (Peter's yawning); she is impolite in offering
comments (the many references to shouting); she berates the efforts of the boys (Sally
herself admits to 'my moans and groans'); she accuses the boys of lack of interest, but
doesn't involve them in policy-making:

'the BOYS' don't . . . listen to what we say and just ignore us . . . they just don't seem
intrested . . .   (Sally)

Sally hasn't let us make a single decision yet . . .   (Gideon)

She is insensitive to the opinions of the boys and unprepared to negotiate or compromise:

We have also changed the play a bit and 'the BOYS' don't like it.   (Sally)

More than the others, Sally seems to have been consciously affected by the mixed gender
grouping, commenting on problems from the first lesson:

. . . its harder to work with the other sex for they always talk and don't listen to what
we have to say.   (Sally 22.09)

Her initial opinion is repeated today, almost word for word:

. . . they always muck around or don't listen to what we say and just ignore us. (Sally)

The view of Sally as shrew is, however, unfair, or at least only a partial view. In Sally can also
be seen an eager, hard-working pupil, keen to get on and do well and frustrated by the
apathy or wilful disruptiveness of others in her group. She will do whatever she can to push
the project forward:

anyway after my moans and groans I think over all we have done QUITE a good job
although it has been painful.   (Sally)

There is no suggestion that Sally relishes her self-appointed role as the team coach – indeed, quite the opposite. Sally and Anne realize, and admit, that they are not handling things well:

> I don't think it is all the boys fault it does not work out. Me and Anne can be bossy at times. (Sally)

> The boys don't like the idea much mind you me and Sally are being a bit bossy.
> (Anne)

It is easy to see that things could have been better if the group had collaborated more fully; but what is impossible to gauge is if things would have been worse without the misplaced but well-intentioned dynamism of Sally. James, the least emotive of the diarists, concedes:

> Despite this [*the arguments; RG*] we have done a lot of work. (James)

Another step forward from the week before is that, even though there appears to be more conflict, there is a greater ability to contain and resolve the conflict within the group:

> Today we tried to do the play. There was a lot of diasagreement. Gideon and James giggled and made stupid comments all the way through. Now it is getting to the point that if the play is worth doing with the boys. We spent forty minutes trying to get it right. At 2.00 after alot of arguing Gideon behaved himself. (Anne)

There will be no further representations to the teachers; indeed, had Sandy not watched the rehearsal last week, the entire project might have passed without the intervention of a teacher. Of the combined total of 3307 words in the group's diaries, just 97 words make any reference to the teachers (2.9 per cent). Only 5 diary entries (4 of them on one day) from a group total of 47 entries refer to the teachers.

Lesson ten: Thursday, 13 October, 1988

The angst and recriminations of yesterday are replaced by a straightforward account of tasks accomplished:

> We have done a wall display . . . (Peter)

> Today we worked on our wall display. (Gideon)

> Today we worked on me and Annes wall display . . . (Sally)

> Me and Sally worked on a wall display. (Anne)

> This lesson I arranged my wall display . . . (James)

Members of the group have clear short-term aims for future work:

> . . . hopefully we will be doing the play again next lesson . . . (Sally)

For homework I will finish copying James timetable so that James can put it on his wall display.   (Gideon)

During the lesson, the boys have worked as a trio, quite separately from the duo of girls – although they have all been engaged on a group task, the production of displays for the final presentation. Sally, who has written most about the perceived problem of working with the boys, ascribes the success of the lesson to this separatism:

> . . . today was the best day so far . . . for we hardly worked with the boys . . .   (Sally)

Gideon and James do not mention the work-pattern of the lesson, whilst Peter and Anne both record that the boys and girls have worked apart, but make no further comment:

> We have done a wall display James and Gideon and me.   (Peter)

> Gideon, Peter and James worked by themselves today.   (Anne)

Whilst they may have been working as distinct sub-groups, it seems they were working in close proximity to each other, for Peter notices and records:

> and Anne and Sally mest up two prittsticks.   (Peter)

There is some discrepancy about the partnership of the boys' display. Peter mentions 'a wall display'; Gideon refers to both 'our' and 'his [*James'*; *RG*] wall display'; James refers to 'my wall display'. It seems likely that, without the guiding influence of the girls, that it is James who emerges as the leader-figure for the boys:

> We have done a wall display James and Gideon and me.   (Peter)

> Today we worked on our wall display. For homework I will finish copying James timetable so that James can put it on his wall display.   (Gideon)

> This lesson I arranged my wall display and Peter and Gideon wrote up some information for me. Peter drew a picture.   (James)

There is an air of optimism after the conflicts of the previous lesson. Anne reiterates James' comment about the amount of work that has been done and Sally looks forward to working as a whole group during the next lesson:

> Looking on it, it seems wev'e both done a lot of work on this project.   (Anne)

> . . . hopefully we will be doing the play again next lesson . . .   (Sally)

However, the group is so volatile that one wonders what will happen next.

Lesson eleven: Tuesday, 18 October, 1988

[*Visit of artist, Sue Lewington. No diary entries.*]
The visits of three adults other than teachers is an important part of the project. They provide an extra stimulus. They are professional experts in the forms of presentation towards

which the cooperative group is working. They provide an interim audience for pupils' work. They act as consultant advisers with no decision-making authority. They provide an opportunity for a dialogue between adolescents and adults, different from the power-balance of school or home relationships. The pupils benefit from professional advice without the intervention of the two English teachers.

Lesson twelve: Wednesday, 19 October, 1988

The metaphorical blood-letting of two lessons ago becomes a reality:

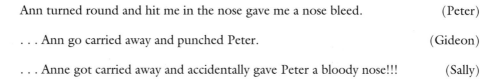

> Ann turned round and hit me in the nose gave me a nose bleed.   (Peter)

> . . . Ann go carried away and punched Peter.   (Gideon)

> . . . Anne got carried away and accidentally gave Peter a bloody nose!!!   (Sally)

> While doing the violent play, I gave Peter a nose bleed (accidentally).   (Anne)

Too much need not be made of the physical incident itself. There is a consensus that it was not deliberate in any premeditated sense. Peter took himself off to the medical room, but did not report to a teacher. This seems to have been one of those incidents that parents will be familiar with when children become over-excited when playing games (although, of course, the group members are not children, they do seem to regress when 'working' together). However, the fragile group dynamics that allowed such an incident to happen are interesting, and as a symbol of the degeneration in the ability of the boys and girls to work together, the incident is noteworthy. It is literally a slap in the face and marks the end of any real attempt to collaborate as a group.

The lesson starts with the resumed rehearsals for the imminent end-of-project presentation:

> we acted out our plays in the drama room and we had done our big play the cort case and then James and I done our talk and then we done the play with the theifs in the big store . . . (Peter)

> Today we tried to do our talks and plays . . . (Gideon)

> Today we TRIED to go through the whole presentation . . . (Sally)

> Today we tried to time the presentation. (Anne)

Thus, the lesson started with an agreed aim, but soon ran into problems:

> . . . but got nowhere. (Gideon)

> . . . but it did not work . . . (Sally)

> But didn't get very far. (Anne)

The reasons for this are, by now, well-documented: the boys' resentment at the girls' attempt to organize things, and the girls' exasperation with the boys for acting facetiously:

Sally changed every other word again . . .   (Gideon)

Peter was being a pain and so was James . . .   (Sally)

Amongst the quarrelling and the confusion and frustration and general tomfoolery, Anne hits Peter. To be fair, she was in-role at the time:

> . . . we done the play with the theifs in the big store and halfe way through Ann turned round and hit me in the nose gave me a nose bleed.   (Peter)

> While doing the violent play, I gave Peter a nose bleed (accidentally).   (Anne)

It seems that Anne's punch was just an escalation of the mayhem of a rehearsal that involved a struggle between a store-detective and a shop-lifter. In mitigation, Anne writes:

> mind you Peter did thump me on the back.   (Anne)

Both Gideon and Sally see the incident as a spur-of-the-moment accident:

> . . . Ann go carried away and punched Peter.   (Gideon)

> . . . Anne got carried away and accidentally gave Peter a bloody nose!!!   (Sally)

Afterwards, things got even worse:

> Sally took to shouting and comletely lost her temper.   (Anne)

> Peter was the worst and he got a bit angry with Anne after the ACCIDENT!   (Sally)

> Peter went to the medical room with a nose bleed while James went to his guitar lesson
> (Gideon)

The girls show no sympathy for Peter, nor any remorse for their actions, although Sally does admit that 'me and Anne were a bit bossy'. Indeed, there is a suggestion that, one way and another, it has not been a completely unenjoyable experience:

> So overall we had an exciting day full of events.   (Sally)

> That put Peter, James and Gideon in their place!   (Anne)

Lesson thirteen: Thursday, 20 October, 1988

Today's entries read as an epitaph for the project. There are no references to ongoing groupwork, although the three diarists who make entries all refer to pair work:

> James and I whent up to Chaple Street to see T. Clancy but he is away on holiday so we went across to the co.op and asked if we could have a job for Gideon James and I for about half an hour in Dinner times   (Peter)

> . . . our pair work has tooken of at last . . . Our pair work is delivering leaflets about antivivasection. (Sally)

> The work willbe completed in the holidays, me and Sally are going to deliver some leaflets. (Anne)

It is interesting that when Peter refers to the group, he now means only himself, James and Gideon:

> James and I whent . . . and asked if we could have a job for Gideon James and I . . . so he said could we come ~~bak~~ back ~~to mor~~ tomorrw dinner time and then we could see if we could get a job there for our group . . . (Peter)

Peter has also helped James and put some time in on his individual work:

> . . . I have helped James do his wall display and have done some of the write up on my single project. (Peter)

Sally also mentions her individual work:

> I will be doing my indivual work over half term as well as our pair work. (Sally)

Like Peter and James, Sally and Anne have spent lesson time on their wall display:

> Sally and I finished the wall displa. (Anne)

All three comment on the group project:

> I think its a good project but it just the girls that are a pain because they altered all the scrips (e.g. Ann, Sally). (Peter)

> I don't think I can stand another week with Peter, Gideon and James although I will try! (Sally)

> Sally and I are glad it has ended, we didn't get on with the boys and totally fed up. (Anne)

The project ends with the boys and girls still making real attempts to complete their pair work in their own time: 'in Dinner times' (Peter) 'in the holidays' (Anne), but making no attempt to work together for the group presentation. Perhaps surprisingly, Sally is the only one to refer to the possibility:

> I don't think I can stand another week with Peter, Gideon and James although I will try! (Sally)

Sally is also discreet in her criticisms of the boys:

> Overall we all tryed to work well for exceptions. And I won't mention any names
>
> (Sally)

Anne and Peter don't have the same coyness. Predictably they blame each other:

> I think its a good project but it just the girls that are a pain because they altered all the scrips (e.g. Ann, Sally).   (Peter)

> Peter didn't do anything, all are efforts in vain to get Peter working was useless. (Anne)

Both Anne and Sally express misgivings about the final presentation:

> . . . our play is a bit rusty . . . I don't think we will be ready by a couple of weeks time.
> (Sally)

> I don't think we will be ready to talk in front of the class. The play is still abit rusty.
> (Anne)

Although Sally and Anne have previously admitted to feeling that they have been over-assertive group members, Anne's only suggestion for improvement in the future is:

> If we had to do this project again it would have to be somebody quiter and didn't complain.   (Anne)

Lesson fourteen: Tuesday, 1 November, 1988

The group make their presentation to the class. Afterwards they are asked to prepare a brief end-of-course statement that they all agree on:

> The play was a mess! Because we didn't get on and nobody put enough effort into it. If we had agreded on anything we could very likely got alot more work done and got alot more organised.

When I first read the diaries, in 1988, my initial reaction was very similar to the group verdict expressed at the end of the project. It was only when I had become much clearer about educational citizenship that I was able to question the unstated but very strong criteria for 'success' that the pupils and I had been using at the time of the *Breaking Down the Barriers* project; and to begin to see what the pupils had achieved and how I, as their teacher, had failed. I failed to make clear the learning agenda: that an important part of the learning would be to do with planning, negotiating, adapting, being resilient and being of good humour. I failed to promote skills success rather than content success: to have made clear to the pupils that evidence of learning, of 'work' was as much revealed by the way in which they conducted themselves, talked to each other, met deadlines, resolved arguments, solved problems, as it was by the amount of written work produced. I failed to aid the learning process by illuminating the learning agenda to the pupils and pointing out the positive learning gains that underpinned what may have seemed frustrating and non-productive sessions.

At the time of the project, I had vague, well-intentioned notions of people getting on with other people, deciding what they wanted to do and doing it. I'm sure I felt that if pupils could see that they could work in this way it might lead them to feel greater self-esteem and a realization that they had the right to some say about what should happen during their school years and thus get some grip on their later lives as citizens. As to the skills required, I really don't think I had any idea. When talking to the pupils I would use unexamined and unhelpful buzzwords like 'commitment', 'self-discipline' and 'motivation'. With no precise ideas about either the learning agenda or the skills necessary for meeting that agenda I was limited as to how much I could aid the learning process for particular groups. I put my faith in the free will and fresh nature of the child that is the basis of the 'out of chaos comes forth creativity' doctrine of libertarian education as promulgated by progressive independent schools (such as Summerhill, 1924–date; Dartington Hall, 1920–1987; Beacon Hill, 1927–43; Sands, 1988–date), 'free schools' that had some state funding (such as Scotland Road Free School, Liverpool, 1972; Saltley, Nottingham and Brighton Free Schools, 1974; the White Lion Free School, Islington, 1977) and the very few state schools that have experimented with libertarian education as a whole-school policy (such as Braehead School, Fife, 1967; Countesthorpe College, Leics. 1973; Summerhill Academy, Aberdeen, 1974; William Tyndale School, Islington, 1975; Sutton Centre, Notts., 1977).

Now I can see why we (the teachers and the pupils) felt that the project had failed. Our judgments were based almost solely on an evaluation of the product of a knowledge-based curriculum, that is to say, that even though we were eager to experiment with new ways of learning, we applied the old criteria to assess the project. Almost inevitably then, the project had failed for us because the product did not match the quality ('The play was a mess!') or the quantity ('we would have . . . got a lot more work done') that both the teachers and the pupils associated with a 'normal' curriculum, the kind of curriculum that surrounded these few lessons. Yet a substantial amount of important learning was taking place, that was either unrecognized or undervalued by the pupils, and not properly explained and supported by the teachers because we had not developed assessment criteria appropriate to the new forms of learning with which we were experimenting. It was sometime later that such criteria of assessment, in the form of the twelve factors of independent learning, were formulated.

The time spent in lessons during the *Breaking Down The Barriers* project was about the same as the total lesson time of Josie and Emily, as described in Chapters 2 and 3. If an analysis is made, using the twelve factors of independent learning, it can be shown that the members of The Outfit had far greater opportunities than Josie and Emily to develop the qualities of educational citizenship, albeit, and admittedly, in an unstructured and poorly supported way. I believe that many positive things about independent learning were evident in the work of The Outfit, if only in embryonic form, and that much more was achieved by the group than they recognized at the time. Their reflection in the interview three years later is more positive.

The interviews with the members of The Outfit shed some new light and confirmed some findings: the statements, by members of The Outfit that gender conflict was enjoyable; that the group, by and large, still had negative feelings of success; but nevertheless, and seemingly contradictingly, all members of The Outfit whom I interviewed felt that the project was the most enjoyable and memorable event in their school years:

James: That was about the only thing I ever remember doing in school I really enjoyed.
Anne: Yeh, it was a really good experience, I mean you don't normally think of things, you know, what did I do, but this one does definitely stick in your mind. And it was good educational value even though you didn't learn anything, you learnt how to work with other people. That's the main thing.

Sally: And it's a good idea because you usually find that boys stick to boys and girls just stick to girls so this got you all involved together.

The interviews also confirmed (to my relief, having invested a lot of time in transcribing and analysing them) that the diaries were a faithful and accurate description of events and feelings:

Rhys: Were you honest in your diaries, generally do you think? That's the other thing, maybe the diaries are just a pack of lies.
Anne: No.
James: It was honest.
Sally: I always wrote what I really felt.

ANALYSIS OF THE THE OUTFIT DIARIES USING THE TWELVE FACTORS OF INDEPENDENT LEARNING

Factor 1: collaborative groupwork

The Outfit conforms to the guidelines of a collaborative group in number and gender, and has consolidated its identity by giving itself a name. During the first lessons, work is initiated and, despite the absence of one member (Anne), the work seems to have proceeded successfully, Gideon and Sally taking on the organizing role. The group is proving adaptable to changing circumstances.

Soon, however, the group enters a second, less positive stop–go phase in its inter-relationships. Although the group has clear shared ideas of what it wants to achieve, by the third lesson the discussion process is proving painful for Gideon and Peter. However, by the next lesson (29.09.88), the planned play seems to have strengthened the sense of partnership, for it is a common task that requires the active involvement of all members of the group. The difference of opinion over Gideon's work has been resolved. Peter and James are collaborating on a further piece of work. The beginning of the third week (04.10.88) sees a major split within the group, a split between Sally and Anne; and James, Gideon and Peter. This is not necessarily a simple gender division; it could be a rejection by one section of the group of a minority that has established itself as the creative, organizational, legislative and judicial authority within the community. By the next lesson, there has been some resolution (05.10.88). The group seems to have collaborated well, overcoming the potential disruptions of Gideon's torn written work and the girls' ultimatum about learning lines or being dismissed from the play. They have completed a good deal of work and have clear notions about what more needs to be done. They are capable of shifts of emphasis within the group: for instance, the inclusion of Gideon within the pair work, the adjustments needed between the script-writers and the actors.

On Thursday, October 6, the project reaches the halfway point. The Outfit has now been working together for three weeks, and has another three weeks before the presentation. Despite disagreements and some personality clashes within the group, they still look as if they will be able to complete their presentation which is now to include two plays, two talks, two displays and a folder of work. What I think is impressive is that the group are continuing to work with each other, even though it is quite clear that there are conflicts within the group.

These conflicts, which centre around the play Sally and Anne have written, leads to a third phase in the group's relationships. The group seems to have polarized into two distinct sub-groups: the boys and the girls. There is antagonism between the two factions. The girls regard the boys as sloths, the boys regard the girls as viragos. Nevertheless, the two sub-groups have not separated, nor are their aims different. The dissension appears to be based on a misunderstanding of attitude and behaviour. Meanwhile, work continues on the whole-group tasks of the two plays as well as the pair work of the talks and displays, and Gideon's solo work. Whilst the exasperation felt by both sides is overt, it is controlled within some unarticulated code. The group is autonomous in that it requires no outside controls for it to function, although it is clear that within the group there are differences of opinion about the best way in which to function. The group seems to be coming to terms with its complex character and is becoming more patient and skilled at finding solutions that all can agree. The following lesson (13.10.88) the group collaborates on a joint task, the production of displays for the end-of-project presentation, but has divided into two sub-groups to get the work done. The sub-groups show a clear gender divide: all girls and all boys. The group has worked in the same physical area and plan to work together during the following lesson. This way of working seems to be efficient: everyone mentions work accomplished, no-one refers to arguments.

However, the next lesson (19.10.88) signifies the final phase in the dissolving relationships. The group no longer seems able to collaborate. Today's lesson degenerates into argument and violence and reinforces the gender split. The only positive point to make is that there was some kind of agreement that their difficulties would not be reported to any authority figure. There is no working partnership, but both girls do refer to presenting the play, and even though they have misgivings, it appears that some form of whole-group presentation will take place. The group seems to have learned little about working together: there is a polarity of views – the boys think the girls too domineering, the girls think the boys not compliant enough.

I think the members of the group are to be commended for although they obviously experienced great difficulties they continually sought to resolve them without outside assistance. Even when relationships broke down, they reached an accommodation that allowed them to fulfil the project outcomes. Greater teacher support, not so much in resolving problems, but in pointing out that they were to be expected, might have helped, as might a written code of conduct, agreed by the members of The Outfit.

Factor 2: cooperative groupwork

There is no real evidence of any sense of cooperative group work other than the references (12.10.88) by three members of the group to the breaking of the cooperative code by Sally chewing gum. The awareness of a cooperative purpose might have helped the group fulfil its aims; the knowledge that other groups were experiencing similar problems might have offered a reassuring perspective. The cooperative theme is not a sufficient bond for this collaborative group.

Factor 3: individual responsibility

During the first lesson (22.09.88) all the members agree to carry out tasks by the next lesson, tasks that must be accomplished if the next lesson is to follow the agreed format. The group has divided into two pairs and Gideon, who will work alone. It is not clear if this is a pattern that will continue or whether these divisions are solely for the purpose of accomplishing the tasks agreed so far. By the second lesson (27.09.88) Peter feels that he is not pulling his weight, but is not castigated by the others. Only Sally mentions that Peter is the one member of the group not to have completed his first piece of work. Sally is industrious and resourceful: in the absence of Anne, it would have been easy for her to have sat back and announced that she couldn't do anything because 'her' partner was away. Instead, she works with Gideon and plays a central role in organizing the group's activities. In the third lesson (28.09.88), despite the unease that Gideon and Peter obviously feel about the decision making process, the group is still functioning, with Gideon agreeing to make a written contribution. Members are showing individual responsibility in continuing to work out of school-time (they have set themselves homework for the second week running). Again, Peter appears to have no contribution to make.

After this, there are fewer examples of individual responsibility, although they can be found throughout the project. Everyone learns their lines for the group play (05.10.88) Gideon is agreeing to the group's code and is carrying out some share of the tasks, but does not appear to be doing so in a particularly responsible manner. (06.10.88)

How clear is the group's code? Has it been defined in discussion? Are there certain rules and procedures that have been decided upon? Is there a written statement of the code? I doubt it. I think that if the group had given time to this at the beginning of the project, much of the arguing might have been avoided. At least there would have been a set of laws, agreed by the group, that could have been used to control behaviour or to arbitrate dissensions.

Halfway through the project (12.10.88), although there has been much metaphorical flexing of muscles and stamping of feet, there is still some powerful force holding the group together. There seems to be a strong individual responsibility felt by each member to protect the group's integrity and autonomy from the intervention and control of outsiders. Within the group there is obviously a vigorous debate about controls and commitments.

However, the phony peace and occasional border skirmishes of the remainder of the project are marked by an individual responsibility to the self and the sub-group, rather than to the group as a whole. This is due to friction between the sexes, which in turn may have been caused by task allocation, rather than task sharing. Had the boys contributed more to the script of the play, and the girls to the police research, then there may have been more common ground and less territorial aggression.

Factor 4: pupil-designed tasks

This factor will be discussed under the sub-headings of partnership versus ownership, initiative, negotiation and range of outcomes.

Partnership versus ownership

The group has been completely free to find its own focus within the cooperative theme of *Breaking Down The Barriers*. In their first diary entry four of the group refer to the project as 'a good idea', the other writes of 'a good project'. Thus, within the group there seems to be a common sense of shared partnership of the tasks they have designed to fulfil the project outcomes: *a topic for presentation to an audience of your choice. The presentation must include a literary and an oral component.* There are also possibilities for pairs or individuals to feel a sense of ownership of some part of the group's work: Peter and James' interview, Gideon's own written piece. By the second lesson, though, this unity is weakened, for Peter is feeling a lack of partnership of the collaborative group project: he is dissatisfied with what he has done; he is the only one not to have completed a piece of work. The disagreements of the next lesson reinforce the diminished sense of partnership felt by Peter and Gideon.

The play seems to re-establish a sense of whole-group partnership of the project, probably because all the group has been involved in the decision making. However, ownership passes to the play's authors, Sally and Anne. Perhaps they should have offered the script as a working draft that needed to be accepted or revised by the whole group during rehearsal. This is a good example of how task allocation can split a group and how task sharing can unite one.

There seems to be a collective sense of partnership of the presentation to the primary school. The rehearsals for the play, even with facetious disruptions, seem to have re-established the sense of shared partnership that appeared threatened. Peter refers not to 'the acting' but to 'our acting'. Gideon seems to have least sense of partnership. His behaviour suggests this, as well as the small amount of work he has contributed compared to the others, and also his muddling-through attitude to the pair and individual work. To put that more positively, at least he still is muddling through: he hasn't given up. Perhaps Anne and Sally have assumed too great a sense of ownership, so excluding others from being able to feel equal partnership.

I would say that on one hand there is a problem of partnership: all the diaries suggest that the girls feel that they have a greater sense of ownership, excluding the boys from decision making. Gideon shows in his comments that he wants a greater involvement. On the other hand, one could argue that the group is showing very strong corporate feelings of partnership: despite disagreements over important and trivial matters (the audience involvement in the play, Peter's tiredness, Sally's gum-chewing), the group shares a common aim and seems to be committed to resolving problems without help. On a positive note, one could say that they feel a partnership of their problems. The central difficulty within the group seems to me to be that the girls present themselves as having the exclusive ownership of the solutions to their shared problems.

Initiative

During the first lesson, the group has shown considerable initiative in finding a focus, allocating tasks, identifying an audience, establishing a format for the final presentation, beginning research within the community, planning deadlines for the first piece of work (the next lesson) and planning the format of the next lesson. The group continues to show initiative throughout the project. James and Peter (it is impossible to evaluate the value of each boy's contribution) show a great deal more initiative than they give themselves credit for in securing the written interview with the community policeman. The group regularly sets itself self-imposed homework and works out of lessons, at lunchtimes and in the evenings. The movement away from traditional language tasks for an English lesson ('writing up information') to more creative forms of expression (the plays, talks and wall displays) shows initiative. The girls show commendable initiative in writing the play in their own time and then hand copying scripts for the boys (although they would have shown more initiative by getting it photocopied). In the second half of the project, when relationships are strained, there is still a strong sense of initiative; the work continues to expand and develop: a second play, a second talk (by Peter and James), displays. The presentation is ambitious, involving displayed written work, lectures and plays. This multimedia approach is commendable and shows a breadth of vision about what the group can achieve despite its problems.

Negotiation

I take negotiation to mean conferring with a view to compromise and agreement where there are differences of opinion. The diaries record no explicit evidence of negotiation within the group during the first lesson, but neither is there evidence that there is one leader and decision-maker. As all agree that the project is 'good', I suspect there must have been some negotiation about the focus. There must also have been negotiation about who was to do what for the first piece of research so that the three pieces of work complemented each other: library research, interview and a factual essay. In the second week, with the absence of Anne, it was necessary to 'organise the group out'. This was done successfully. At the end of the lesson, the group decided on the format of the following day's lesson.

The lesson of the 28 October is characterized by heated discussion. Peter and Gideon regard the discussion as argument, James, Anne and Sally, as negotiation. In the following lesson, no matter what kind of interaction led to the destruction of Gideon's work, it must have required a high order of negotiative skills to resolve the discord, so that the lesson ended with Gideon still a committed member of the group. The ultimatum about the play, delivered by Sally and Anne to the boys, is the antithesis of negotiation (04.10.88). This does not mark the end of whole-group negotiation, but there is now more of an emphasis on negotiation within sub-groups. Gideon, James and Peter agree to complete pair work as a trio. Anne mentions a need to establish a running order for the presentation with all the group involved in discussion. I think that Gideon may well have negotiated with James and Peter about their diary entries concerning him. There is obviously a lack of negotiation between Gideon and the girls. He feels he is being victimized, they feel he is sabotaging their efforts. For the first time (06.10.88) they consider adult intervention, presumably because they are unable to talk the problems through and resolve them for themselves.

However, during the final part of the project there is a lot of evidence of negotiation: the shortening of the boys' talk, the change in the play to involve the audience, the resolution of a disagreement that lasted for 40 minutes. There must have been some negotiation for the group to have agreed not to work together as a whole for a while (although the sub-groups work adjacent to each other). This temporary cooling-off period was effective: work for the whole-group project was produced and Sally, usually the most resistant to working with the boys, is looking forward to the whole group working together when rehearsals for the play resume. It is worth noting that rehearsals are to resume: the group has not abandoned their presentation after yesterday's dissension.

The group makes some very sensible and pragmatic decisions in an attempt to resolve their internal conflict; however, their negotiating skills lack sophistication and the group often descends to personal argument between the genders which confuses discussion of issues and is a powerful reinforcement of Sally's notion that the best work is done when the boys and girls work separately.

Range of tasks

The range of tasks that the group takes on is impressive and encompasses a broad English curriculum: diaries, interviews, library research, notes, argumentative pieces of writing, play scripts, scripts for talks, questionnaires, information collated, summarized and written up, group discussion, shared reading of each other's work, a written piece on the history of the police force by Gideon, a written piece on the modern policeman by James that will form an introduction (to the folder of work? the play? the talk?), props for the play, cards for the play, introduction for the play, drafting and redrafting, the rehearsals, the learning of parts, folders of written and artwork, and wall-displays including text and supporting visual material. All of these tasks are completed and the presentation takes place.

Whilst it is possibly the task allocation and resulting ownership of the play that causes conflict, there is also evidence of task-sharing throughout the project. The process of the first pieces of work is within the two pairs. The product of the first pieces of work will be shared by the whole group in the next lesson. The workload has been shared so that more is accomplished (they're not all going to interview the policeman). Gideon and Sally shared the responsibility for reorganizing the lesson structure; James and Peter shared the visits to the police station; Gideon and Sally shared a workspace, although they worked on their own tasks; James and Peter shared the results of the questionnaire with the others in the group. There is the collaborative work of Sally and Anne; and the shared topic of James and Gideon, although individually written. All five members have speaking parts in the play, so there is a shared responsibility: one person who has not learned the lines will prevent the other four from rehearsing. On October 5, Anne writes that 'we' – obviously meaning everyone in the group – need to plan the end-of-project presentation.

Thus, there is much that the group share; what they don't seem to be sharing is a common level of commitment, but perhaps that is impossible in any group. They need to share *with* each other their concerns *about* each other in a more positive way.

Factor 5: pupil-designed assessment

In the follow-up interview with members of The Outfit, they stated that they had made no assessment of their work. The diaries suggest otherwise. In fact, a wide range of assessment took place throughout the project, even though this was not recognized by the pupils. In the first lesson, they plan to make a group assessment of James' and Peter's police interview. In the second lesson, Peter makes a written self-assessment of his contribution to the group in his diary; and Sally records a written evaluation of Peter and James's questionnaire. During the second week of the project, an assessment of ideas for the play is made in a whole-group discussion, and each member of the group makes an individual written assessment of this process in their dairies. On September 29, an oral assessment of Gideon's report on the police force is made during the lesson by Gideon and at least one other member of the group. This assessment leads to a negotiated statement of future intent. There is whole-group oral assessment of the play script (04.10.88), followed two days later by an individual written reflection by Gideon. On October 5, four members of the group record a written summary of their opinion of the project so far. As well as the progress of the work and the quality of various tasks, the contribution of members of the group is assessed. Peter, Sally and Anne make written statements about Gideon's attitude after group discussion involving Gideon. Over the course of two lessons, James and Peter's talk is assessed, using a form of successive approximation during which the talk was watched, commented upon, and refined. The process involved peer-assessment, self-assessment and the assessment of an adult other than a teacher (author Nicholas Walker). On October 13, Anne makes a self-assessment, based on reflection and pair discussion with Sally, which she records in her diary.

Perhaps because the members of The Outfit have a limited view of assessment as the grading of written work by an external marker, they do not realize the assessments that they are constantly making. These assessments utilize ipsative, normative and criterion-based references, involve self, peer and external assessors, and take different forms appropriate to the assessment being made.

Factor 6: pupil-negotiated deadlines

The group's time management is good. They soon decide on the clear form of their project outcome and plan tasks accordingly. Their short-term planning is constructive: what each will do by the next lesson (for example, police interview, library research, factual essay) and what the group will do during the next lesson (for example, writing up information, starting on the play). There is also evidence of effective long-term planning: the play and talk to a primary audience at the end of the project. Their planning includes evening homework, lunchtime and holiday work. By October 6, this careful planning is showing dividends: with a fortnight of school time remaining, there seems every possibility that the group will refine its work to a good level of presentation. If the project had been teacher-led, I am sure that few teachers would have outlined such an ambitious programme of work for such a short time, whatever the pupils' age and ability.

Factor 7: pupil-initiated research

The group's literature research is restricted to printed texts, although they do use the public as well as the school library. Their fieldwork research involves the local community. There is no use of electronic data storage systems. The group do not telephone or write letters requesting information. The fieldwork consists of asking the local policeman to complete a questionnaire. No interviews are conducted, nor any surveys undertaken. The group seems to have decided to accumulate sufficient information to inform their plays and talks and then to concentrate their time on polishing the presentation of the information via these performances.

Factor 8: pupil-use of language technology

There is no evidence of the use of language technology.

Factor 9: community involvement and the use of the environment

Research was undertaken at the local library and police station. Naomi Roberts discussed the group's idea for a plot involving a magistrates' court. Nicholas Walker advised on the plays. Sue Lewington made suggestions for the wall displays. Pupils from the local primary school were to act as an audience for the plays, and the group intended to involve the audience in the play. The questionnaire for PC Rowell included the environmental issues of graffiti, vandalism and litter.

Factor 10: a sense of audience

The group has a clear sense of audience for their presentation – pupils from the local primary school. As the work progresses they refine their target audience to an infant class. During the project, three adults other than teachers and one teacher act as an audience for work in progress. Comments in the diaries also suggest a sense of the reader as audience. There is a clear purpose to the presentation of the work to an audience: to inform on their chosen subject in an entertaining way. The style of presentation is well-defined: a multimedia presentation of written and performed work. The group shows critical awareness in suiting the presentation to the the age of the audience, considering a Year 2 class more appropriate than a Year 6 class. The audience will participate in the presentation by acting as the jury in the courtroom play concerning drunken driving.

Factor 11: presentation in various forms

The group presents a wide range of work in various forms that encompasses a broad English curriculum and gives opportunity for all members of the group to contribute both to developmental work and the summative presentation. As the diaries were freely offered to me, they can be considered part of the presentation of the group's work, along with a written folder, two wall displays, two talks and two plays. The printed outcomes include chronological and non-chronological texts in the following genres: autobiographical, critical and reflective (the diaries), narrative and dramatic (the play scripts), transactional (the questionnaire), descriptive (James's piece on the daily routine of a police constable), discursive and factual (Gideon's work), persuasive (one of the play scripts puts the case against drunken driving and the other warns that crime does not pay), factual (the library research, writing up information, the scripts for the talks, James' and Gideon's pieces comprising the history of the police force, details in the plays and in the displays). The oral outcomes cover formal and informal registers and a variety of purposes and styles: peer discussion, argument, resolution, planning, criticizing, appeasing; discussion with adults; learned scripts for informative lectures and dramatic presentations to a real audience; rehearsals. There were no video or audio recorded outcomes. There were wall displays that included redrafted written work and artwork.

Factor 12: reflexivity

The keeping of the diaries is part of a reflective process, and there are examples from each writer of a capacity for self-criticism. The diaries reveal how members of the group would approach another project differently. What is lacking is a clear ontology and epistemology for reflection: the members of The Outfit are overly critical of their efforts.

Conclusions

The main conclusion to be drawn from participant observation of the project, a commentary upon the group's diaries, a retrospective interview with members of the group, an analysis of The Outfit's achievements in the light of the twelve factors of independent learning and a comparison of The Outfit's conclusions with those of groups involved in later projects (in which the 12 factors were more explicitly understood by teachers and conveyed to pupils) is that independent learning appears to be a natural activity for pupils who are given the freedom to structure their own learning, but that the clear application of the 12 factors, far from inhibiting or restricting the independence of a collaborative group, can enhance the development of educational and global citizenship.

The second conclusion is based upon an analysis using the 12 factors of independent learning of the equivalent curriculum time spent by The Outfit and Josie, all Key Stage 3 pupils. The conclusion is that, even at its worst, independent learning offers more educational opportunities relevant to citizenship and the workplace than the normal presentation of the National Curriculum does at its best.

The third conclusion is that independent learning, whilst rejecting a knowledge-based curriculum, enhances the management rather than the memorization of knowledge. During this short project, members of The Outfit researched, collated, selected and presented an area of knowledge that held a personal interest for themselves and which was related to the social environment in which they lived. This approach to knowledge seems to me to be much more purposeful and relevant than the decisions imposed upon Josie and Emily about which eclectic areas of knowledge – often completely distanced from any peopled environment with which they could identify – they were forced to study (by option choices, by teachers' choice of texts, by examination syllabuses, by the strictures of National Curriculum subjects and by categorizing knowledge to different ability sets).

5 Educational citizenship in action

Independent learning projects

The purpose of independent learning projects was to collect data on teaching and learning styles across the five to sixteen age range that might be regarded as promoting educational citizenship. The projects took two forms: cross-curricular, cross-phase projects; and secondary phase projects in one National Curriculum subject (English). Most English projects spanned one full term; the cross-curricular projects encompassed a full school year. Term-long independent learning projects took place in each of Greenshire's comprehensive schools, usually with the involvement of three or four classes. Around 4500 pupils were directly involved in these projects. Year-long projects took place in 27 schools (15 secondary and 17 primary), often with whole-school involvement. Around 2500 pupils were directly involved in these projects. In total approximately 7000 pupils, spanning the age and ability range of the National Curriculum, and 250 teachers, were involved in independent learning projects between 1988 and 1994. During the first phase (1988–1990), 14 projects were undertaken, during the second phase (1990–1991), 24 projects, and during the final phase (1991–1994), 19 projects. During these three phases the factors of independent learning evolved, were developed and applied. Although the 12 factors of independent learning differ greatly from the 10 subjects of the National Curriculum, both attempt to bring a structure to the classroom experience of pupils that allows comparability between different sites; and both share the same aims, those of the 1988 Educational Act 'to promote the spiritual, moral, cultural, mental and physical development of pupils at school and of society, and to prepare pupils for the opportunities, responsibilities and experiences of adult life'.

All the projects were based upon the concept of educational citizenship, although a clearer explicit understanding of the classroom application of this concept developed throughout the three phases of the research with the identification and refinement of the 12 factors of independent learning. From the second phase onwards, at staff meetings prior to the inception of a project, the 12 factors were discussed and copies distributed. Before the start of every project, I addressed any class that might choose to be involved and the same procedure was followed. Meetings with parents, governors and whole-school staff conformed to the same pattern. A list of the factors was used to orientate any visiting observers. Each project was undertaken at the request of the school, generally from the head of English, sometimes by individual teachers, sometimes by headteachers. No teacher or pupil was involved who did not wish to be. During a project all involved in the research partnership (pupils, parents, teachers, observers) were regarded as equals and encouraged to express their opinions about independent learning. I have already discussed the philosophical differences between independent learning and the normal presentation of the normal curriculum. Another significant difference, at an organizational level, was that independent learning was developed as a local partnership characterized by the mutual trust of all involved and was very much a consensual process. This was in direct contrast to teachers' strongly-held views that national reforms had been imposed by a centralized government that either ridiculed or ignored the views of those who would have to implement the National Curriculum in the classroom.

All of the projects were based on the premise that pupils should be allowed to study whatever they wanted, in whatever way they wanted, in partnership with whomever they wanted. This premise was inevitably subject to some limitations, mainly to do with the legal obligations of the teachers and the timetable of the school. For instance, pupils were dissuaded from undertaking activities that were clearly dangerous; if working off the school premises they had to return in time for their next lesson; and their choice of partners was sometimes limited to the pupils in their class (although they could arrange to work with adults other than teachers during lessons and with other pupils outside lesson time).

All of the projects shared the same five outcomes. Each collaborative group of pupils chose their own subject of study but were expected to aim towards these five outcomes, which are listed with no sense of hierarchy:

1   a short video (around five minutes), researched, story-boarded, filmed and edited by pupils, with editing to include computer-generated titles and credits, insert-editing and audio-dubbing where necessary, including theme music, sound effects and voice-over commentary where required;
2   a magazine (or pamphlet, brochure, booklet) preferably drafted and published using a range of word-processor and desktop publishing software; the contents to include a variety of writing, both individual and collaborative: descriptive, discursive, explanatory, narrative, poetry;
3   a short live presentation (five–ten minutes) prepared for a particular audience; the presentation may be one of, or a combination of, the following (or something entirely different): lecture or demonstration, using technological and other audio-visual aids as appropriate, mime, play, poetry-reading, song, storytelling, dance;
4   a project bibliography of texts referred to by the members of the collaborative group, including databases and other research reading, visual texts, poetry, fiction, drama, factual and reference texts; the bibliography to include a review of some texts, with criticisms, comments and suggestions;
5   a diary of the project kept by each pupil that need not be shown to anyone else; diary might include ideas, drafts, memos, deadlines, group's code of conduct, and reflections on problems encountered and group relationships.

The video, the magazine and the live presentation should show a clear sense of audience and would usually be presented to that intended audience.

Other members of the the Greenshire Advisory Team were involved in some projects, notably the Outdoor Education Team, the County Multicultural Education Advisory Teacher, members of the County Music Service and English Advisory Support Teachers. Technical support for video and audio-recording was provided jointly by the English and Performing Arts Advisory Teams. All of these personnel acted as catalyst or participant observers, as did the research partners of pupils and teachers. The research projects were referred to by Greenshire teachers as 'independent learning projects' and the work as a whole became known under the collective title of The Independent Learning Project. LEA funds were made available for personnel and equipment and a support team was established.

Although I was involved in every project, I was certainly not the lone director. In the projects that spanned a term's lessons, I usually spent one day a week working alongside teachers and pupils in the classroom, thus was present for only a third of the project lessons. In year-long projects, I would typically spend a day each half-term with a project school. My role was to help establish projects and then to monitor and support them, giving teachers and pupils the space and time to explore independent learning in their own ways. Other than my own classroom involvement, I offered support via project newsletters, organizing meetings of project teachers from different schools, arranging for teachers and pupils to visit other schools, providing in-service training courses, and chairing end-of-project debriefings.

In this research programme, each step in the process is clearly linked: the postulation of the likely attributes of global citizenship; the construct of educational citizenship intended to develop the attributes of global citizenship; the development of a pedagogy intended to enact educational citizenship – independent learning; the refinement of the implementation of independent learning via clear procedures of operation – the 12 factors; and the construction of practical outcomes, flexible enough to accommodate the five to sixteen age and ability range, but uniform enough to allow comparable assessment procedures to be developed. During the five years of the fieldwork research, conducted upon multisites, teachers, pupils, parents and school managers were consulted at all times. This seems to me to be a much more considered, valid and reliable way of investigating curriculum development than by basing it upon a political ideology that is now largely discredited (Thatcherism), making a host of untested *a priori* assumptions about how such an ideology can be applied to education, and then railroading through legislation to impose an untried curriculum upon a profession united in opposition to the intended changes.

Because of the encouragement to classes to organize in groups that may choose to work in their own way on self-selected topics, I doubt that it is possible to give a defining picture of an independent learning project. With this caveat in mind, I consider the following three descriptions to be fairly typical of the experience of an organized and committed collaborative group – and organization and commitment were typical of the vast majority of groups and classes. The first description is written by a teacher of English, the second by the pupil members of a collaborative group, the third by an independent observer from the Mini-Enterprise in Schools Project.

ANOTHER DAY IN PARADISE

David-John, Gemma, Harry and Martha were Key Stage 3, Year 8 pupils at an urban comprehensive school, and at the time of the project, in the summer term of 1990, were all thirteen years old. As a collaborative group, the four pupils chose to undertake a study of homeless people in their locality, a town of about 25,000 inhabitants. After much discussion within the group they decided that they would like to write a short script about a day in the life of two homeless adolescents and to video-record the film in the town. Their intended audience was the local adult community.

The opportunities for purposeful speaking and listening were already extensive: the original idea-sharing within the group until a consensus was reached; and then the need to persuade me (the class teacher) that their idea was feasible. I arranged an interview for the group with the headteacher, whose permission was required for the pupils to work and film off the school premises. The group decided to send their most articulate member to the head and spent some time preparing for the interview, coaching Martha, their representative, drafting her exposition and hot-seating her for possible questions. Body language, dress, form of address, register and style of speech were discussed and practised.

At this stage, the first part of a considerable programme of factual research was undertaken, the group feeling that their case would be strengthened if they appeared well-informed at the head's interview. The final presentation to the head was based around two discovered facts: that, apart from London, their town had the highest per capita homeless population, and that 75 per cent of this population was of local origin. The headteacher gave permission for the filming, subject to the written approval of the two shopkeepers and the hotel manager on whose premises the group intended to film, the permission of parents, and the attendance of a responsible adult carer when the group were on location.

Telephone conversations took place, meetings were arranged with, and letters sent to, all those involved (including the parents) and a schedule organized, all by the pupils themselves.

The group had by now amassed a great deal of information that went far beyond the original local focus and included research on contemporary destitution in Africa, the dust bowl depression of middle America in the 1930s and the British history of the Poor Laws and the workhouse. Choosing what material to base further work on for the magazine that the group intended to publish was a formidable task and required a high order of selection, comprehension and summary skills.

At about this time (early June), the group began to feel that their original objectives were being lost, and that the experiences of the local homeless were being overlooked. With adult supervision, each member of the group spent a morning with a different homeless person (in one case, a couple). Their experiences were recorded on video, on pocket audio-recorders, in note form and, perhaps most vividly, in their memories.

None of this material appeared in the final video; somehow, the group felt that this cheapened the trust the homeless had shown in them, particularly as the video was to be viewed by the local public. In discussion, I suggested that, with the subjects' permission, there were ways in which the material could be handled sensitively, but the group was adamant: words such as dignity, integrity, fairness were used. (*It might be felt that the group was rejecting the notion of the local homeless as research subjects and responding to them as fellow members of the research partnership of the project. RG*)

However, transcripts were taken, some of which were written up in interview or article form for the magazine. This highlighted to the group the ways in which language changes as it moves from one form to another and is used for different purposes with different audiences. On a rather more mundane, but nevertheless important, level, there was much discussion about punctuation and spelling, the excision of expletives, the retention of slang.

This work led to narrative, descriptive and poetry writing as the pupils now felt able to empathize, without the sentimentality of ignorance, with the homeless. The magazine also contained factual articles placing contemporary homelessness in an historical perspective, and clearly argued discursive pieces outlining possible solutions to 'the problem'. There was lively debate about what constituted the problem and whose problem it was. After all, one of the people interviewed had said that he wouldn't swap his lifestyle at any price. So did he have a problem? Or did conventional citizens have problems coming to terms with a sub-culture they regarded as anti-social? A pivotal point in the project was the realization that homeless people were as diverse as any other group – beware stereotypes.

The group wrote to the Urban Council Housing Committee (the Chair granted them an interview) and the local representatives of all the political parties, all of whom eventually responded in some form or other. They also visited the local DSS office and a local support centre for the homeless.

I offered suggestions for works of literature as diverse as a revisit to *Gumble's Yard* (which the group agreed created an exciting fantasy of child destitution quite at odds with the reality) and the George Orwell essays *The Spike* and *How The Poor Die*. Gemma later read *Down and Out in Paris and London* and interviewed a local major in the Salvation Army about his opinions of Orwell's criticism of their 'tea and prayers' approach to charity for the homeless. Martha compiled a list of colloquialisms from Orwell's essay and compared them with present day language usage – for instance the shift from tramp to traveller, homeless to rough sleeper, jobless to unwaged, charity to support. The events leading up to the death of Fanny in *Far From The Madding Crowd* were read; and David-John and Harry then compared literary text with a video version of the film.

Their own video was successfully filmed, with Harry and Martha operating the camera and David-John and Gemma starring. The film was edited one afternoon with the help of two members of the county advisory service. The group audio-dubbed the prerecorded sound-track of Phil Collins' song *Another Day In Paradise* on to video and then insert-edited both their live footage and a series of still shots culled from texts discovered during their research. Much use was made of an Atari software package that helped create digitized special effects and a different software program was used for computer graphic titles and credits.

The film was shown to a public audience, followed by a live presentation by the group which included an impassioned plea for greater understanding of the homeless. A demonstration of how to audio-dub and insert-edit so that synchronization is achieved between lyric and visual image, and members of the group welcomed spontaneous questions.

INDEPENDENT LEARNING PROJECT, POLTRICE SCHOOL

This project took place at Poltrice School in the spring term of 1992. The collaborative group members offering their opinions below were in a Year 10 class, so were all fourteen and fifteen year-olds. The class was a 'top set', taught by the head of English. Each collaborative group was allowed to choose its own area of study. This group (The Issue-Hitters) chose Euthanasia. At the end of the project, pupils were asked to complete evaluation forms, after discussion within the collaborative group. In an attempt to show both the diversity and the consensus within the group, I have brought together the comments from each individual evaluation form completed by the members of The Issue-Hitters.

General impressions

Tom: I found the project overall, very interesting. I enjoyed the live presentation and think that our group delivered it very well.

Katy: My first impressions of this project where that this was going to be a waste of time and that I'd be bored all term. As the term went on, however, I got more interested in the topic; more friendly with the others in my group and by the end of the project I was dismayed that the course was completed.

Pam: This project was very enjoyable. It gave us all the opportunity to work as groups on a subject which we were interested in. It also gave us a little experience with the video camera. I think that to begin with we all talk and no action – but this improved and everything soon started to slip into place. I enjoyed doing the live presentation and the video.

Zarah: Generally, I enjoyed this course and thought it was fun. It was a good way of learning new skills, exercising old skills and getting on with other people in the group. As we were all interested in euthanasia before the project, it gave us a good basis and we soon started working fairly well together.

Margaret: there was a very relaxed atmosphere on the Wednesday afternoons but people were not messing about and wasting time. Everyone was getting on with what needed to be done. There was not too much pressure but enough for everybody to understand that they were there to work and there were things to be done. The teachers did not butt their noses in all the time but were willing to give help if necessary. We were told what was expected of us and it was a very enjoyable challenge.

Simon: I enjoyed the project and I found it very interesting. The live presentation went well and it was done well.

What I learnt

Tom: I learnt more about the school computers, how they work and how beneficial they can be to a project. I learnt about euthanasia, of which I knew very little before the start of the project. I learnt how to use the video camera correctly and how to edit and do mixing on video. I got to know other people in the class who I wouldn't normally speak to very often.

Katy: I got to research and find out about a topic I had never really thought about before and I used resources I hadn't made use of previously. I also worked with people I didn't know very well before and used editing equipment I hadn't taken advantage of before. I gained a knowledge of euthanasia and I picked up skills in using the video camera, editing and dubbing equipment.

Pam: I learnt quite a lot from the project – and it wasn't just about Euthanasia. I think that my skills as a group member have improved.

Zarah: I learnt how to use a video camera, how to use the editing suite, how to make a video using the two above. You got to know people better, through group discussions etc., you learnt a number of new skills, it was a fun way of learning about a new topic.

Margaret: I learned things I never knew before: what Euthanasia was, how to use a video camera, the mixing equitment and how to find out more information in depth. We did not sit in a classroom with a teacher supervising all our actions. We were left to think for ourselves. I learnt more by doing this project than I would sitting in a classroom writting essays day in and day out and have a teacher prance about in front of you telling you that you put your semi-colon in the wrong place.

Simon: I have learnt how to use the school computers because it was the first time I have used them. I also learnt how to use the video camera and then how to edit what we had filmed. I have also learnt what Euthanasia means as I didn't what it was before we did the project. The project enabled me to meet other people in our class and get to know them. It also allowed me to use all points of english, like reading books and poetry.

Would you like to do something similar again? If so, why?

Tom: I would like to something similar again because it was very educational but interesting at the same time. It was not a waste of a term as it was very enjoyable and really good.

Katy: Definetly. This project expanded our minds and made us consider the plight of other people. It educated us in IT and taught us humility and to hold our tongues! We tought us how to put across our views in an adult manner.

Pam: I would like to do something similar again. It's a really good way of learning. Learning to discuss and work at things as a group rather than an individual is much more fun and you can really start to see how other people think.

Zarah: Yes, I would like to do something like this again. I became a lot closer to the people I worked with, read a lot of books that I wouldn't normally have read, and found out a lot about euthanasia.

Margaret: Yes I would because I learn more this way and I feel that it is important to learn how to apply your knowledge just as much as it is to be continuously learning. It is important to learn how to get on with people because that is what is important out in the big wide world!

Simon: I would like to do something similar again because it was good fun and everybody worked to get the project finished.

OUR BACKYARD

This project took place in the same school year (1990) in two different schools: Tavyford in the spring term and Poltewan in the autumn term. Mixed ability classes in Years 7–10 (eleven to fifteen year-old pupils) were involved. The following analysis was made by John Stock, author of *The Enterprising Classroom* (1991).

Management of projects

The projects were conceived and run by Rhys Griffith (Senior Advisory English Teacher) and Andy Lineout (County Music Service), with assistance from technician Tony Stone. On one day each week classes ranging from Year 7 to Year 10 each spent a double period on the project, plus voluntary lunch hour and after school work. The centre of activity was the school drama studio, which clearly had advantages over a normal classroom area.

Main aims

  i   To involve pupils in an English with music project to produce videos which touched on the local community and environment.

  ii   The videos were to be produced by pupils working in groups of four, self-selected.

  iii   Subjects were to be of their own choice, but had to be instructive, useful or entertaining to other young people or to adults. Some videos might prove marketable to members of the community and parents, but this was not of prime concern.

  iv   The end of the enterprise was to be an evening presentation and demonstration by pupils of their work.

  v   In Poltewan's case some of the tasks were more focused toward creating a literary content, both for the video and in the group production of an accompanying magazine as well as the completion of a personal, reflective diary.

Resources

Rhys and Andy were able to bring into school additional video cameras, VCRs, computers, synthesizers, keyboards and tape-recorders. This constituted a much larger resource than most schools could amass internally. Cooperation with other schools or with LEA resource centres would be necessary to run a similar event.

Features and requirements

Each video had to meet the following conditions:

- to have computer graphics, titles and credits;
- to have a sound-track, using synthesizers or prerecorded and edited audiotape;
- to have dialogue and/or commentary.

Further requirements were that:

- preparatory work had to include story-boarding and scripting;
- after production, videos were to be edited;
- some filming was to be done outdoors;
- there had to be community involvement;
- work had to be cooperative. Groups had to ensure fair access to available resources by operating a disciplined booking system.

Teachers acted throughout purely as resources and consultants. Every step was pupil-led. There was no formal training in the use of equipment. Groups and individuals had to seek help as they perceived the need. Pupils with certain skills or previous knowledge helped others, teachers intervened only if the possibility of damage from misuse of equipment appeared likely. The creative process was left entirely to pupils.

Methodology

To the independent observer, it was striking that at the beginning and end of 'lesson' periods, no instructions were issued by teachers. In fact, neither teacher was heard to address the whole class at any time. The work proceeded from lesson to lesson quite naturally under the ownership of the pupils.

Outcomes

The level of teamwork was high, and there was intense involvement. There was a high degree of initiative and enterprise, self-motivation, self-discipline and group awareness. There was a general willingness to take decisions, and put themselves on the line. The confidence and assertiveness that gradually developed seems to relate directly to the environment and atmosphere in which the pupils were working. Some of the scripts used in the videos were imaginative, and included some original poetry.

Presentation

The presentation and demonstration of work and working methods to a gathering of parents and teachers, some from other schools, took place at the end of the 12 weeks. Pupils demonstrated their mastery of the equipment and their creativity was encapsulated in the range of videos produced. Their confidence and skill in demonstration were evident and a clear outcome of their sense of ownership of the whole project. The actual products – videos and a wide range of written work used in their production – were of high quality.

Debriefing

Part of the above evening presentation was used as a debriefing session which took the form of a discussion between pupils, teachers, observers and parents. A number of pupils evaluated their project honestly and informatively in a way which reinforced their learning experiences.

Conclusions

This was a model of the type of project which could be undertaken by any English department which could gather about itself sufficient equipment. Collaboration with music/creative arts departments would be almost essential.

National Curriculum

A wide range of National Curriculum attainment targets was addressed, especially in the area of Listening and Speaking skills, but also Writing. Daniel Fisher, head of English at Tavyford, envisaged that further work, creative and factual, would emerge from his school's project. The emphasis on literary content at Poltewan demonstrated that enterprise work could be the stimulus for such work at all levels of the Writing attainment target. The reading/research was an added bonus.

English National Curriculum attainment targets, level statements and provisions from programmes of study observable in this project

Attainment Target 1 – Speaking and Listening
Level 3b, c, d; Level 4c, d; Level 5b;
Level 7a, b, c; Level 8b; Level 9a.
Programmes of Study – General Introduction Provisions Nos. 3, 4
Programmes of Study – Key Stages 2–4 Numbers 6, 8.
Programmes of Study – Detailed Provisions – Key Stages 3/4 Numbers 17, 18, 19.

Attainment Target 2 – Reading
Level 4; Level 5; Level 6

Attainment Target 3 – Writing
Level 5; Level 8
Programmes of Study – Key Stages 3/4 Number 24
General Provisions of Key Stage 4 Number 31

The descriptions above give some idea of how teachers, pupils and professional observers regarded the term-long independent learning projects that took place during English lessons in comprehensive schools. I want now to present two examples of cross-curricular, cross-phase independent learning projects that spanned the subjects of the National Curriculum and involved pupils across the five to sixteen age and ability range. John Stock's analysis shows that independent learning projects offer full opportunities for the development of National Curriculum skills, but I prefer to use the twelve factors of learning as a tool of analysis. This offers consistency and comparability with the curriculum analysis of Josie (Chapter 2), Emily (Chapter 3) and The Outfit (Chapter 4).

MINORITIES: OCTOBER 1989 – JULY 1990: ANALYSIS USING THE TWELVE FACTORS OF INDEPENDENT LEARNING (TABLE 5.1)

Table 5.1 Details of schools involved in the Minorities cross-curricular, cross-phase independent learning project

School	Phase	Age-range	No. of pupils
Carnmore	Secondary	11–12	32
Stonall	Secondary	12–13	26
Cedric Harvey	Secondary	12–13	80
St Ilda	Primary	10–11	36
Lanyon	Primary	9–11	67
Totals	2P + 3S = 5	9–13	241

As well as developing independent learning, this project was intended to develop an awareness of the citizen's rights and responsibilities in a multicultural society. Preliminary classwork in the winter term of 1989 was followed by a residential course for teachers in the spring term, during which experiences were shared and a class-based project was planned for the summer term. Six schools were originally involved, with one class (and teacher) from each participating in the project. Each class was divided into six groups of pupils. Each group in each class studied one of the following minorities: the aged, youth, those having a disability, travellers, the poor, non-indigenous residents of Greenshire. It was agreed that the project should embrace local, national and international issues and that pupils should be encouraged to conduct their own active research within the local community, meeting representatives of the minority groups. When one school had to withdraw from the project, one of the other schools contributed a second class, so that the equilibrium was maintained. Two of the schools (but three of the classes, therefore approximately half the pupils) were in the primary sector, three in the secondary. All were schools in the same administrative district of Greenshire. The pupils were from Years 5–8 (nine to thirteen-year-olds). Pupil representatives from each group in each school met at a central venue, for a whole day once each week, to work in partnership with the other five pupils from the other five schools who were studying the same minority. During the central venue days, therefore, each group of six consisted of a pupil from each participating school, and each group spanned the nine to thirteen year old age-range. Figure 5.1 attempts a graphic representation of this process. One school class (Carnmore) has been highlighted, and one collaborative group within that class, to depict inter-relationships generated by the central venue days. All the other groups in all the other schools were simultaneously engaged in the same interaction. Figure 5.2

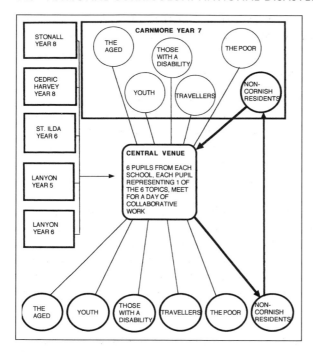

Figure 5.1 The interaction of individual pupils, groups of pupils, classes and schools during the Minorities cross-curricular, cross-phase project for 9–13 year olds (October 1989 – July 1990)

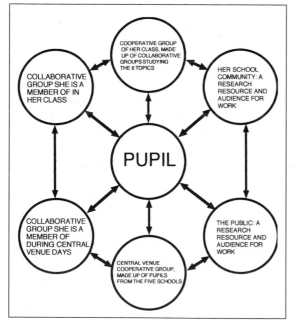

Figure 5.2 Interactions intended to promote collaborative groupwork, cooperative groupwork and the individual responsibility of pupils during the Minorities cross-curricular, cross-phase project, (October 1989 – July 1990)

indicates the possibilities of individual, collaborative and cooperative interactions for every pupil involved in the project.

Around 240 pupils were actively involved, although many more were audiences to presentations, both in individual schools and at the public performance. The project ended with a whole-day multimedia presentation, by the pupils, to the public, staged at Westwood Town Hall. The interactive presentation included demonstrations of equipment, screenings of video programmes made by pupils, lecturettes, song and dance, plays, poetry readings, music and exhibitions and displays of pictorial and printed information.

Factor 1: collaborative groupwork

All involved pupils worked in small, mixed-gender collaborative groups.

The method of group selection varied from school to school, but the two predominant criteria were either friendship and/or the choice of a particular minority for study. Lucy Wing, the County Multicultural Advisory Teacher for Greenshire, described the process in her report to the education committee, entitled *Minorities: A project to develop multicultural awareness and independent learning*:

> Rhys Griffith and myself took a lead lesson with each class. During this lesson we allowed time for the pupils to divide themselves into groups and select their preferred cultural minority to study. We specified, with explanation, that the group must have a gender mix. We explained the project to them, how it was structured and their role and responsibility. Finally by the end of the lesson the pupils were getting to know us. We hoped this would boost their confidence to come to the central venue days with less trepidation.

Most pupils also formed collaborative groups with pupils from each of the other schools during the six central venue days, on which pupils from each school met and worked together. John Stock, author of *The Enterprising Classroom: English Case Studies*, included in his book an evaluation of the Minorities project, in which he observed:

> This was an unusual project of rather daunting complexity. In order to involve the maximum number of children in the project, the plan was to draw pupil delegates successively from particular teaching groups in all the participating schools. These delegates attended central activity and training days held at the most centrally placed of the schools. On each day, delegates went through learning experiences using various resources in relation to one of the multi-cultural themes they had chosen. They became familiar with video and music-producing equipment. They brought ideas from their own schools to develop, and they carried back their experience and skills to those schools. Delegates then disseminated their acquired skills, knowledge and ideas to their teaching groups in their own schools. Work was carried forward in the schools; and then different delegates were then allocated to the next central day, and so on. Approximately 50 children attended each central day, so it can be seen that a very large number of children eventually participated in the enterprise.
>
> (Stock, p. 16, 1991)

Teachers also worked in collaborative groups during the planning stage, at a residential in-service course, and on central venue days.

Factor 2: cooperative groupwork

There was a responsibility on the part of the collaborative groups within each class to various concentric cooperative groups: their own class; the cooperative group of pupils across the five schools that were studying the same minority and whose combined efforts would be represented in the open day at the end of the project; the cooperative group of pupils and teachers from all five schools; the cooperative group of all who would be present on the open day, including the public audience; the cooperative group of each minority being studied, representatives of which worked with pupils; the cooperative group of the research community, to whom those involved held a responsibility for the accuracy of their own research.

Stock commented on the equilibrium between different groups:

> Pupils developed a high degree of communication skills as the project progressed. Teachers in the different schools remarked on the skill with which delegates instructed others in their acquired techniques and knowledge. As far as possible, Teacher-Leaders acted as resources, the emphasis being on pupil-led learning and enterprise. Collaboration between different age-groups was remarkable.
>
> (Stock, p. 17, 1991)

Factor 3: individual responsibility

Each pupil had the responsibility, at the outset, of deciding whether to be involved in the project at all. Within independent learning, individual responsibility has a two-fold meaning. It both implies the individual's responsibility to herself and her responsibility to the other individuals in the many collaborative and cooperative groups of which she is a member. This duality of responsibility underpins a letter to the Senior Inspector for Primary Schools by the headteacher of Lanyon school:

> I think the children of Lanyon School have been privileged to have taken part. They have studied six minority groups in their immediate area, worked with unknown children from other schools, used the video camera, made music, etc., etc., worked with the Advisory Staff, other teachers and ancillaries, talked to parents, interviewed adults – the list is endless. They have integrated their curriculum, their souls and their minds one with another.
>
> (Headteacher, Lanyon)

The final sentence above draws attention not just to the cooperative nature of independent learning, but to pupils having a personal stake in their education, and to the duality of affective and cognitive development – characteristics of educational citizenship.

Factor 4: pupil-designed tasks

Pupils, in collaborative groups, designed their own research tasks – some of which involved the whole group, some duos or trios within a collaborative group, some individual assignments. One group, from St Ilda, visited Nancledwrack Special School for a day and the pupils worked and played together. Games, including a football match, took place, and one St Ilda pupil was able to introduce his brother, a Nancledwrack pupil, to his friends. The pupils made a video of this visit, which includes interviews with pupils about how their feelings, opinions and attitudes had been challenged. A group of Lanyon pupils arranged to meet Alex, a traveller. This meant co-opting the help of parents and driving around the district until they spotted Alex's familiar horse-drawn caravan and were able to ask his permission for an interview. The interview was later conducted, video-recorded and edited.

A pair of Year 8 girls from Cedric Harvey school wrote and recorded two songs about growing old, and performed the songs live at the open day. Other examples are mentioned below under Factors 7 (Pupil-initiated research) and 9 (Community involvement and use of the environment).

Factor 5: pupil-designed assessment

Pupils planned the content and course of their collaborative groupwork. 'Normal' formal teacher assessment involving alphabetical or numerical gradings was suspended during the project. Some teachers attempted some assessment of some of the work of a collaborative group, by formulating a negotiated statement with the members of that group. Pupils decided what work to submit for the open day. In a sense, the public made the final assessment, data that were not systematically collected. The project was intended to encourage the development of pupils' ipsative and reflexive assessment (see Factor 12).

Factor 6: pupil-negotiated deadlines

Pupils negotiated their own collaborative group deadlines within the time limits imposed by the timetable of the project: the starting date, the central venue days and the date of the public presentation. Pupils often worked outside of lesson time to meet their own deadlines between central venue days, particularly in the recording of interviews or other video images that could be edited with advisory support at the central venue days.

Factor 7: pupil-initiated research

As the idea of a project to study minority groups in the locality was originally suggested by a planning group of teachers who had attended an in-service training course, it is not accurate to claim that the pupils were completely unrestricted in their area of research: their research had to relate to the project (the same point is true of Factor 4: Pupil-designed tasks). However, all pupils chose, on an individual basis, whether they wished to take part in the project, and pupils made suggestions as to which minorities might be studied before the class-based work of the project began. A collaborative group of teachers made the selection of the six minority groups chosen for study. Pupils chose which of these their own collaborative group would study and then initiated their own research. They were supported by teachers and other adults. The open day programme records:

> Everything on exhibition is the result of the pupils' own research, design and production.

For further examples, see Factor 9 (Community involvement and the use of the environment). Pupils' research involved fieldwork as well as a survey of the field literature. Telephone calls were made, letters sent, documentation collected, audio, video and photographic images were recorded, visits were made to members of the minority groups within their own environment, and representatives of minority groups attended the central venue days and also visited individual schools. Authoritative figures who had some specialist knowledge of a particular minority group were also consulted and interviewed.

At central venue days, local and national papers were available and groups were encouraged to identify examples of how different groups are represented in the media.

Copies of the current Radio and TV Times provided a reference for relevant television programmes for pupils to watch or record. Telephone directories and Yellow Pages provided a mechanism for making useful contacts for information. A range of fiction and non-fiction books, that could be borrowed by pupils, provided a source of information and still images. Handouts on bias within texts were freely available to pupils and were given to teachers.

Factor 8: pupil-use of a range of language technology

A wide range of technology was used both to gather data, and to process the data for presentation. On the central venue days, all pupils had an introduction to the technology that was available, some of which could be borrowed by pupils between central venue days. Their expertise was developed through hands-on experience in the commission of real tasks, working together collaboratively to eliminate technical gremlins, and sharing expertise and achievements with other collaborative groups. Technical assistance was offered, if requested by groups, by members of the the Greenshire English and Performing Arts advisory teams, but decision making was entirely left to the pupils. Technology used by pupils included: amplifiers, audio-editing equipment, audio-recorders, computer-graphics systems, electric guitars, electronic sound effects units, keyboards, microphones, microphone stands, multi-track audio-recording equipment, overhead projectors, photocopiers, slide projectors, speakers, still cameras, synthesizers, televisions, tripods, video cameras, video-editing equipment, video-recorders, word-processors.

Factor 9: community involvement and the use of the environment

This factor underpinned the entire project. The theme of the project was the local community and environment, the research was conducted within the local community and environment, and the project culminated in a presentation to the local community, from a venue within the local environment.

> Members of various minority groups attended the Central Days, and were interviewed on video by the pupils. Opportunities were provided for the pupils to go out into the local community to visit members of the minority groups. Having researched the topics, pupils exchanged information and opinions, and raised awareness of a whole range of multicultural aspects of the local community.
>
> (Stock, pp. 16–17, 1991)

Some brief examples are:

TRAVELLERS:

interview with Alex, a local Romany; interviews with the manager of a travelling fair, one of the sideshow owners and the twelve-year old son of one of the fairground workers;

YOUTH:

Nicki, a punk, and her friend, a lone parent, and the friend's infant daughter, spent a whole day at the central venue, working with pupils; a group went to the Department of Social Security and interviewed manager Adam Kelly;

THE AGED:

pupils spent an afternoon at the Westwood Age Concern Day Centre talking, playing cards and drinking tea with the people there; a group of pupils met and talked with the residents of Bucklington House residential home who gave them a guided tour of the home; many pupils interviewed grandparents and neighbours;

THE POOR:

a representative from *Breadline* attended a central venue day; Jane Cordle from the DSS attended a central venue day; Sean, an unemployed punk spent a whole day at the central venue (and also worked with the youth group); a group of pupils interviewed homeless people in Westwood;

NON-INDIGENOUS PEOPLE LIVING IN GREENSHIRE:

pupils conducted vox pop interviews in the streets of Westwood and Stonall; pupils interviewed estate agents and Job Centre personnel; pupils filmed evidence in the environment around them (multinational stores, fishing industry at Lynn Cove, tourists, etc); Cassie Spender, a Cedric Harvey parent and newcomer to Greenshire, spent a whole day working with pupils at the central venue;

THOSE WITH A DISABILITY:

Keith, a fourteen year old who had profound hearing impairment, spent a day at the central venue, accompanied by his friend and interpreter (another fourteen-year-old boy), working with pupils; on a research expedition in Westwood, pupils filmed hazards and facilities for the blind and those in wheelchairs; pupils met and talked with a man who has a car especially adapted for his needs, and inspected the car.

Factor 10: a sense of audience

There was a clear sense of audience: the local community; and a clear sense of purpose about the presentation to that audience: to challenge stereotypical attitudes and to raise awareness of the reality of life as a member of a minority.

Factor 11: presentation in various forms

> Back in their own schools pupils created a wide variety of written and creative arts work in preparation for the Exhibition.
>
> (Stock, p. 17, 1991)

The open day featured a range of presentations, brief examples of which, designated by the minority group that was the subject of study, are:

TRAVELLERS:

an ongoing live 'Question Time'; a pupil-produced video featuring an on-location interview with Alex, a Romany, beside and inside his caravan; another pupil-produced video featuring interviews with members of Rowlands Funfair; a slide-show about travellers with factual commentary provided by pupils; and displays of poems, posters and collages;

YOUTH:

a display of acrostic poems, collages, pictures and posters; a 3D display of poetry; a pupil-produced video of an interview with a teenage single parent; a pupil-produced video of an interview with an unwaged punk-rocker; a drama presentation, repeated at intervals throughout the day;

THE AGED:

display of poetry, writing, posters; an audiotaped interview with inmates of a rest-home; a pupil-produced video of old people contributing within the community; a pupil-produced video of old people interviewed at a day centre; a paper sculpture depicting the extended family; a musical rap.

THE POOR:

display of poetry, collages, posters, written work; display entitled *Living On A Tight Budget*; a dramatized video about the homeless, set to music; musical rap, dance presentation, rock-band of pupils and teachers, performances of all of which were repeated throughout the day;

NON-INDIGENOUS PEOPLE LIVING IN GREENSHIRE:

displays of pupil-produced photo-picture stories, collages and poems; an audiotape of pupils' poetry; a 20-minute drama and poetry presentation, repeated at intervals throughout the day; a musical rap, also repeated at intervals; a display of black and white photographs taken by pupils;

THOSE WITH A DISABILITY:

picture collage, written work, posters; pupil-produced video of a day in the life of a severely handicapped boy in a special school (a brother to one of the collaborative group who made this film); a video and drama performance, repeated throughout the day.

The programme for the open day, given free to all who attended, had the following:

> Please feel free to ask children or staff as many questions as you like – Don't miss the opportunity to have a go with the audio, video and computer technology.

John Stock commented both upon the quality and range of the pupils' work and the confident interaction between pupils and adults:

> The final enterprise, the exhibition for parents and the public, was very well received. The level of work in various media was of a high order. Notable was the confidence of the pupils in communication with visitors to the exhibition. Some of the videos were highly artistic and well-produced. Some excellent poetry and written work was on view. There were also poetry readings, playlets, lecturettes, songs, dance, posters, photographic displays, booklets, audio tape and collections of objects. All were pupil-produced.

(Stock, p. 17, 1991)

Factor 12: reflexivity

The principal purpose of the project was to encourage reflexivity: the sense of a personal stake in society and a critical and self-critical examination of one's attitudes and actions. This aim is described by Wing in her report to the Greenshire Education Committee:

> Firstly, inequality, prejudice and injustice are realities within our own community. Certainly it is essential that these issues are raised appropriately in relation to racism and how it operates within our society. However a greater understanding of this may be achieved if pupils and teachers have had the opportunity to identify how these issues are reflected in their local community.
>
> Secondly, that multicultural education aims to promote and respect interest in and celebration of cultural diversity and individual difference as positive, non-threatening and enriching aspects of life. In short, to develop a positive open-mindedness and to replace irrational prejudice with informed opinion and knowledge.
>
> The aim of equality and understanding is as important in the rural south west as it is in inner-city London. We all have our own ethnicity and culture and as such are part of the multicultural society.
>
> Rhys Griffith and myself took a lead lesson in each class. This involved working through the concepts of 'minority', 'prejudice', 'inequality', etc. We introduced challenging questions e.g. Is 'minority' always about numbers? Which minority group members have a choice whether or not to be part of that group? What are gypsies like? Have you ever met one? etc. Gradually pupils' attitudes and opinions began to emerge.
>
> (Wing, p. 3, 1990)

The structure of the project, with pupils moving away from their own familiar surroundings and friends, and working with a mixed-gender group of pupils of different ages from different schools, was intended to offer the opportunity for the pupils themselves to experience at a personal level, and to reflect upon, what it felt like to be a minority of one.

Video recordings of pupils at work show reflexivity, as do observers' notes on the work of collaborative groups and the pupils' own artifacts. The following quotations are from pupils talking to each other in collaborative groups during the project. They were overheard and recorded in note-form by Griffith and Wing:

> I was frightened of him when he walked in. I think it was his punk hairstyle and big boots. But he was really nice and friendly and dead quiet. (Ten-year old Lanyon pupil describing his first meeting with Sean, the unemployed punk)
>
> All gypoes wear big gold ear-rings and they are dirty with dogs.
> Alex hasn't got a dog –
> My dad's got an ear-ring because he's a fisherman –
> You can't say all –
> There's dogs up Cavensey and they're not gypsies – (Collaborative group of nine to thirteen year-old boys and girls from different schools, studying Travellers, at a central venue day)

They were really fun to play with. When we scored a goal they were really pleased and didn't get cross. They've got some really good skills.

> (Eleven-year old St. Ilda boy describing a football game with pupils at Nancledwrack Special School)

I think fifty is old.
Don't be stupid, my mum's fifty!
(Laughter.)
Old people are best at telling things from their memories –
Yeh – but when I was interviewing her, she started to ask me questions and I got confused . . .

> (Pair of Carnmore twelve-year-old girls discussing a visit to Westwood Day Centre)

When my voice squeaked, it made me laugh!
(Laughter.)
It's because you were too far away from the mike –
No, it's because he was too near, isn't it?

> (Mixed group of eleven to thirteen year-old Cedric Harvey pupils discussing the audio-dubbing of a spoken commentary on to an edited videotaped interview with Alex the Traveller)

Conclusions

The Minorities project offered evidence that a scheme of work based upon the twelve factors of independent learning was practicable with older primary school pupils and young secondary school pupils. The structure of the project encouraged pupils to throw off any traces of dependent learning to which they may have been subject during 'normal' lessons and to become independent learners.

CENTENNIAL: OCTOBER 1990 – JUNE 1991 ANALYSIS USING THE TWELVE FACTORS OF INDEPENDENT LEARNING (Table 5.2)

Table 5.2   Details of schools involved in the Centennial cross-curricular, cross-phase independent learning project

School: no. of pupils	Phase	Age range	Decade of study	
Pruddock	Primary	7–11	1901–10	60
Clayport	Secondary	14–16	1911–20	100
Marketmoor	Primary	7–9	1921–30	72
East Green	Primary	7–9	1931–40	34
Three Lanes	Primary	8–11	1941–50	31
Barmouth	Secondary	11–12	1951–60	120
Shearpool	Primary	5–11	1961–70	175
Dore	Secondary	12–14	1971–80	90
Higher Strand	Primary	7–11	1981–90	63
Tavymouth	Secondary	12–13	1991–2000	31
Totals	6P + 4S = 10	5–16	1900–2000	776

As well as developing independent learning, this project was intended to develop pupils' awareness of the changing nature of citizenship over time but of the enduring sense of community.

After a planning term in the winter of 1990, ten schools (six primary, four secondary) studied a different decade of the twentieth century during the spring term of 1991. Schools decided their own approaches, some schools choosing to focus on one or two events in 'their' decade, whilst others spanned the whole 10 years. Some schools limited their cross-curricular involvement to three or four subjects, others embraced the whole curriculum. Some schools targeted particular classes, other included the whole school. It was stipulated that the study should embrace local, national and international issues and that pupils should be encouraged to conduct their own active research within these communities.

In the summer term, each school distilled their research to a six-minute presentation. Enhanced with large-screen video images, pyrotechnic effects and stage sound and lighting systems, a continuous multimedia presentation of the pupils' perceptions of the twentieth century was performed to an audience of 2000 at a public theatre, situated centrally in Greenshire. Over 750 pupils were actively involved, although many more were audiences to presentations, both in individual schools and at the public performance.

Factor 1: collaborative groupwork

Centennial involved primary and secondary schools across the whole LEA. It also involved more than one class within most of the schools, and a wide age and ability range of pupils. A wide range of schools offered the possibility of observing a wide range of practice. During the course of the project, I made visits to working classrooms in each of the schools. Although pupils in all schools worked in collaborative groups during the project, in only two schools did pupils work exclusively in the same collaborative groups, without teacher intervention, throughout the project. The common pattern of the observed lessons was for lessons to begin and to end under the orchestration of the teacher, and for the rest of the time to be devoted to collaborative groupwork. Teachers also made it clear that on occasions they taught whole-class lessons. For some of the teachers, extended collaborative groupwork was a new venture and, understandably, they were cautious about committing themselves to a whole term's work in this medium. For pupils in the secondary sector, it was not possible to work consistently in the same collaborative group on a cross-curricular project because of the different grouping systems used for different subject lessons. The criteria for the formation of collaborative groups did not always adhere to the mixed gender model, although there were some mixed gender groups in every class observed. Whatever the variations between schools, at some stage all pupils had the opportunity for collaborative groupwork.

It was interesting to note that teachers, particularly those new to team-teaching or the partnership that cross-curricular work requires, commented on the collaborative groupwork of the *teachers* involved in the project.

> Working with both primary colleagues from schools of vastly different sizes and colleagues from comprehensive schools, created an understanding of the factors and constraints under which they had to work, in coordinating this project in their schools.

> (Headteacher, Pruddock)

We feel Centennial has been very worthwhile for Clayport School. By adopting a team-teaching approach both pupils and staff were able to experience a liberating effect. One member of the staff commented – 'I hadn't realised how isolated one can become'.

(Acting Head of English, Clayport)

What did Centennial achieve? From a personal viewpoint I worked closely with two members of the staff I had not known well before. We enjoyed the collaboration and the foundation was laid for future cross-curricular projects.

(Head of drama, Tavymouth)

Factor 2: cooperative groupwork

The spirit of working with others, perhaps initially germinated through the collaborative groupwork, appears to have been enhanced by the feeling of belonging to an expanding series of concentric cooperative groups: one's own class, any other classes in the school actively involved in *Centennial*, one's own school and community which acted as an audience for in-house presentations, all the schools which contributed to the final public presentation.

The reaction from staff, pupils and the local community was totally positive from the beginning and in their final evaluation, everyone was gratified to have been involved and all felt they had learnt so much.

(Headteacher, Pruddock)

They worked as a team, helping and supporting one another. The Year 6 children were very protective towards the Year 3 children, especially at the theatre. Everyone who wanted to be part of the performance was included.

(Project Coordinator, Shearpool)

The pupils learnt the necessity of working with us and with each other to create a worthwhile achievement . . . They appreciated the opportunity to observe other schools' work, to note their approaches to the project and compare it with their own.

(Head of drama, Tavymouth)

Today we got ready for filming. One problem that we had to face was that Ruth was away, and she had one of the main parts so we had to rearrange it a bit. We asked Donna from another group to stand in. We started filming at about three o' clock, first with Brian and then with Richard.

(Elspeth, Year 9 pupil, Dore)

Factor 3: individual responsibility

Several teachers commented upon the individual responsibility shown by pupils in their commitment to the cooperative group, particularly in the pressurized atmosphere of the public presentation, which involved 800 pupils on stage, performing to an audience of

2500. Pupils from all ten schools met for the first time during the afternoon, and had the one and only rehearsal before the evening presentation.

> The rehearsal for our decade was a disaster. The overhead microphones did not pick up the children's voices and after a second run-through with the children speaking as loudly as they could I decided that we would have to reroute all their moves so that they could speak into the standing microphones, one either side of the stage. Weeks of patient rehearsing appeared to have been wasted but I reckoned without the professionalism of the children. In the evening they sailed through their performances perfectly in their new positions. I was very, very proud of them.
>
> (Years 2–4 class teacher, East Green)

> The children rose to the occasion, many taking responsibilities previously unthought-of. In retrospect, maybe we all learnt to rely more on our own abilities and less on others. I think that all the children gained a tremendous amount from the experience.
>
> (Teacher i/c Language Development, Shearpool)

Factor 4: pupil-designed tasks

There were many examples in every school of pupil-designed tasks, both concerning pupil initiated research (often fieldwork in the local environment, involving the local community), and each school's contribution to the final presentation. Pupil-designed tasks were not always executed exclusively by pupils: there were occasions when collaborative groups of pupils co-opted adults, including teachers, to assist them. Examples of pupil-designed tasks are given under Factor 7 (pupil-designed research) and Factor 11 (various forms of presentation).

Factor 5: pupil-designed assessment

Some of the work produced by pupils was later used for formal assessment in GCSE examination (Years 10 and 11 pupils, Clayport). In the main, though, the influence of Factors 4, 7 and 11 (pupil-designed tasks, pupil-initiated research and various forms of presentation) mitigated against the lone authority of the teacher as marker. Pupils were likely to negotiate with a range of informal, but informed, assessors: peers in collaborative and cooperative groups, teachers, parents, members of the local community. The overall impression, based upon researchers' observations, was that assessment in the sense of the teacher awarding grades or marks was suspended during the project; but that a great deal of reflexive assessment – that was not always recognized as such – took place in the form of discussion, comment, evaluation for future action, planning, and other shared talk.

Factor 6: pupil-negotiated deadlines

Pupils negotiated deadlines within the time limits of the starting date of classroom work and the final performance.

> The need to work within a time constraint at first appeared irksome but emerged finally as an enjoyable challenge. Secondly, although this was a curriculum project, the pupils involved also worked in lunch hours and after school. They did so, not through any

teacher pressure, but because they wanted to. Any scheme which generates this level of care and commitment must be counted a success.

(Head of drama, Tavymouth)

Factor 7: pupil-initiated research

Centennial was based upon the premise that pupils initiated their own research (albeit within the confines of their school's chosen decade, over which they had no personal choice), and that fieldwork took place within the local community. Thus, all schools provided a rich seam of data for this factor. Other examples are given under Factor 9 (community involvement and use of the environment).

> Today we decided what subject we were going to do for our project – 'THE 1970's'. We all agreed on Sam's idea for our title – FASHION AND FACTS IN THE 1970's. Our idea is based on fashion in clothing and music, plus major events of the decade. We thought we could show how fashion was influenced by music and pop-stars e.g punk rock, New Romantic era. We hope we can achieve our aim by: a) interviewing people who were alive in this decade; b) research into the subject using libraries, humans and general knowledge.
>
> (Lizzie Martin, Year 9, Dore, writing about the pupil-initiated research of her collaborative group)

> East Green: Work has been organised on a individual basis: each pupil is to research one historic event of international significance with, if possible, its effects on the local community. Audrey has written to all the school's parents and is currently compiling a 'research register' of people that pupils could contact and interview.
>
> (Excerpt from Centennial newsletter, February, 1991)

Factor 8: pupil-use of a range of language technology

Primary and secondary pupils used videocameras and audiorecorders during fieldwork interviews (Pruddock, Marketmoor, Tavymouth, others). Some pupils had in-school access to videoediting equipment and made their own video programmes (Dore, Tavymouth). Some pupils filmed their peers and this footage was incorporated into the public presentation (Tavymouth, Clayport, Marketmoor). Some schools recorded pupils singing for inclusion in the public presentation (Pruddock, Shearpool, Higher Strand). Computers were used by pupils for word-processing (all schools), for creating titles and credits for video programmes (Dore, Tavymouth) and for e-mail (Three Lanes, Pruddock, Barmouth). Telephone calls were made by pupils in pursuit of information and to make arrangements for fieldwork (all schools). A more passive, but important use of technology was the watching of television and video programmes pertinent to the research field (all schools). All pupils contributed to the planning and directing of the video sequence that was projected during their own school's six-minute contribution to the public presentation. This invariably required the selection and editing of appropriate background music, using reel-to-reel or cassette recorders. Pupils from every school were involved in discussions about the positioning of microphones, the lighting plot and the use of pyrotechnical effects as appropriate to their contribution to the presentation.

. . . interviews with octogenarians were taped . . .

(Teacher i/c English, Marketmoor Juniors)

We regularly word process our stories for display purposes. We then used the Campus 2000 equipment to transmit the traffic survey results to other schools.

(Class teacher, Three Lanes)

The English curriculum was extended and enhanced through the integration of information technology and media. The word-processor and 'Caxton Press' were utilised to create magazines and newspapers, all pupils learned how to use the video cameras and computer graphics for film credits and they were able to participate in the final editing and addition of soundtracks and graphics using the video mixer.

(Head of English, Dore)

I have really enjoyed working on the Centennial project. I have learnt how to use the computer graphics and the video camera, technical ideas I have never had the chance to be involved in before.

(Frankie, Year 9 pupil, Dore)

This term the children are collating this work [*their own childhood memories, RG*] on a database called Decade. It should give clear indications of statistical growth trends.

(Class teacher, Higher Strand)

Factor 9: community involvement and the use of the environment

This factor underpinned the entire project. The theme of the project was to reveal the myriad and interconnected cultural communities and environments of Planet Earth during this century; and how, increasingly, we belong to a global community living in a shared environment and that everyone has a citizen's responsibilities to care for both the community and the environment. Much of the research was conducted within the local community and environment, on the basis of 'Think global, act local'. The project culminated in a presentation to the community of Greenshire, from a venue at the centre of the county. The presentation both expressed the collaborative and cooperative power of those involved and symbolized the potential of other apparently widely diverse groups to work together to a common outcome for a common benefit.

One of the most remarked-upon features of this factor was how it synthesized with Factor 2: cooperative groupwork. There are many examples of how the researched in the local community actively contributed to the research, becoming part of the cooperative group. A parent gave cookery lessons each Friday afternoon at Pruddock School, using recipes from an Edwardian book brought in by a pupil. Parents at Pruddock sent in a vast number of artifacts, some of which remained on permanent loan, so that the school was able to establish its own social museum. The school held its own end-of-project presentation for the local public. Tavymouth pupils wrote to local, national and international figures and organizations for predictions of events to include in their forecast of the 1990s. The Shearpool project was community based with most of the research concentrating on how national and international events during the 1960s affected life in and around Shearpool and how some of those effects are still evident today. Like Pruddock and Tavymouth schools, Shearpool made an end-of-project presentation to the local public. Local senior citizens who could recall the 1920s were interviewed by Marketmoor pupils, using video and audio equipment, and one of the teacher's fathers visited the school to talk about his memories of schooldays in the 1920s. With the involvement of the local community, East Green school established a research register of people that pupils could interview. Many written reminiscences were sent to East Green school by grandparents and others. This data was used as a stimulus to factual and narrative work by the pupils. A parent collated this material and a booklet, with illustrations, was produced and copies made available to the local public. Higher Strand pupils wrote to Prince Charles, who responded by letter and enclosed a seed catalogue. The owner of a private mine visited the school, one parent donated a piece of the Berlin Wall to the project museum and a study was made of the lifeboat service and in particular, the Penlee lifeboat disaster of 1981.

> I have quoted at length what we did, because it backs up the excitement, enthusiasm and parental involvement in the work. Only on Friday a school governor, Elaine Wood, lent me her copy of Jean Metcalfe's *Twenties Childhood*. The adult enthusiasm is still snowballing and these spinoffs are great. That parents and children have researched books together, neighbours and greatgrandmothers (octogenarians) have taped their memories which were listened to, and still people are coming forward to share a forgotten memory, is surely a testimonial to the value of the work.
>
> (Teacher i/c English, Marketmoor)

> The children, almost without exception, got a great deal from this project. They enjoyed learning about the period and especially talking to grandparents and friends who lived in it. The personal memories that many people wrote about so readily were more evidence of the community's interest in the project.
>
> (Class teacher, East Green)

> We were trying to find out about Shearpool High Street in the sixties. We asked Mrs. Baker because she lived in Shearpool High Street. She gave us lots of information. Now we know lots of shops that are not there now. In 1965 the Coop was still there but the inside was different. Grocery was on the left and clothing was on the right. The Library building was still there but it was just a hall used for Whist Drives.
>
> (Felicity and Theresa, Year 5 pupils, Shearpool)

Factor 10: a sense of audience

There was a clear sense of different audiences: other pupils in the school, the local community, members of the public from across Greenshire. Most of the ten schools made different presentations to all of these audiences. Shearpool held an open day that culminated in a Sounds of the Sixties disco for parents and children. Barmouth held a 1950s 'High School Prom' with a live rockabilly group, parents and pupils dressed in period clothing and the school catering staff providing soda-pop, milk-shakes and hot-dogs. East Green held an open afternoon for the public to view an exhibition of pupils' work and locally collected artifacts. During an idyllically sunny May afternoon, present-day East Green pupils and ex-pupils – including some who had attended the school in the 1930s – talked together before sharing a high tea on the lawns in front of the two-class granite school, which overlooks a wooded valley of the River Wyvell. Pruddock pupils and teachers, dressed in Edwardian costume, had a day of Edwardian lessons, which was open to the public. During breaktime, pupils played Edwardian games in the school yard, before eating an Edwardian school dinner. In the afternoon they talked to three nonagenarians who had attended their school during the first decade of the century.

> On the 14/3/91 we got changed into Edwardian clothes. First we put on white shirts, collars and we had black socks which came up to our knees. First the reporter came and took photos. Soon Mr Griffith came around with a video camera to record us. Our first lesson was an object lesson about a daffodil. Half way through Richard made a spelling mistake and a blot so Mrs Winters gave him the dunces cap but they were only acting. After that we did poetry. We learned a poem called daffodils. Then we had scripture At playtime I played leapfrog. After dinner we had drill. Then we interviewed old people. Then we watched the video. It was one of the best days of my life.
>
> (William, aged nine, Pruddock)

The final presentation to an audience of 2500 at a public theatre, required not just a sense of audience, but, as rehearsal time was limited, a sense of individual responsibility to that audience and to other pupil presenters:

> In less than 100 minutes, a performing arts collage of 100 years revealed itself: a snapshot in time of 800 pupils' feelings about the 20th Century. As this was the first time all the pupils had met each other, it was an interesting occasion. During the afternoon, we had a quick run-through and then settled back to enjoy the show, with each school being able to see its 'own' decade set in the context of the whole century.
>
> (Greenshire Education Newsletter, Summer, 1991)

Factor 11: presentation in different forms

Over the ten schools, just about every form in which it is possible for pupils to present their work was observed. Written work included stories, poetry, discursive and factual articles, and empathic descriptions (hand-written as appropriate to the text by biro, quill, chalk, fountain pen or brush; or word-processed using a variety of software). Writing was presented in different forms: in stapled booklets, facsimiles of brochures and magazines, on 'parchment', aged with cold tea and burnt at the corners. Some booklets were photocopied and multiples distributed or sold in the school locality. Displayed visual work included posters, paintings, drawings, photographs, tracings, sketches, paper and wooden sculptures, and exhibitions of period artifacts. Recorded work included video programmes that ranged from simple vox pop interviews to highly sophisticated edited programmes, audiotaped recordings of interviews and reminiscences, and the recording of pupils' singing. Apart from the use of electronic text for word-processing, computers were used to print out e-mail and questionnaire forms, and to compile database information. Work was also presented in dance, mime, tableau, play, poetry reading, lecture and song.

Perhaps more important was the evidence of range of presentation within each school, so that no pupils would be disbarred from contributing to the project. Pupils at the Shearpool Special Unit created a life-size, three-dimensional tableau of space exploration and built a representation of a lunar module which they used in the public presentation. Year 10 'bottom set' [sic] pupils at Clayport produced poems and essays for the school display.

Less able pupils quickly realised that they had much to offer and there was a commensurate improvement in the quality of their work. In Humanities these pupils produced startling and provocative propaganda posters and were prepared to discuss, in depth, complex issues such as class structures and relate this knowledge to themselves and the 1990's. In Linguistics, I discovered that a very bottom set was capable, aided by a National Geographic video, of writing detailed and atmospheric essays and poems on The Titanic and aspects of her fate. At the other extreme, my Year 11 (top set) produced coursework of such quality and depth that I decided to elevate the status of *Animal Farm* from a wider-reading text to that of a set text for GCSE examination. This improvement must be attributable to the cross-curricular links that placed greater emphasis on the context of the book and the purposes which stimulated its author.

(Acting head of English, Clayport)

Factor 12: reflexivity

The principal purpose of *Centennial* was to encourage reflexivity: the sense of a personal stake in society and a critical and self-critical examination of one's attitudes and actions. This is the least observable of the twelve factors and therefore the hardest for which to gather evidence. What are more readily observable are learning practices and teaching techniques that are intended to develop reflexivity. Collaborative and cooperative groupwork (Factors 1 and 2) give the opportunity for pupils to talk freely and discuss what they want, to justify their ideas for tasks, research or presentation, to negotiate with others – so that pupils may develop the capacity for critical and self-critical thought and an appropriate speech register for articulacy. Individual responsibility, pupil-designed tasks, pupil-negotiated assessment and deadlines, and pupil-initiated research (Factors 3–7) give the opportunity for pupils to feel a personal stake in their education. Community involvement, the use of the environment and a sense of audience (Factors 9 and 10) gives the opportunity for the subject of study to be related to the peopled environment in which pupils live, encourages empathy and requires social and ethical viewpoints to be formulated and moral decisions to be made. The use of a range of language technology and presentation in various forms (Factors 8 and 11) is intended to give all pupils the opportunity to make their own statements via the media most appropriate to them. Thus, all the other factors have a role to play in developing reflexivity. The example of a Year 8 class at Tavymouth (which had the 1990s as their decade of study) illustrates a synthesis of the following factors of independent learning: collaborative and cooperative groupwork, individual responsibility, pupil-designed tasks, pupil-initiated research, a sense of audience, presentation in various forms, reflexivity:

This project has forced one [cooperative] group into becoming soothsayers and crystal balls are few on the ground in Tavymouth. There has, however, been much humour and speculation during brain-storming sessions. *Tomorrow's World* has suddenly acquired new devotees and current new stories are analysed to try to determine where events might lead them. Specific items such as entry into Europe, the opening of the Channel Tunnel and the next general election have been placed under the microscope. The [cooperative] group has debated trends in such diverse areas as clothes, music and religion.

The students [in collaborative groups] have worked with dedication to create this programme and varying responsibilities have been assumed. Some have worked on models, others have composed graphics for future television channels or music to back the various items. Ingenuity has been expended in acquiring costumes and props to be used during the show. The style of presentation which mixes live theatre with video film has given them an appreciation of various communication styles. Two of the [cooperative] group have become avid watchers of television presenters as they attempt to capture that professional gloss. Another is studying the Queen in order to open the Tunnel and yet another is preparing a speech in French.

The benefits have already appeared. The group's ability to connect the work of different disciplines and appreciate how they complement each other has been heightened. They have become a cohesive team working well together and supportive of each other's efforts. They look forward to the day and the performance but the process of creation has clearly become an enjoyment in itself.

One final thought – these pupils have had a term in which to create this experience. They will then have near a decade to observe the nineties as they unfold and reflect on how accurate or otherwise their predictions have been.

(Head of drama, Tavymouth)

There is also evidence that reflexivity was explicitly encouraged in other schools (as well as implicitly, through the application of the other 12 factors):

They [pupils] made critical judgments, took constructive criticism and amended their performance accordingly.

(Class teacher, Shearpool)

It was noticeable that these pupils were bringing a much wider awareness to bear on the relevant issues in both Faculty areas. In Humanities these pupils produced startling and provocative propaganda posters and were prepared to discuss, in depth, complex issues such as class structures and relate this knowledge to themselves and the 1990s.

(Acting head of English, Clayport)

When I chose the 1930s as East Green School's decade I had not realised how many parallels there would be with the present day. The more I researched the more similarities I discovered. Unemployment, poverty, homelessness, war, even the IRA planting bombs in London stores. The children at East Green are not deprived in any way and many of the things that we have learnt have, I think, made them appreciate their good fortune while, at the same time, giving them the feeling that history repeats itself.

(Class teacher, East Green)

The pupils decided to concentrate on youth culture in the 1970s. How did music and fashion influence each other? How did they relate to major national and international events? The 1970s was the decade in which these Dore pupils were born. 'Just what were we born into?' they asked themselves. 'What was it like for our parents who were embarking on adult life?'

(Head of English, Dore)

Conclusions

Centennial offered further evidence to suggest that independent learning can apply in many areas of the curriculum, to all ages of pupils in statutory state education, and to pupils across the full ability range.

Subjects in which work took place in the primary sector were: art, cookery, craft, creative writing, dance, design and technology, drama, English language, English literature, geography, geology, health education, history, information technology, mathematics, media studies, music, physical education, religious education, science.

Subjects in which work took place in the secondary sector were: art and design, design and technology, drama, English language, English literature, food technology, French, geography, history, information technology, mathematics, media studies, modern languages, music, physical education, science.

Independent learning, as expressed through this project, was regarded as educationally effective by teachers and other professional observers, and felt to offer benefits for both cognitive and affective development. Involved pupils expressed enthusiasm for this way of working in lessons, and parents and other members of the various schools' communities praised both the process and the product of the project.

> As a teacher I gained a great deal of personal satisfaction from the project. Rather like Topsy, it just grew and grew. One aspect seemed naturally to promote another until it appeared that it was taking up twenty-fours a day.
>
> (Class teacher, East Green)

> The most outstanding event in the last school year came when Mrs. Tapper's class of Year Three and Year Four children were accepted to take part in Centennial.
>
> (Excerpt from 1991 Governors' Report to Parents, East Green)

> I loved the classroom work. It was a sudden challenge. I state again, it felt good to be part of something bigger.
>
> (Teacher i/c English, Marketmoor)

> The feedback I got from parents and governors was totally positive. They much appreciated the experience the pupils had enjoyed. My pupils greatly enjoyed doing the topic work and with the theatre presentation, had an experience they will never forget.
>
> (Class teacher, Three Lanes)

> Parents, governors and the pupils themselves all hailed it as a very positive learning experience.
>
> (Project Coordinator, Barmouth)

> Brilliant.
>
> (Parent, Shearpool)

> When asked to evaluate the Centennial project and the final theatre show, the overwhelming response from all involved was one of real enjoyment and achievement.
>
> (Head of English, Dore)

What an eye-opener! A marvellous way of nourishing minds young and old.

(Governor, Higher Strand)

The evening helped to put back the 'magic' of working with children & to encourage me to work towards the importance of the child at the heart.

(Primary adviser for Greenshire LEA)

Centennial: an inspirational effect on the schools.

(Senior inspector for primary schools in Greenshire)

In presenting us with *Centennial*, all those responsible for it are demonstrating that creativity must never be superseded in schools by conformity, as the principal virtue of the teacher. On the contrary, an approach to learning through imagination, exploration and – as this evening – presentation, becomes more vital than ever if an imposed curriculum is to be given life and breath, and to nourish young minds.

(Excerpt from the introduction to the theatre programme, May 1991, by the Chief Inspector for Schools, Greenshire LEA)

6 What the pupils say: a survey of 11 to 16-year-old pupils

Getting pupils' opinions was both very easy and extremely difficult. It was easy because, during independent learning projects, I worked alongside the pupils as an equal member of the cooperative group and over the course of a successful project, due to the nature of independent learning, a trusting and easy-going relationship developed so that pupils, teachers and other observers were happy to discuss in critical terms educational citizenship and independent learning. It was difficult because of the sheer volume of data that could be collected; the need to ensure that data collection was uncontaminated by feelings of personal loyalty to either myself, other teachers or the concept of independent learning itself, whilst allowing the full range of expression; and the need to find forms of evaluation that did not exclude less literate pupils from expressing their opinions.

EVALUATING THE DATA

Volume of data

The five outcomes of an independent learning project generated enormous amounts of valuable research material: project diaries, bibliographies, magazines, videos and live presentations (many of which were videorecorded). Considering that the case study of one collaborative group (The Outfit) took me about six months to transcribe, collate, analyse and present my conclusions, it can be seen that had I collected the project diaries of the 7000 pupils who undertook independent learning projects, the research could never have been completed. But this data was just the tip of the iceberg, for I also experimented with a variety of ways to collect not just the artifacts of independent learning, but to gather the opinions of those involved about the process of a project. Because the projects were very open, involving members of the community as well as professional educational observers, there was no shortage of people keen to express an opinion. Table 6.1 shows the wide range of sources.

Range of expression

I was aware that each of these sources would bring a different perspective to bear, which was useful and a recognized technique of research in the critical paradigm, but this raised two further considerations. First, different observers would be viewing a project through the lens of different epistemologies. To give a simple example: a pupil may regard an independent learning project as good because they enjoyed more freedom than within their usual

Table 6.1 Sources of data collection

- Pupils involved in independent learning projects in their English lessons;
- pupils involved in cross-curricular independent learning projects;
- teachers involved in independent learning projects in their English lessons;
- teachers involved in cross-curricular independent learning projects;
- advisory teachers involved in independent learning projects in English lessons;
- advisory teachers involved in cross-curricular independent learning projects;
- observers of independent learning projects in English lessons;
- observers of cross-curricular learning projects;
- observers of end-of-project presentations.

Observers comprised: advisers, advisory teachers, ancillaries, caretaking and maintenance staff, carers, catering staff, cleaning staff, clerical staff, ET trainees, headteachers, HMI inspectors, LEA inspectors, lunchtime supervisors, members of the senior management team, parents, prospective parents, prospective pupils, road-crossing supervisors, SEN staff, school deliveries personnel, teachers from other departments, teachers from other schools, technical staff, visitors to the school, YTS trainees.

curriculum: a teacher might regard a project as good because the quality of pupils' written work improved; I might regard a project as good because I believed that pupils were being offered a greater chance to develop the qualities of global citizenship (and that the quality of artifacts was a much less important consideration than the quality of interpersonal relationships); a parent might regard a project as highly suspect because it didn't seem like classwork as she remembered it as a pupil; a member of a school senior management team might feel distinctly uneasy because independent learning did not fit with the back-to-basics ethos being promulgated by government. How did one balance these viewpoints? Second, how did one develop data collection methods that enabled each different group to express themselves to the best of their ability and also find some consistent method of data collection that allowed collation, comparison and analysis of data from different sources? The problems were resolved by trial and error as various forms of data collection were tried, considered, amended or discarded (Table 6.2).

Non-exclusive forms of data collection

Another problem was quality of data, in terms of depth. For instance, the vast majority of parents and pupils were enthusiastic and made very positive comments, but at a superficial level. Methods had to be found to allow pupils to analyse their learning, to think, talk and write about it in ways that many had never done before. Of course, independent learning should do this anyway in its concern for the development of a critical disposition, reflexivity, moral awareness, a concern for social justice – not just 'out there', but applied to the work of the collaborative and cooperative groups on an explicit and acknowledged basis within their own social environment. Nevertheless, a major part of the research process was to experiment with different forms of data collection in an attempt to find ways for *all* pupils to voice their opinions as profoundly as possible.

There is only enough space in this book to show that the research partnership was aware of these three problems, but not to elaborate upon how we solved them. The emphasis in this text is upon reporting what pupils thought and said, rather than offering a full analysis of how they were enabled to express themselves. For a detailed account of how these problems were resolved, readers are guided towards Chapter 3: 'Research method and procedure' in *Independent Learning and Educational Citizenship* (Griffith, 1998). Suffice to say that a range of forms of evaluation were tried and developed that satisfied the research

Table 6.2 Methods of data collection

Open evaluations:	• pupils' group responses to independent learning projects; • pupils' individual responses to independent learning projects; • teachers' responses to independent learning projects; • teachers' responses to INSET courses; • observers' responses to independent learning projects; • responses of advisory support teachers involved in independent learning projects.
Guided evaluations:	• pupils' individual responses to independent learning projects; • teachers' responses to independent learning projects; • teachers' responses to INSET courses.
Multi-choice questionnaires:	• completed by pupils undertaking independent learning projects in English lessons; • completed by teachers on INSET courses.
Written response questionnaires:	• completed by pupils undertaking independent learning projects in English lessons.
Lesson notes by:	• pupils involved in independent learning projects; • teachers involved in independent learning projects; • advisory support teachers involved in independent learning projects.
Videotapes of:	• work produced by pupils; • work produced by teachers on INSET courses; • pupils working; • pupils reflecting on independent learning projects in English; • pupils reflecting on cross-curricular independent learning projects; • end-of-project presentations by pupils; • interviews with pupils.
Audiotapes of:	• pupils' work; • pupils reflecting on independent learning projects.
Photographs of:	• pupils' work; • pupils at work during independent learning projects; • teachers on INSET courses.
Examples of work:	• produced by pupils during independent learning projects in English lessons; • produced by pupils during cross-curricular independent learning projects; • produced by teachers on INSET courses.

team within Greenshire, and external adjudicators at Exeter and Nottingham universities, that the research data were authoritative and valid.

The previous chapters in this book that have dealt with the classroom experience of children have been based on case studies, and despite the sound arguments for their generalizability, I also wanted to find a way of collecting data that would permit some form of statistical representation, whilst at the same time allowing the voice of the individual child to be heard. This chapter reports the findings of a questionnaire that was completed by 514 pupils (239 boys – 46.5 per cent; 275 girls – 53.5 per cent) who undertook independent learning projects between January 1991 and July 1992 in ten comprehensive schools in Greenshire. These schools can be grouped chronologically (see Table 6.3).

The questionnaire was intentionally subjective: it asked pupils to express their opinions, feelings, emotions. The format was not restricted in the way that a multi-choice questionnaire must inevitably be (in that it provides a selection of possible answers, as envisaged by the compiler, and invites the respondent to choose one or more of them). The questionnaire format was guided: a broad question and a space for a response in the pupil's

Table 6.3 The three groups of Greenshire comprehensive schools in which the independent learning questionnaire was used

Group 1 schools (Spring Term, 1991)
Castlefort, Cord, Dore, Saltair

Group 2 schools (Winter Term, 1991)
Ashbridge, Ashfordton, Stonall

Group 3 schools (Spring and Summer Terms, 1992)
Carnmore, Coppersand, Poltrice

own words. The questions were based on pupils' suggestions and the phrasing was approved by groups of pupils from each Group One school (Castlefort, Cord, Dore, Saltair – Spring Term, 1991).

From September 1988 to December 1990, pupils' responses to prototype independent learning projects had been collected in a variety of ways: video and audiorecordings (Budleigh, Poltewan, Tavymouth, Southbay, Penmouth, Axton, Benallick), project diaries (Venturers, Marketmoor, Carnmore, Stonall), end-of-project evaluation forms of differing format (Tavyford, Axton, Stonall, Marketmoor, Carnmore, Woodcoombe, Poltrice, Pemburton, Venturers). Common sense analysis had revealed that pupils can often be inconsistent in their statements, or hold views that seem contradictory. Such comments can be confusing to the research analyst; and their form is not conducive to a systematic analysis that might clarify ostensible contradictions or inconsistencies. Yet without more precise information about independent learning, it would have been irresponsible to have formulated a questionnaire that allowed only tightly defined responses, and which might have excluded the voicing of undefined but important aspects of the pupils' experience. This hesitance to restrict, inhibit or guide responses led to the construction of a questionnaire about independent learning, in which no question used the phrase 'independent learning' and no question referred specifically to any of the twelve factors of independent learning. Whilst this would make the data processing and analysis more complicated, it avoided a superficiality of response, and effectively mitigated against the possibility of researcher bias. It was hoped that the style of the nine questions would also overcome the etymological and epistemological difficulties referred to above and allow all pupils the opportunity to comment freely. With these considerations in mind, a format was decided upon, in collaboration with pupils and based upon earlier data collection, that was regarded as being as open as possible, given that the returned data were intended to provide some statistical evidence for a generalization.

Completed questionnaires were returned by 94 per cent of the target population. The pupils spanned the eleven to fifteen age range (25 per cent Year 7, 36 per cent Year 8, 24 per cent Year 9 and 15 per cent Year 10) and the full ability range. Some classes were setted, some mixed ability. Pupils from 'top' sets and individual needs classes took part in the project and completed the questionnaire. Pupils born in Greenshire and non-indigenous pupils were represented, as were pupils from family backgrounds across the social scale. Despite these variables (and others such as school ethos and facilities, the expectations and expertise of teachers, and the quality of advisory team support), there is a consistency of opinion expressed in the questionnaire. Local fluctuations are hard to detect. As a broad indication of consistency, a eudemonic test was applied: an examination of the spread of pupils who expressed either enjoyment or dislike for the project.

Eudemonic comments were not specifically solicited in the questionnaire. Any expressions of approval or disapproval were volunteered in the Advice or Comments section: *Any final comments, opinions, suggestions, thoughts?* Only 4 per cent of the population responded negatively. Seven pupils (four boys and three girls across Years 7–10) wrote that they disliked the project; two from Ashfordton, two from Ashbridge and three from Poltrice. Twelve pupils (seven boys and five girls across Years 8–10) advised others not to do the project: one from Cord and four from Saltair (Group One schools, Spring Term, 1991), four from Ashfordton (Group Two school, Winter 1991), one from Poltrice and two from Coppersand (Group Three schools, Spring and Summer Terms, 1992). Thus, pupils who expressed negative views are fairly evenly distributed between girls and boys across the project age-range and from schools in each time-phase of the project. There is an equally wide distribution, across school and age-group, of the 81 per cent of pupils who wrote that they had enjoyed the project, that it had been fun and educational and who advised others to work hard and to enjoy the project (15 per cent of the questionnaire respondents wrote neither positive nor negative comments). This was a consequential finding, offering confirmation of the evidence provided by cross-curricular, cross-phase projects that independent learning is not a pedagogy that only suits a particular section of the school population, but is a form of learning accessible to all, capable of supporting the less able and extending the more able.

Other data suggest that the findings of the questionnaire are representative of all the pupils who were involved in independent learning projects – not just those pupils who completed the questionnaire.

Between 1990 and 1994 an independent learning project with English advisory team classroom support, lasting for either half of a term or a whole term, was undertaken in every secondary school in Greenshire. Although the questionnaire was administered in only ten of the 31 secondary schools, observation notes, examples of pupils' work and end-of-project evaluations were collected from every school. The salient points that emerge from these secondary data are consistent with the findings of the questionnaire: both sets of data corroborate each other. In short, over 7000 pupils, during a five year period between 1989 and 1994, were involved in independent learning projects in Greenshire; this questionnaire sampled a representative body of those pupils, at a proportional rate significantly higher than that stipulated for professional opinion poll surveys.

In the same way that Chapters 2 and 3 were intended to illuminate to the reader a typical week of the conventional presentation of the National Curriculum from the pupil's point of view, and Chapter 4 attempted to reveal the thoughts and feelings of pupils engaged in an independent learning project, this chapter records pupils' reflections upon independent learning, using their own words to illuminate statistical representations drawn from the whole population. As in previous chapters, my commentary accompanies the unfolding story.

An analysis of the nine database fields for the questionnaire (one for each question) reveals that there are four consistent aspects than occur in all the fields, that is, four aspects of independent learning that are referred to in response to every question on the questionnaire:

- group dynamics;
- time management;
- the technology used in videomaking;
- other project outcomes (the magazine, the live presentation and the diary).

These aspects of an independent learning project occur repeatedly in responses throughout the questionnaire, and the information elicited by different questions allows a multifaceted picture of the aspects to emerge. The four aspects can be seen to have two different emphases:

- one for the process of the project (group dynamics and time management);
- one for the product generated by the project (videomaking and the other project outcomes).

These two emphases of a project, the process (based upon the twelve factors of independent learning) and the product (based upon the project outcomes) have a symbiotic relationship: the commitment to a product provides a practical focus for a process intended to develop the attributes of global citizenship. Analysis of the cumulative data of various forms of pupil evaluation, participant observation by researchers, teachers, other professional and non-professional observers, and a critique of project artifacts strongly suggests that the process of independent learning, when successful, leads to a higher quality of product than teachers would expect from a conventional pedagogy. In short, independent learning enhances the traditional skills of a knowledge-based curriculum whilst also developing the characteristics of the ideal global citizen – critically reflective, ethically concerned with social justice, and capable of exercising personal control.

WHAT WAS THE HARDEST THING YOU HAD TO LEARN?

Figure 6.1 shows the distribution of responses to Question One: *What was the hardest thing you had to learn?* Two aspects of an independent learning project dominate the responses. One of these aspects concerns process (group dynamics, 40 per cent), the other, product (videomaking, 43 per cent). Figure 6.2 shows the distribution of responses by gender. It can be seen that girls and boys place a different priority on process and product, with girls making more references to group dynamics and time management (process) than boys; and boys making more references to videomaking and other project outcomes (product) than girls. Figure 6.3 crystallizes this difference: about a third of the boys found the process aspects of a project the hardest thing they had to learn, compared with around half the girls.

These data might appear to suggest that, because they find the process aspects of the project harder, girls are 'worse' than boys at groupwork; and, similarly, that boys are 'worse' than girls at achieving outcomes. However, the cumulative and inter-related data from the questionnaire, other forms of pupil evaluation, the conclusions of teachers and other observers, and my own participant observation in every secondary school in Greenshire does not support this view. A more informed interpretation of the data might be that, in response to this question, pupils are identifying the aspects of the project in which they were most concerned to succeed; and that boys were more engaged by the product challenge and girls by the process challenge.

The differences are differences of emphasis rather than of fundamental attitude – a large number of boys (32 per cent) do identify groupwork as the hardest thing they had to learn

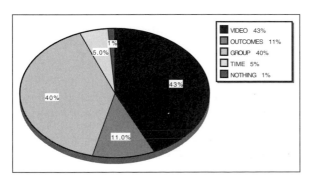

Figure 6.1 What was the hardest thing you had to learn? (All responses)

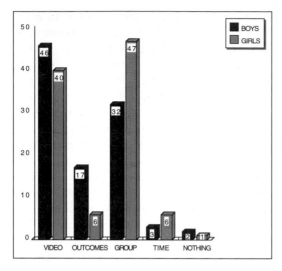

Figure 6.2 What was the hardest thing you had to learn? (Responses by gender)

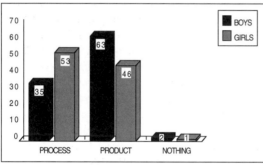

Figure 6.3 What was the hardest thing you had to learn? (Gender responses to process and product skills)

and a large number of girls (40 per cent) identify videomaking as the hardest thing they had to learn. There is no exclusive realm of the project that can be definitively labelled 'male' or 'female'; but there is a tendency that runs as a theme through the questionnaire that clearly indicates that girls are more regardful of social and personal relationships, the citizenship benefits of independent learning; and that boys are more functional and task-oriented. This can be seen in Figure 6.3: the majority of girls express their concern with the process skills of independent learning, the majority of boys with the product skills.

Despite these differences, boys and girls seemed to have few problems, caused solely on gender grounds, of working together in collaborative groups. Only 3 per cent of the pupils (4 boys and 12 girls) found that avoiding or resolving gender clashes within the collaborative group was the hardest thing that they had to learn. Indeed, one might postulate that a collaborative group that could capitalize upon the complementary strengths and interests of both boys and girls would be more effective than a single gender group of either sex. Whatever the complexities of group dynamics – relationships, allocation of responsibilities, working conditions, adhering to schedules – collaborative groupwork *per se* is not regarded as a negative experience. Only 1 per cent of the pupils (two boys and two girls) wrote that adapting to working without a teacher directly controlling the group's activities was the hardest thing they had to learn. Relationships with teachers seems to have been good: only three pupils (all Year 9 girls from Coppersand, in the same group) referred to a problem of 'getting on with the teacher' or 'teacher's complaints'.

The majority of pupils who found groupwork the hardest thing that they had to learn referred to 'cooperating', 'working together as a group' and 'getting on with the group'. A Year 7 girl from Coppersand (457) wrote that the hardest thing she had to learn was 'GETTING EVERYONE TO Coperate with others'. For a Year 10 girl at Poltrice (400) it was 'To co-operate with the rest of the group'. A Year 8 boy at Castlefort (015) wrote that learning 'About working together as a group' was the hardest thing he had to learn, a view shared by the Year 10 Stonall boy (286) whose response was 'working together as a team'. 'Getting on with each other' was what one Year 9 boy at Coppersand (509) found hardest, as did the Year 9 girl at Ashfordton (230) who wrote, 'I thought the hardest thing was to get on with everyone throughout the space of time'.

Yet only 2 per cent of the pupils commented that avoiding or resolving arguments was the hardest thing they had to learn. Only one pupil, a Year 8 boy at Cord (050), wrote about the problems of motivation; for him 'motivating others in my group' was the hardest thing. Not one pupil referred to group members messing around in response to this question. Thus, despite the real difficulties of collaborative groupwork *for pupils working in this way for the first time*, it seems that genuine and successful attempts were made to work productively and harmoniously. Pupils are clearly aware of the elusive qualities of effective groupwork. They use words such as discipline, compromise, patience, responsibility, justice, trust. 'Discipline – working during lessons' was the hardest thing for a Year 10 girl from Stonall (289), as it was for the Year 8 girl from Poltrice (371) whose response was 'to keep our group in order'. For a Year 8 Castlefort girl (013) the key to collaborative success was 'To give up or compromise on ideas' or, as this Year 8 Cord boy (061) put it: 'How to compromise with people in our group'. A Year 10 girl at Poltrice (392) exclaimed that the hardest thing she had to learn was 'Patience! Working with people you don't get along with'. A Year 8 boy at Poltrice (363) referred to 'the importance of responsibility', and a Year 8 boy at Saltair (092) to 'group justice'. The hardest thing a Year 10 boy at Poltrice (409) had to learn was 'TO TRUST OTHER PEOPLE TO DO THINGS'.

Pupils may have encountered difficulties, but the project experience appears to have revealed to them how improvements could be made in the future. Were pupils given the opportunity to learn independently more often, then they might develop, by successive approximation, the skills that some were only able to identify during their first independent learning project.

WHAT WAS THE MOST IMPORTANT THING YOU HAD TO LEARN?

Figure 6.4 shows the distribution of responses to Question Two: *What was the most important thing you had to learn?* The same aspects of process (group dynamics and time management) and product (videomaking and other project outcomes) that were seen in the analysis of the responses to *What was the hardest thing you had to learn?* are present here. A cross-referenced search of the two database fields 'hardest' and 'mostimport' revealed that 95 pupils referred to groupwork in their responses to both *What was the hardest thing you had to learn?* and *What was the most important thing you had to learn?* Thus an interface group comprising 19 per cent of the questionnaire population is revealed: that group of pupils who found constituents of groupwork to be both the hardest and the most important things that they learnt. Of this group, 59 (62 per cent) are girls and 36 (38 per cent) are boys. Another interface group of 40 (8 per cent of the questionnaire population) consists of

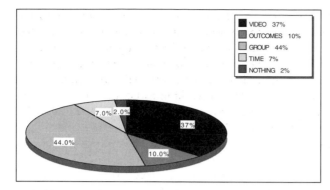

Figure 6.4 What was the most important thing you had to learn? (All responses)

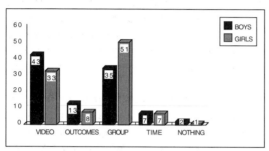

Figure 6.5 What was the most important thing you had to learn? (Responses by gender)

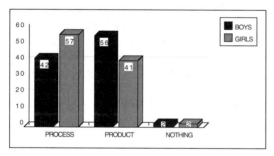

Figure 6.6 What was the most important thing you had to learn? (Gender responses to process and product skills)

those pupils who found using a videocamera to be both the hardest and most important things that they learnt. Of these pupils, 18 (45 per cent) are boys and 22 (55 per cent) are girls. One pupil, a Year 10 girl at Ashfordton (246), regarded time management ('Best use of time' and 'Make the best of time') as the hardest and most important things that she learnt. It could be said of such groups (on the interface between 'hardest' and 'most important') that they are typified by pupils who respond positively to learning challenges.

The gender imbalance towards the process and product skills of independent learning noted in the analysis of the question *What was the hardest thing you had to learn?* is also apparent in the responses to this question, with 51 per cent of the girls stating that group dynamics was the most important thing they learnt, compared to 35 per cent of the boys. Conversely, 43 per cent of the boys regarded videomaking as the most important, compared to 33 per cent of the girls. Figure 6.6 crystallises the process and product difference between boys and girls: the girls' percentages are an inversion of the boys'.

Of the total of 497 responses to the question *What was the most important thing you learnt?*, 30 per cent specified the following constituents of groupwork: working as a group or in a group, cooperating, getting on with the group or all contributing, working with others or working together. Only five pupils (1 per cent) felt that overcoming arguments was the most important thing that they had had to learn and only one pupil thought that learning not to mess around was the most important thing. These nugatory references to discord suggest that misbehaviour or quarrelling were uncommon, and that pupils can adapt quickly to the responsibilities of independent learning. This opinion is endorsed by the tiny number of pupils (1 per cent) who wrote that working without a teacher was the most important thing they had to learn: for the vast majority of pupils, the withdrawal of the didactic, decision-making teacher was simply not seen as an obstacle to learning.

Only one pupil refers to a gender clash, a Year 8 girl at Poltrice (372) who felt that the most important thing that she had learnt was 'never to work with boys (Brian)'. This observation is balanced by the only other reference to the gender issue, from a Year 8 girl at Carnmore (413) who felt that the most important thing that she had learnt was that 'you got to work in mixed groups with boys and girls'. Although friendship was the most-used criterion for group formation, only two pupils (0.4 per cent), both boys, felt that working with friends was the most important thing. Later analysis of the 'most enjoy', 'different', 'advice' and 'comments' database fields (see below) will show that this criterion underwent considerable reassessment during the project.

Even in this early stage of the analysis of the pupils' opinions about independent learning, some of the arguments that those resistant to collaborative groupwork deploy, as a tattered intellectual laager of defence for their preferred 'chalk-and-talk' pedagogy, are exposed as the shibboleths they truly are. If the questionnaire responses are accorded credibility, then it must be accepted that, within the specific conditions of an independent learning project in which the twelve factors of independent learning are clearly applied, pupils are quite capable of working under largely unsupervised conditions; that groups will not disintegrate into a chaos of dissent and inertia; that girls and boys will not automatically polarize into single-sex groups; and that pupils will not inevitably choose to congregate with their friends motivated by an irresponsible desire to waste time and mess about. Moreover, as the analysis of the next question will indicate, and the observation of project teachers confirms, pupils set for themselves tasks and standards more demanding than those which teachers would ordinarily impose upon them.

WHAT DID YOU MOST ENJOY ABOUT THE PROJECT?

Figure 6.7 shows the distribution of responses to Question Three: *What did you most enjoy about the project?* The two emphases of process and product are clearly visible in the four aspects that once again dominate the pupils' responses. The idea of giving a framework to the project, of certain common cooperative outcomes, irrespective of what choice of subject each collaborative group made, is endorsed, with 73 per cent of pupils stating that they most enjoyed either the videomaking (47 per cent) or the other project outcomes (26 per cent). The constituents of group dynamics that pupils most enjoyed were: being allowed off the school premises to film and conduct research amongst the community in the local environment (8 per cent), collaborative groupwork (7 per cent), and the freedom to set their own agenda (5 per cent). Fifteen pupils (3 per cent) most enjoyed every aspect of the project, six pupils (1 per cent) enjoyed nothing about the project, five pupils (1 per cent) most enjoyed completing the outcomes and three Year 10 boys at Stonall most enjoyed being able to set their own deadlines.

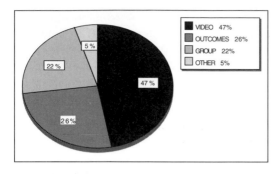

Figure 6.7 What did you most enjoy about the project? (All responses)

Figure 6.8 shows the distribution of references to the question *What did you most enjoy about the project?* by gender. The gender divide is again apparent, with 55 per cent of the boys most enjoying videomaking compared with 40 per cent of the girls. More girls than boys most enjoyed group dynamics: 24 per cent of girls and 19 per cent of boys. Particular constituents of groupwork that were mentioned were working in or as a group, working together and working with others. Only four pupils (0.7 per cent – one boy and three girls) mentioned that working with friends was what they most enjoyed about the project. The opportunity to engage with the local community and environment was noted as the most enjoyable part of the project by 45 pupils (8 per cent – 24 boys and 21 girls), a fairly even gender balance. However, of the 27 pupils (5 per cent – eight boys and 19 girls) who most enjoyed the freedom to plan their own learning that the project allowed them, more than twice as many girls responded than boys.

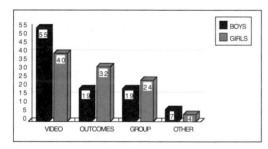

Figure 6.8 What did you most enjoy about the project? (Responses by gender)

Girls clearly enjoyed the written and oral aspects of the project more than the boys, with 32 per cent of girls stating that they most enjoyed other project outcomes compared to 19 per cent of the boys. The constituents of other project outcomes most noted in response to this question were: research, watching the finished videos and live presentations, performing the live presentation, the magazine, drawing, acting and interviewing. Of these, both 'magazine' and 'research' show a gender imbalance. Of the 29 pupils (6 per cent) who most enjoyed research 27 were girls; of the 16 pupils (3 per cent) who most enjoyed compiling the magazine 11 were girls. Whilst it would be wrong to extrapolate from these figures and pronounce upon the project as a whole, certainly within the confined area of research and magazine-writing, girls exhibit a greater enthusiasm than boys for the self-organization and sheer hard work that these two constituents of an independent learning project require.

As Figure 6.9 demonstrates, the gender imbalance that associates boys more with the product and girls more with the process of the project is not as great as in the questions *What was the hardest thing you had to learn?* and *What was the most important thing you had*

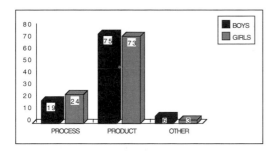

Figure 6.9 What did you most enjoy about the project? (Gender responses to process and product skills)

to learn? There is no simple gender polarization along product and process axes. However, the accumulating data from the first three questions indicate that there is a tendency for girls to be more aware, both positively and negatively, of the personal and social relationships incumbent upon independent learning; and for boys to be more focused upon the completion of functional tasks, particularly those involving the use of language technology.

Three interface groups are revealed: pupils who most enjoyed what they found hardest, pupils who most enjoyed what they considered most important, and pupils who most enjoyed what they considered to be both the hardest and the most important things they learnt.

Interface group: pupils who most enjoyed what they found hardest

An interface group of 82 pupils (16 per cent of the questionnaire population) most enjoyed what they found hardest to learn. This group comprised 37 boys (45 per cent) and 45 girls (55 per cent). Of these pupils, 58 (71 per cent) – 29 boys and 29 girls – specified videomaking as the particular aspect of the project that they had found both the most enjoyable part of the project and the hardest thing that they had to learn; 20 pupils in this interface group (24 per cent) – 6 boys and 14 girls – specified group dynamics; and four pupils (5 per cent) – two boys and two girls – specified other project outcomes, all of a non-literary, oral nature: the live presentation, 'acting' and 'interviewing'.

The existence of this group is further evidence that a proportion of pupils involved in an independent learning project will be stimulated by its inherent challenges of problem solving, overcoming difficulties and adapting to new areas of learning. It is doubtful if this group is an isolated entity; it is more likely that it exists at one end of a range, the other end of which is populated by pupils who most enjoyed what they found easiest to learn. If this is so, then there are more pupils – possibly a majority – who most enjoyed what they found hard, but not the hardest thing, to learn. A common exhortation to other pupils in the Advice and Comments sections of the questionnaire (see below) was to 'work hard and enjoy the project'. Pupils like independent learning not because they regard it as a soft option, but because it provides a learning challenge.

Interface group: pupils who most enjoyed what they considered most important

An interface group of 116 pupils (23 per cent of the questionnaire population) most enjoyed what they considered to be the most important thing that they had to learn. The existence of this interface group is more predictable: one would expect people to feel positively towards something they value. This group comprised 59 boys (51 per cent) and 57 girls (49 per cent). Of these pupils, 69 (59 per cent) – 43 boys and 26 girls – specified videomaking as the particular aspect of the project that they had found most enjoyable and most important; 30 pupils in this interface group (26 per cent) – 10 boys and 20 girls – specified group dynamics; and 17 pupils (15 per cent) – 6 boys and 11 girls – specified other project outcomes, 15 of the 17 responses being for the catch-all keyword 'work', signifying that it was the work of the project in general, rather than a specific constituent of it, that these pupils considered most enjoyable and most important. Although the gender make-up of this group is evenly balanced, the tendency for boys to associate more with the product of the project, and girls with its process, is evident in the responses within this interface group to videomaking and group dynamics.

Interface group: pupils who most enjoyed what they considered hardest and most important

An interface group of 45 pupils (9 per cent of the questionnaire population) most enjoyed what they considered to be both the hardest and the most important thing that they had to learn. This group comprised 23 boys (51 per cent) and 22 girls (49 per cent). Of these pupils, 32 (71 per cent) – 19 boys and 13 girls – specified videomaking as the particular aspect of the project that they had found most enjoyable, hardest and most important; 13 pupils in this interface group (29 per cent) – four boys and nine girls – specified group dynamics; and no pupils specified other project outcomes. Although the gender make-up of this group is evenly balanced, further evidence for the association of boys with product and girls with process is revealed in the responses within this interface group to videomaking and group dynamics.

That almost half of the questionnaire respondents (48 per cent) most enjoyed that which they found hardest and/or most important can be seen as a powerful incentive to learning and as an endorsement of independent learning which requires a personal and reflexive commitment to the learning process. Teachers and other observers invariably commented on the high levels of intrinsic motivation that pupils displayed and upon the raised standards of work produced. They contrasted this with the condition of the normal classroom, in which pupils usually most enjoy what they find easiest and least enjoy what they find hard, and in which pupils generally exhibit no sense that the syllabus has any indigenous importance nor any personal relevance – points that emerged from the tracking of Key Stage 3 and 4 pupils as described in Chapters 2 and 3. In independent learning projects, pupils consistently identify both the social skills of citizenship (group dynamics) and the technical skills of the contemporary workplace (the use of a range of technology) as aspects that they regarded as most important and most enjoyed (even when they found them the hardest to learn). These aspects, conspicuously absent from the normal classroom experience of the National Curriculum (see Chapters 2 and 3) are an integral part of an independent learning project. It can be claimed that there is a greater correlation between the pedagogy of independent learning and the aims of the Education Reform Act (1988) than there is between the usual presentation of the Natural Curriculum and ERA.

WHAT DID YOU LEAST ENJOY ABOUT THE PROJECT?

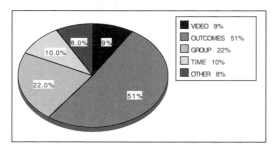

VIDEO 9%
OUTCOMES 51%
GROUP 22%
TIME 10%
OTHER 8%

Figure 6.10 What did you least enjoy about the project? (All responses)

Figure 6.10 shows the distribution of responses to Question Four: *What did you least enjoy about the project?* About a quarter of the pupils stated that they most enjoyed group dynamics and three-quarters that they most enjoyed the project outcomes. These two aspects also dominate the field for 'least enjoy' and therefore one might have expected an inversion of the 'most enjoy' figures, with about three-quarters of the population stating they least enjoyed group dynamics and a quarter of the population stating that they least enjoyed the project outcomes. There is no such inversion. In fact, the percentages for group dynamics are very similar for both fields: 22 per cent of the pupils most enjoyed group dynamics and 22 per cent least enjoyed group dynamics. Although there is a greater difference between the two fields for project outcomes, the figures are still relatively close: in answer to Question Three, 73 per cent of the pupils most enjoyed the full project outcomes (including videomaking); in answer to Question Four, 59 per cent least enjoyed the full project outcomes.

An explanation of why it appears that pupils, in more or less the same numbers, both most enjoyed and least enjoyed the same aspects of the project can be provided by examining the following six propositions.

1   Some of the pupils may have both most enjoyed and least enjoyed the same aspects of the project, in which case the *same* pupils will respond with the same answers to both fields.
2   Alternatively, whilst some pupils most enjoyed certain aspects of the project, similar numbers of different pupils may have least enjoyed the same aspects, in which case *different* pupils will respond with the same answers to both fields.
3   There is also the possibility that there may have been shifts of emphasis within aspects, that it is different constituents of group dynamics and project outcomes that are most and least enjoyed – for instance, references to group dynamics in answer to the question *What did you most enjoy?* could refer to positive constituents of groupwork, such as 'team plus working as a group' or 'team plus working together', whereas references to group dynamics in answer to the question *What did you least enjoy?* may be negative, such as 'team plus arguing' or 'team plus messing'.
4   Shifts in gender may also contribute to the apparent inconsistency. For – an exaggerated – example, it may be that the pupils who most enjoyed group dynamics were all girls and those who least enjoyed this aspect were all boys.
    Other factors that may have had an effect are:
5   the age of pupils (for instance, Year 7 pupils may have responded to the demands of independent learning more – or less – favourably than Year 10 pupils); and
6   the population and ethos of different schools in responding to independent learning.

When these six tests are applied to the aspect of group dynamics, the following points emerge.

1   There is an interface group of six pupils (1 per cent – three boys and three girls) who both least and most enjoyed groupwork. This small number suggests that the element of inter-relationship (the same pupils most and least enjoying the same aspect) is not significant as a partial explanation for the similarity in the figures in the 'most enjoy' and 'least enjoy' fields.

2   Therefore, it is the element of diversity (different pupils most and least enjoying the same aspect) that has an effect. Apart from the six pupils in the interface group, the pupils who responded to group dynamics as the most enjoyable part of the project are different pupils from those who found group dynamics to be the least enjoyable thing. Thus, once the small interface group of six pupils is excluded, a range is established with 21 per cent of the pupils least enjoying group dynamics, a different 21 per cent most enjoying group dynamics and the remaining 58 per cent of the population lying somewhere between the two.

3   An examination of the constituents of group dynamics shows that there are also shifts in emphasis. The list of 'team' responses in the 'most enjoy' field is led by the following three keyword phrases: 'team plus working in a group', 'team plus working as a group', and 'team plus working together'; whereas the list of 'team' responses in the 'least enjoy' field is led by the following three keyword phrases: 'team plus arguing', 'team plus [putting up with] members' and 'team plus [lack of] planning'. Thus, it is different constituents of group dynamics that are most and least enjoyed.

4   There is not a gender shift between the figures for who most and least enjoyed group dynamics. Of the 121 pupils who most enjoyed group dynamics, 40 per cent are boys and 60 per cent are girls. Of the 115 pupils who least enjoyed group dynamics, 45 per cent are boys and 55 per cent are girls.

5,6 Significant fluctuations between age groups or schools are not detectable.

An analysis of the responses to project outcomes in the 'most enjoy' and 'least enjoy' fields reveals a similar pattern to that of group dynamics. Inter-relationship is not significant (although there is an interface group of eight pupils who most and least enjoyed the same constituents of the project outcomes). The shift in emphasis within an aspect is a more potent influence. When videomaking is viewed separately from other project outcomes, then the shift is clear: 47 per cent of the pupils most enjoyed videomaking, falling to 9 per cent who least enjoyed it. This is reflected in a converse shift in the responses to the other project outcomes: 26 per cent of the pupils most enjoyed the other project outcomes rising to 47 per cent who least enjoyed them. This set of figures is much closer to an inversion of responses between the two fields, with videomaking falling nearly 30 per cent from 'most enjoy' to 'least enjoy'. This shortfall is transferred to other project outcomes (rising 20 per cent from 'most enjoy' to 'least enjoy') and time management (increasing by 10 per cent), with group dynamics remaining constant at about 22 per cent.

Figure 6.11 shows the constituents that make up the responses to other project outcomes. The figures refer to percentages of the number of references to other project outcomes, and not to a percentage of the full questionnaire population; for instance, of a total of 260 references to other project outcomes, 80 were to the diary, which equals 30 per cent. It is apparent that traditional tasks (both written and oral) constituted the least popular aspect of the project. This can be interpreted as further confirmation that pupils like to be

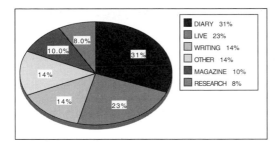

Figure 6.11 What did you least enjoy about the project? (Constituents of other project outcomes)

challenged. There is a much stronger correlation between what pupils found to be the hardest and the most enjoyable aspects of the project than there is between familiar tasks and enjoyment. It is maintained that the length of the projects (a full school term) and their intensity (every English lesson) mitigates against the Hawthorne Effect (in which any change is initially regarded favourably because of its novelty). These findings have implications for the teaching of English. In this questionnaire, pupils may well be rejecting the traditional English curriculum in preference for modes of language development that they find more stimulating, more empowering and more relevant to their own interests and forms of expression.

Figure 6.12 shows the distribution of references to Question Four *What did you least enjoy about the project?* by gender. The gender divide is less than for the previous three questions, although girls show less resistance than boys to the diary and the magazine and express more concern for time management. This relative unity of opinion is seen clearly in Figure 6.13 which shows the gender distribution of process and product references to the question *What did you least enjoy about the project?* Only five pupils (1 per cent – three boys and two girls) least enjoyed the whole project. This group is outnumbered by the 30 pupils (6 per cent – 17 boys and 13 girls) who enjoyed everything and the four pupils (1 per cent – one boy and three girls) who least enjoyed the fact that the project had to come to an end.

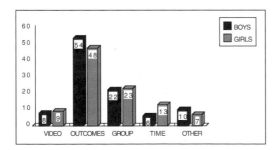

Figure 6.12 What did you least enjoy about the project? (Responses by gender)

Figure 6.13 What did you least enjoy about the project? (Gender responses to process and product skills)

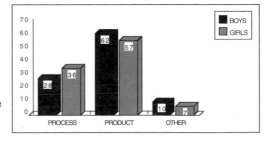

WHAT WOULD YOU DO DIFFERENTLY IF YOU WERE DOING THE PROJECT AGAIN?

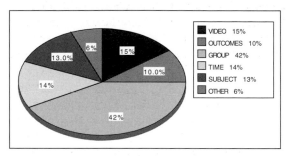

Figure 6.14 What would you do differently? (All responses)

Figure 6.14 shows the distribution of responses to Question Five: *What would you do differently if you were doing the project again?* Group dynamics is the aspect that draws the greatest number of responses, nearly three times as many as for videomaking or time management. Choice of subject, hitherto hardly mentioned, has 13 per cent of pupils referring to it. The other project outcomes that pupils would handle differently are: the live presentation, the diary, writing, interviewing, research and the magazine. Pupils would like more time with the video equipment, particularly the camera; and pupils would organize or plan their time better to avoid being rushed. Nineteen pupils (4 per cent) would do nothing differently, seven pupils (1 per cent) would do everything differently and seven pupils (1 per cent) would not do the project again.

Ninety nine pupils (19 per cent – 42 boys and 57 girls) would change the personnel in the group. However only 6 per cent of pupils would make a change because of dissent within the group: 14 pupils (3 per cent – seven boys and seven girls) would make a change because of arguments within the group; nine pupils (2 per cent – five boys and four girls) would change because they 'didn't get on with' the group; and seven pupils (1 per cent – four boys and three girls) would make a change because of group members 'messing about'. Two conclusions may be drawn from these statistics. First, the figures suggest that there was very little quarrelling or misbehaviour in the collaborative groups, during term-long projects that required group members to plan and execute self-designed learning strategies that would enable each group to achieve a series of demanding outcomes. Nearly 95 per cent of the pupils, if they were doing the project again, would not change the group personnel because of an inability to work together due to personal antagonism. The majority of suggestions were concerned with improving the quality of groupwork through procedural rather than personnel changes. Second, the figures demonstrate a commitment to collaborative groupwork despite – or perhaps because of – the demands that it makes upon pupils. Ninety-nine per cent of pupils wanted to be involved in collaborative groupwork in the future. Pupils who referred to changes in groupwork practice, but not to personnel, stated the need for better organization and planning, for group members to make a more conscious effort to 'get on with' and 'talk with' each other, to 'cooperate' and 'concentrate' and avoid 'arguing', 'messing' or 'panic', to 'work together' with 'all contributing'.

Pupils referred to working with a wide range of people to further develop collaborative skills. A Year 7 girl at Ashfordton (205), in a mixed group of four, formed because pairs of pupils were required by the teacher to select a pair of the opposite gender to form a collaborative group, wrote that she would 'Work with different people because I don't want to work with the same people and I would like to see how well I get on with other people'. A Year 10 girl at Stonall (302), in a mixed friendship group of five pupils, would 'Choose different people to work with because we were all friends'. Others referred to altering the size of groups, with recommendations for both increasing and diminishing the number of group members. A Year 10 girl from Ashfordton (252), in a friendship group of five girls, would 'Be more organised and a smaller group because we could then produce and even better project'. However, a Year 8 boy from Poltrice (352), in a friendship group of three boys would 'Be better behaved and have a bigger group because we where messing around'.

Few pupils wished to change the make-up of groups on the grounds of gender: seven pupils (1 per cent – three boys and four girls) in mixed groups would make changes, although not necessarily to single-gender groups; and six pupils (1 per cent – one boy and five girls) in single-gender groups would change to a mixed group. A Year 7 boy at Coppersand (451), in a mixed group of six pupils, chosen in consultation with the teacher, wrote that he would 'Go in a differ group because the girls had most of the say'. A Year 8 girl at Poltrice (372), in a mixed group of four, chosen by the pupils themselves, wrote: 'I would not work with the boys. The boys boss you around to much'. A Year 7 girl at Ashfordton (217), in a group of four girls, formed when two couples joined together, wrote: 'One thing I would be with some boy's and some people I didn't know all that well. Because you seem to get on better with people you don't really know and girls always fight in groups'.

Although pupils wanted the right to an unrestricted choice of whom to collaborate with, only one pupil (a Year 7 girl from Coppersand (442), in a mixed group of four, chosen in consultation with the teacher) stated that what she would do differently would be to work with friends. Other pupils specifically wrote that they would not work with friends again, or suggested improved criteria for group formation. A Year 7 boy at Dore (127) wrote: 'If I tried to did this project again I would choose the groupe more matualy instead of personally. When we choose the groups friendships came first and matuerity second'. Another Year 7 boy at Dore (133) wrote: 'If I did it again I would choose a group with mixed skills, because we had a group full of people who all wanted to do the same things'. Some pupils would change groups because they had the confidence to explore different experiences, like the Year 7 Poltrice girl (329), in an all-girl friendship group, who wrote that she would 'do a different subject with a different group because I would like a change'.

Of the 67 pupils who wanted to change the subject the group had chosen to study, 40 were boys (60 per cent) and 27 were girls (40 per cent). Many of the comments are vague and refer to a choice of subject that is 'different' or 'more interesting', 'better' or 'good'. There are more specific and helpful suggestions: choose a subject you like or are familiar with, choose a subject that has lots of information available upon it, choose a topical subject, take your time in making a choice.

Figure 6.15 shows the distribution of references to the question *What would you do differently if you were doing the project again?* by gender. Girls (49 per cent) were more concerned than boys (34 per cent) to make changes to group dynamics and to time management (girls: 15 per cent; boys: 12 per cent). Boys were more concerned with changes to the content of the project (videomaking, choice of subject, other project outcomes). This difference is clearly illustrated in Figure 6.16 which shows the gender distribution of process and product references.

Figure 6.16 indicates that, when asked to state in what way or ways pupils would make changes to improve an independent learning project, there is a tendency for girls to associate improvement with a higher quality of personal and social skills (process) and boys to

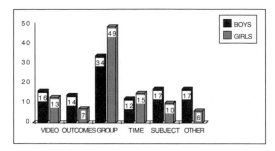

Figure 6.15 What would you do differently? (Responses by gender)

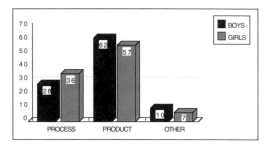

Figure 6.16 What would you do differently? (Gender responses to process and product skills)

associate improvement with production and performance (product). These data corroborate the emerging trend that has been detected from earlier responses. Girls appear to perceive success in terms of relating, boys in terms of doing. For girls, an independent learning project would be better if people got on better; for boys an independent learning project would be better if people produced better artifacts. Girls relate. Boys function. However, as has been stated before, these are differences of degrees, not absolutes. There is much more common ground between the sexes than is perhaps generally recognized.

WHAT COULD THE TEACHERS INVOLVED (INCLUDING ME) DO TO IMPROVE THE PROJECT?

Figure 6.17 shows the distribution of responses to Question Seven: *What could the teachers involved (including me) do to improve the project?* The large group of 66 pupils (14 per cent – 33 boys and 33 girls) who responded to this question with the word 'Nothing', provide what can be interpreted as a glowing testimonial or a dismissive evaluation of the role of the teacher: either teachers could do nothing to improve the project because it was perfect, as was their contribution, or teachers could do nothing to improve the project because it was abysmal and their influence worthless. Profiling these 66 respondents suggests the former.

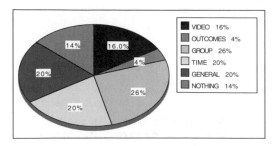

Figure 6.17 What could the teachers involved (including me) have done to have improved the project? (All responses)

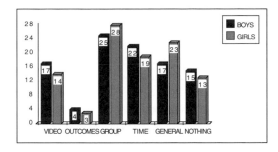

Figure 6.18 What could the teachers involved (including me) have done to have improved the project? (Responses by gender)

There is a schism amongst the references to group dynamics. Of the 122 responses to this aspect, 54 pupils (10.5 per cent – 18 boys and 36 girls) wanted more teacher support and 37 pupils (7 per cent – 19 boys and 18 girls) wanted less teacher intervention. Those wanting more support requested that teachers 'spend more time with groups', particularly to 'check' on progress, to give 'more advice on groups' plans' and more help to 'groups without any ideas'. Those pupils wanting less intervention asked for the opposite: 'less help' and 'more freedom' for groups; and also 'less whole class talk' and more opportunities for groups to work 'off school premises'. The other main concern expressed by pupils who responded to the aspect of group dynamics was that they should have the right to choose their own groups.

Generally, pupils' comments about the role of the teacher were to cast her in the role of audiovisual technician, providing more equipment for videomaking and being available to 'demonstrate', 'explain more fully' or 'help with editing'. The main constituent of time management that pupils felt that teachers could help with was to 'allow pupils more time' to complete the project. Figure 6.18 suggests that both boys and girls hold similar ideas on the role of the teacher, and exemplifies the trend for boys to be more concerned about the product of a project, and girls the process.

WHAT ADVICE HAVE YOU FOR OTHER PUPILS STARTING THE PROJECT?

Figure 6.19 shows the distribution of responses to Question Eight: *What advice have you for other pupils starting the project?* The majority of responses refer to group dynamics, time management and choice of subject, which is not surprising, because these are the aspects that have most exercised the pupils during their own projects. Of these, group dynamics and time management (61 per cent) are process aspects of the project. The product aspects (choice of subject, videomaking and other project outcomes) only account for 18 per cent of the responses. Fifteen per cent of pupils offer exhortations that can be distilled to the

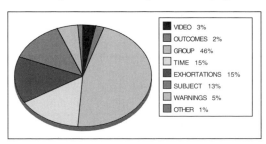

Figure 6.19 What advice have you for other pupils starting the project? (All responses)

phrase 'work hard and enjoy yourself' and 5 per cent of pupils offer warnings either to be cautious or to avoid the project. Figure 6.20 shows that, whilst the tendency for boys to be more closely associated with the product, and girls with the process of the project is still clear, there is no gulf between the two sexes, for both identify the same aspects. The exhortations and warnings percentages reiterate the girls' greater enthusiasm for the project. Of the 203 responses concerning group dynamics, 82 (40 per cent) are from boys and 121 (60 per cent) are from girls. The advice on groupwork centres around organization, choice and conduct.

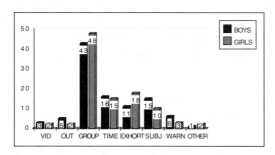

Figure 6.20 What advice have you for other pupils starting the project? (Responses by gender)

Pupils' advice: organization of collaborative groups

Of the 93 pupils who advise that groupwork needs planning and organization, 29 (31 per cent) are boys and 64 (69 per cent) are girls. Careful thought is advocated before decisions are made and actions taken. 'Think about it alot' advised a Year 7 boy at Cord (028). 'Prepare everything in advance', and 'Plan it out well' suggested a Year 8 boy (050) and a Year 9 girl (075) also from Cord. 'PLAN!!!' emphasized her classmate (083). 'PLAN what you are going to do before starting filming else you will end up in a right mess!' urged a Year 8 girl from Saltair. A Year 7 boy at Dore (132) warned about the danger of over-elaborate planning: 'plan but not much plan'. A Year 8 girl at Dore, however, felt that pupils should 'Plan each day from the start'. A Year 9 girl at Stonall (284) advised: 'plan the project very carefully and stick to that plan'.

Some pupils gave helpful advice of a more specific nature. A Year 9 girl from Dore (165) was clear about what planning should entail: 'Plan who does what and when there to do it', a view shared by the Year 10 Stonall girl who wrote: 'Plan the project well and make sure everyone knows exactly what their doing'. A Year 9 boy at Ashfordton (221) suggested tackling the different outcomes chronologically; his advice was 'To get on with the magazine and Presentation Before the video', a view echoed by a girl classmate (233), but with a different order of priority: 'Do the video 1st then do your paperwork'. A Year 9 girl at Stonall (268) explained why planning was so important: 'you should Plan very carefully because you could go wrong and ruin everything', an opinion endorsed by the Year 7 girl at Dore (142) who wrote: 'Be aware of problems even little problems can be hard to fix'. A Year 9 girl at Coppersand (488) warned that plans should be clear and practical: 'Make sure you understand what you are doing'. Whilst most of the pupils who mentioned planning advised that a plan must be made before any work was started, a Year 10 girl at Poltrice (392) advocated that pupils 'don't waste any time planning – start working straight away'. A Year 10 girl at Stonall (310) wanted the best of both worlds: 'Start working right away. & plan thoroughly'. Eighteen pupils stressed the importance of making a good start.

The references to group organization tended to be shorter and rather more cryptic: 'be orginised' (046 Year 8 boy Cord), 'get organised' (107 Year 8 girl Saltair), 'be orginised from the beginning' (180 Year 9 girl Dore), 'organised your work and good luck' (265 Year 10 girl Ashfordton), 'Get organised' (285 Year 10 boy Stonall), 'Work hard and get organised' (317 Year 9 girl Ashbridge), 'Get organised' (325 Year 7 boy Poltrice), 'Organisation' (413 Year 8 girl Carnmore), 'Organisation is the key' (465 Year 8 boy Coppersand). Organization may well be the key, but clues to what constitutes 'being organised' are hard to find in the questionnaire responses, possibly because the state of 'being organised' is self-evident to pupils. Profiles of the pupils who referred to group organization suggest that the concept of organization is seen as a fusion of good planning and then the orderly execution of the plans. This execution is dependent upon careful time management and an equal sharing of the workload within the collaborative group.

Pupils' advice: choice of collaborative groups

The second strand of advice about groupwork concerns the formation of groups. The first principle is epitomized by this Year 7 boy at Ashfordton (203): 'Choose your own groups'. Given that right, the most common advice concerned working relationships within the groups. 'Try to get on with your people in your group' wrote a Year 8 boy from Cord (047). A Year 8 girl at Carnmore (421) advised: 'Act sensible about the whole project. Also don't row, and try to communicate with people. And if you don't like something just go along with it'. Pupils are more likely to get on if they 'choose people you like' or 'people you can work with' or 'people you trust'. These working relationships are not necessarily the same as out-of-project friendships. 'Never work with you best friend' advised a Year 8 girl from Poltrice (373).

Pupils' advice: conduct of groups

The third strand of groupwork advice offered concerns the conduct of groups. Having made an appropriate choice of members and planned the group's schedule of work, pupils should begin work quickly and continue to work at pace. 'Get started on solid work soon, don't talk for ages about what to do', warned a Year 9 girl from Ashfordton (222). 'I haven't got much advice', wrote a Year 7 girl from Cord (019), 'but I would tell them to get things done quickly'. 'Work fast', counselled a Year 9 boy from Coppersand (509). 'Don't take your time!' was the tip from a Year 8 boy at Saltair (101). Arguments are to be avoided: 'Don't argue with your group as it gets you nowhere'. (001 Year 8 girl Castlefort). Messing around is also admonished: 'Do not mess around or you will not finnish in the short time'. (116 Year 8 boy Saltair). Pupils should 'work hard and work together' (423 Year 8 boy Carnmore), or as his classmate (428) put it: 'put your brain in go and put as much efert in as you can in your plan. comunicate with yure grupe'. As the project develops it is important that all members of the group should make an equal contribution: 'ORGANISE – EACH PUPIL TO HAVE A TASK' (318 Year 9 girl Ashbridge); 'Don't leave to late and get a good plan worked out for each person' (090 Year 9 girl Cord). Members should 'help each other' (156 Year 8 boy Dore), 'learn to work in a group and try to cooperate well' (473 Year 8 girl Coppersand), and if necessary 'BE PATIENT' (044 Year 7 girl Cord). They will need to 'stay calm if something goes wrong' (036 Year 7 boy Cord).

Pupils' advice on time management is basically to organize and plan so as to meet deadlines. On choice of subject, the advice is to take time and choose carefully a clearly defined subject that the group likes. Other suggestions are that the subject should be interesting, easy, and have lots of information available.

ANY FINAL COMMENTS, OPINIONS, SUGGESTIONS, THOUGHTS?

Figure 6.21 shows the distribution of responses to Question Nine: *Any final comments, opinions, suggestions, thoughts?* Figure 6.22 shows the distribution of references to the Final Comments section by gender, and again displays the tendency for girls to associate more fully – but certainly not exclusively – with the process of the project and boys with the product. The first four questions (*What was the hardest thing you had to learn? What was the most important thing you had to learn? What did you most enjoy about the project?* and *What did you least enjoy about the project?*) were designed to generate useful information about the project. This final question, like three other questions (*What would you do differently if you were doing the project again? What could the teachers involved (including me) do to improve the project? What advice have you for other pupils starting the project?*) had been intended to give the opportunity for pupils to offer constructive criticism of the project. Whilst the last question succeeded in this aim – it was often used to emphasize a point made in response to an earlier question – it also prompted many unsolicited expressions of enthusiasm.

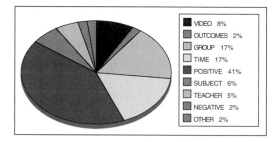

Figure 6.21 Final comments (All responses)

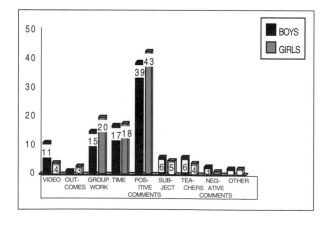

Figure 6.22 Final comments (Responses by gender)

The phrasing of all the questions considered in this analysis had intentionally not been aspect-specific, thus all references to group dynamics, videomaking, time management, other project outcomes, choice of subject, exhortations and warnings, had been the pupils' own, uninfluenced, unguided, voluntary expressions. I suggest that this increases the significance of the number of positive comments expressed by pupils. They were not asked whether they liked the project or not, or whether they considered it educative; but given a chance to make any final comment they wished, 41 per cent of pupils took the opportunity to praise the project and 2 per cent of pupils to denigrate it. (These pupils do not represent the only pupils who felt praise or denigration: the percentage represents only those pupils, who, given the chance to make any concluding comments, chose to prioritize their positive or negative feelings as the final point they wanted to make. There must have been others who liked or disliked the project, but felt that videomaking, group dynamics, etc. were specific aspects that they wished to conclude upon.)

Pupils' comments: enjoyment and education

I am going to look in some detail at the attention given by pupils to their enjoyment of independent learning. This is because I believe that there is a causal relationship between education and enjoyment: pupils cannot become educated without enjoying the educative process. This belief lies at the very heart of the liberal/libertarian debate on education, in which the two philosophies become polarized, with a knowledge-based liberal education representing the disciplined virtues of determination, self-denial, effort, of 'work' and a pupil-centred libertarian education representing the carefree indulgences of capriciousness, self-gratification, indolence, of 'play'. In their questionnaire responses, many pupils do not regard education in this simplistic either/or way (either work or play, either enjoyable or educational), but instead comment upon the inextricable connection between enjoyment and education.

'This project was enjoyable and educational. I would like to do this project again', wrote a Year 8 boy from Castlefort (010) 'It was an experience that was very worthwhile and I thoroughly enjoyed it', was the opinion of a Year 10 girl from Poltrice (410). A Year 7 girl at Dore (123) wrote: 'I've learnt a lot and really enjoyed it'. For a Year 7 boy at Poltrice (335) the project 'has been very interesting, educational and overall a pleasure to do', and for a Year 10 girl at Poltrice (397), 'The project was a worthwhile experience and very enjoyable'.

Thus, pupils demonstrate a synthesis between enjoyment and education; and the number of references to groupwork clearly indicate that some pupils perceive education as more than the completion of a series of functional tasks: it also involves learning how to relate to others. That the enjoyment to which pupils refer is characterized by the grim virtue of a dutiful, self-denying and assiduous puritan work ethic is doubtful. Classroom observers' descriptions of pupils involved in independent learning projects often feature words such as activity, exuberance, excitement and energy. A word used by pupils is 'fun'.

Year 8 Castlefort boy (004): 'It was great fun really'.
Year 7 Cord girl (045): 'The project was great fun, thanks to everyone involed'.
Year 9 Cord boy (077): 'It was good fun'.
Year 7 Dore boy (192): 'No comments because it was cool fun'.
Year 7 Ashfordton boy (193): 'It was a good, fun project'.
Year 10 Stonall girl (308): 'Using the video camera was ace fun and I really enjoyed it'.
Year 8 Carnmore girl (413): 'Good, interesting, fun'.
Year 8 Carnmore boy (433): 'It was intresing and it was fun to do'.

Only one pupil commented that the project was not fun, a Year 7 boy from Coppersand (460): 'The video should be a bit more fun. Make a bit more fun for others'. And only one pupil felt that it was fun because he did not have to do any work, another Year 7 Coppersand boy (451): 'It was good fun and 90 per cent of the [time] no one gave me any work to do'. Indeed, pupils expressed the opposite, that the project was fun or enjoyable and involved hard work. 'It was fun to do the project but a lot of work', wrote a Year 7 girl from Coppersand (442). A Year 8 boy from Carnmore (428) recorded that 'This project was hard as well as fun and the end result was good'. A Year 7 Ashfordton girl (194), undertaking an independent learning project during her first term in secondary school, wrote: 'The project was fun but I found it quite hard and I would have rather done it later in the year'. A Year 7 girl at Poltrice (332) wrote: 'I did enjoy it, but you need to work fast and hard', and a Year 7 boy at Coppersand (453) stated: 'I thought the progect was quite hard, I was quite enjoyable. For anybody starting the project work your hardest'.

Something can be fun and difficult. The pupils' definition of fun implies more than meaningless frivolity. Fun seems to encompass in its definition excitement and challenge. Certainly, just as something can be hard and enjoyable, and enjoyable and educational, so it can be fun and educational. 'I thought the project was good fun and very worth while,' wrote a Year 8 boy from Castlefort (015). A Year 9 girl at Cord (080) thought 'this project was a brilliant idea and I would do it again Because you learn alot of things but in a fun way', a view shared by her classmate (084): 'I really enjoyed doing this project and looked forward to the end results. It was a fun and education project'. A Year 10 Stonall boy (285) put it succinctly: 'Good fun, learnt alot. Educational'. For his classmate, a girl (311): 'It was good fun and very educational as we learnt about technology as well as English work'. A Year 8 Carnmore boy (414) and girl (416) wrote respectively that 'It was good fun. We learnt alot. Using the video camera was good fun, it was never boring, I would like to do the same type of thing again' and 'I think it was brilliant fun it was something new that most of us had never done. I think everyone learnt something'.

Whatever the relationship between education and enjoyment, that the project was regarded as educational is indicated by the following comments. 'This project was more than valuable. We had to work on our own, aquire new skills in editing etc and be able to communicate ideas and opinions well,' wrote a Year 10 girl from Ashfordton (245). A Year 10 girl from Stonall (302) believed that 'Over all I was a good project. It was very benefical and we learn alot. We had alot of finished work. We picked a subject we enjoyed and put alot into it'. A Year 10 Poltrice girl (396) wrote: 'I thought this project was a very good idea, involvinging many skills and group work'. The word 'worthwhile' was commonly used, as by this Year 10 Stonall girl (307): 'A worthwhile project which helped certain english techniques, though you did not realize you were doing it eg find information – reading. Using such advanced equipment for the video' or by this Year 10 boy from Poltrice (394): 'The project was a worthwhile use of the time. It could have been better if more time had been allowed for the project'.

Some of the comments give a powerful, but undefined, impression that the project was regarded as a positive experience. 'It's very enjoyable,' wrote a Year 8 boy from Castlefort (005). A Year 7 girl from Cord (032) had 'enjoyed the whole project THANK YOU!!' A Year 7 girl at Dore (125) had 'really enjoyed doing this Project' and a Year 8 girl at Poltrice (374) 'enjoyed doing the project and found it very interesting'. For a Year 8 Coppersand girl (467), 'the project was brilliant'.

Other pupils were more specific, drawing attention to particular aspects of the project. A Year 8 Castlefort boy (002) 'really enjoyed the video work' as did a Year 9 boy at Stonall

(267): 'I enjoyed making the video very much'. Although a Year 9 girl at Dore (174) wrote that 'I have really enjoyed working on this project' and commented particularly that 'it has been really good fun working on the graphics machine', most of the specific references by girls concerned group dynamics rather than videomaking. A Year 9 girl at Cord (079) thought 'this project was really good well organised and it involved team work and suggestions from all of the group'. A Year 7 girl at Dore (144) 'loved the independance'. A Year 9 Stonall girl (284) wrote that 'it was enjoyable work and taught us how to co-operate better and get on in a group' and a Year 8 girl from Carnmore (417) enthused: 'Brilliant, a really good idea. We were forced to be self-motivated. We got on well as a group and also worked well as a group'. A Year 10 Poltrice girl (406) wrote: 'The project was very enjoyable and as well as learning about our chosen subject we learnt to work in groups'. Boys, too, commented on group dynamics and their own personal and social development. A Year 10 boy at Stonall (286) wrote: 'I enjoyed the project, but there were points when I did not like it such as the live presentation. But on the whole I learnt alot about video making and being part of a team'. A Year 10 Poltrice boy (405) was quite clear about the personal benefits he had gained: 'I think the project was very useful to me. It helped me develop many new skills. I also enjoyed the project alot. I also learnt how to work in a group. and became a bit moe confidet at speaking'. A classmate of his, a girl (408) was similarly analytical: 'The project was a great experience for me I learnt a great deal about working with others and technical equipment, aswell as organisation. My insight into prejudice, especially racialism, was greatly increased. It was a very worthwhile exercise.'

Others expressed enjoyment or enthusiasm that was qualified in some way, suggesting that for these pupils the experience need not be completely satisfactory, or successful, for it to be enjoyable. Most pupils' reservations concerned group dynamics and time management. A Year 8 girl at Cord (060) 'enjoyed doing a video learning to use *expensive* equipment' but would 'like a better group to work with'. A boy in the same class (053) wrote that 'We all enjoyed this topic' despite the fact that 'some of my group were pains' and a Year 7 girl at Dore (126) commented: 'I liked inderpendant learning it was fun but it sometimes corsed argument', an opinion presumably shared by her classmate (138): 'A part from the Group I enjoyed it alot'. A Year 10 Ashfordton boy (242) 'enjoyed the project a fare bit but I wish I used my time better' and a girl in the same class (243) also commented on time management: 'I enjoyed it very much but the equipment should be more available and people should use time well and not misjudge it'. A Year 10 girl at Poltrice (392) had this suggestion: 'I really enjoyed the project, but the deadline was too short. I would suggest that we either had less to do, or more time to do everything in.'

Although completing the project outcomes generated feelings of personal satisfaction ('I think the tape was a success.' – 056 Year 8 boy Cord; 'I thought the project was great and we had a brilliant result!' – 081 Year 9 girl Cord), there were pupils who enjoyed the project even though the final product was not a success. 'We enjoyed it although we didn't finish out tape,' wrote a Year 8 boy from Castlefort (003), a feeling shared by two Year 9 girls at Ashfordton (225 and 236): 'The video was fun but we didn't finish it' and 'The use of the vidios was good, but we didn't get ours finished'. A Year 9 Stonall girl (283) expressed similar feelings: 'It was good doing the project and it would be nice to do something like it agian. It was good fun but we didn't finish the video' and a Year 9 Ashbridge girl (318) stated: 'Enjoyed project – shame that not all tasks could be completed'. A Year 8 boy at Poltrice (366) enjoyed the project despite problems with both the videomaking and group dynamics: 'I enjoyed the project but we had alot of arguments with one of our members, and the project was lost so we didn't do onough work that we expected.'

Pupils from all the questionnaire schools expressed a desire to continue working independently. 'I really enjoyed the project and wish we could do it again.' (142 Year 7 Dore girl) 'I am very pleased to do the project I won't mind doing a nother one.' (157 Year 9 Dore boy) 'The idea was good! I'd certainly do it again.' (223 Year 9 Ashfordton girl) 'I thought the project was a good idea and I would really like the chance to do it again.' (278 Year 9 Stonall boy) 'I think this was a brilliant project & I would like to do it again.' (273 Year 9 Stonall girl) 'Can we do it again?' (315 Year 9 Ashbridge boy). Some pupils suggested that a second project would demonstrate an improvement in their abilities: 'I really enjoyed making the video, and I'd love to do it again if I had the chance. I hope you come and do it again to see the difference between the 2 videos,' wrote a Year 9 boy at Cord (071). This Year 8 girl at Castlefort (013) was also interested in comparing her first independent learning experience with a second project: 'I really enjoyed this project so thank you for making it possible to do. I think it would be interesting to do this project again in a few years to see if I would tackle it <u>differently</u>.'

The frontispiece to the questionnaire had explained its various purposes, one of which was *To try and see how we can improve things for other pupils who will be involved in the next stage of the project.* One of the questions (*What advice have you for other pupils starting the project?*) had specifically linked the questionnaire respondents with pupils in other schools. Some pupils returned to this theme in their concluding comments and offered testimonials for the future of the project. 'I think what your doing is a brilliant idea and I highly reccomed you,' wrote a Year 9 boy at Cord (085). 'This project is a good Idea and I think other children should be given a oppertunity to take part in the project,' wrote a Year 7 boy at Dore (129), a comment echoed by a Year 7 girl at Poltrice (331): 'I think it was good and they should do this again with other children'. A Year 10 Poltrice girl commented more soberly (391): 'I believed the project was a worthwhile experience which pupils throughout the county should participate in (although the experience should come before the GCSE course years)'. This was an opinion echoed by many of the Year 10 pupils who were involved in independent learning projects and represented a cruel irony: projects that pupils and teachers endorsed as stimulating and educational in both the affective and cognitive domains were actually regarded by them as a hindrance to performance in the National Curriculum tests at Key Stage 4, the GCSE examinations. Perhaps as a consequence of this view, embedded in these references to future projects appears to be the assumption that an independent learning project is unlikely to make any change to the regular curriculum experience of the pupils. The project was seen to have a finite life-span and a particular personnel. It was an extrinsic event that might visit a school and then pass on, and then classroom life would return to 'normal'. There is no evidence from the questionnaires that pupils feel that their everyday school learning will change as a result of the term that they have spent on independent learning. Indeed, quite the opposite: here is the project epitaph of a Year 7 girl at Cord (044), with four years of statutory education ahead of her, who wrote, in block capitals, that she most enjoyed 'DOING THINGS WHICH I WON'T BE ABLE TO DO AGAIN'.

CONCLUSIONS

Pupils enjoy having control of their education. They express great enthusiasm for independent learning, although they also regard it as more exacting than the process and product of 'normal' National Curriculum lessons. They are stimulated by the freedom of independent learning and respond seriously and responsibly, whilst regarding the experience as fun. The definition of fun seems to embrace both challenge and enjoyment rather than frivolity and irresponsibility.

Pupils identify two clear aspects of independent learning: the process (collaborative and cooperative groupwork) and the product (various outcomes such as the video, the magazine and the live presentation). Girls tend to express a greater interest in, and concern for, the social and personal skills of the process and boys for the functional skills of the product, particularly outcomes that involve the use of language technology. However, this is a difference of degree only. There is no gender schism, the questionnaire analysis revealing more similarities than differences. Despite this imbalance in priorities, mixed gender groups are favoured by the majority of boys and girls. Pupils found the project to be challenging in terms of personal relationships, time management and the completion of the outcomes. The most successful groups were mixed gender groups with five members who were all capable of interacting and forming different cross-gender combinations for different purposes, and who worked harmoniously to produce the full range of outcomes to a standard that they regarded as, at least, satisfactory. Even if not all the outcomes were achieved to the standard that a collaborative group may have wanted, pupils still had a sense of success in planning and executing self-chosen tasks.

Despite the huge differences between conventional lessons and independent learning projects, pupils attempted the transition with enthusiasm and with greater success than failure. Pupils talked enthusiastically about how they would seek to improve certain aspects if undertaking a second project, yet few thought they would. Pupils in Key Stage 4, whilst endorsing the educational qualities of independent learning, expressed concern about neglecting the classroom practices they regarded as good training for forthcoming GCSE examinations: silent, individual work on prescribed texts with regular written tests of memory.

THE VALIDITY OF THE QUESTIONNAIRE

A fuller discussion of the technical aspects of the research can be found in Chapter 3 of *Educational Citizenship and Independent Learning* (Griffith, 1998). I use the term validity in its research sense to mean the accuracy with which the research tool (the questionnaire) recorded the opinions of the research population (the pupils). There are several tests for validity that can be applied. First, responses to the questionnaire were similar from school to school and across the age and ability range of Key Stages 3 and 4 (eleven to sixteen year-olds). Second, questionnaire responses correlated with the responses of pupils gathered in other ways (analysis of project diaries, evaluations, interviews). Third, questionnaire data were consistent with my own and others' findings based upon participant observation of independent learning projects. Fourth, the comments of teachers and other observers corresponded with those of the pupils. Thus, by the use of multifaceted and multi-perspective data collection, common agreements about independent learning provided strong consensual validity for the questionnaire.

It is worth quoting some of those observers to illustrate this consensus. One of the most interesting findings was that pupils value activities that are simultaneously demanding and enjoyable. Teachers used the same vocabulary as pupils to express this point:

> It had, dare we say, been fun to work together as a team. As the sessions continued we could see that the groups were working productively.
>
> (Year Seven teacher, Stonall)

The groups were hard-working, learnt a great deal and had a great deal of fun.

(Year 8 teacher, Cord)

all sessions were hectic, hard-working, worthwhile fun for everyone involved.

(Year 9 teacher, Castlefort)

When I ran residential in-service training for teachers, I structured the courses as compressed independent learning projects, with the course members working in collaborative groups to the various project outcomes. I felt that this was the simplest and most effective way of communicating to teachers the benefits of independent learning. Teachers on these courses enthused about independent learning in the same way that pupils did:

The best – most stimulating – course I've attended. It was relevant, friendly, creative – allowed tons of individuality and yet provided loads of learning opportunities too. An immediate impact on my own work will be giving children more time to produce work, providing more varied stimuli, more use of IT and more multimedia work.

(Primary school teacher)

It was totally brilliant! Hard work but refreshing too! It's recharged the batteries so I'll be more lively and enthusiastic!

(Secondary school teacher)

Stimulating and extending. real learning experience. All parts of the course were useful – but particularly working cooperatively in groups and learning to do new things.

(Tertiary college lecturer)

Tremendously enjoyable. The most worthwhile course I have been on. I found all of it useful. The immediate impact it will have on my work will be to reinforce my enthusiasm for such a diverse way of working – giving choice to the learners.

(Anon)

Teachers and other professional observers noted the personal and social skills associated with the process of a project:

They had matured socially by learning how to work in a mixed group situation with pupils from another tutor group. They had begun to realise that cooperation and making progress involved listening to others and valuing their opinions and ideas. For many of the more naturally shy pupils, the experience had increased their confidence as their contributions had been considered valuable by the rest of the group. Each group had been responsible for planning how the work was to be shared and had learned something about being self-sufficient.

(Year 7 teacher, Stonall)

We've learnt how to use a lot of expensive and impressive machines, but much more important than that is what we have learnt about ourselves and about each other, our skills, our shortcomings, how we get on as a group and what sort of contribution we can make to that group.

(Year 8 teacher, Poltewan)

. . . children had to discuss, negotiate and sometimes arbitrate (!) among themselves and, generally, they reached better standards of cooperation than more usual group work in class generates . . .

(Year 9 teacher, Cord)

Some individuals excelled themselves. Other individuals revealed skills which were previously unknown and therefore unacknowledged.

(Year 10 teacher, Poltrice)

Teachers also commented on the quality of the product – the work produced by pupils for the project outcomes:

The work generated much good writing which might reassure teachers . . . The results now were quite exciting. Pupils were discovering a new voice. They were no longer hemmed in by the ties of prose conventions and words locked in their grammatical contexts and meanings. They were using this limited vocabulary with a freedom that amazed me.

(Year 8 teacher, Cord)

All the outcomes were impressively achieved.

(Year 10 teacher, Poltrice)

Pupils learned new techniques – i.e. handling video equipment, developing organising ability, learning to write letters that were actually sent by post. They worked with enthusiasm and looked forward to each session.

(Year 8 teacher, Poltrice)

Generating ideas posed no problems for the children. Throughout the week ideas pulsed through the class and children rarely took break times, preferring to work in a sustained way throughout the day. They also worked at home bringing work into school to develop with the equipment that they were gradually mastering. Children were using video cameras confidently and were spending hours of sustained work on computer graphics which they used to illustrate their work. The deliberate non-intervention policy of the team coupled with the respect they showed for the children as people and for their ideas did much to foster these attitudes.

(Primary Adviser, observing Year 4 and 5 pupils, Haldon)

They also commented on how independent learning, far from leaving the less able floundering, allowed them to achieve standards that were not typical of their usual National Curriculum performance:

a class of 33 stroppy third years who were notorious among the staff, for being difficult to teach are happily producing some written work for their class folder . . . I feel much more confident with them and consequently the situation is considerably improved.

(Year 9 teacher, Venturers)

We were delighted to note that many of the 'low achievers' appeared to be gaining a great deal from this experience; they were participating confidently in their groups' activities, working with children they had probably never spoken to before this project began: social interaction was not just a maxim but a reality. The amount of ideas and writing grew steadily with each session – much to our relief.

(Year 7 teacher, Stonall)

This from the point of view of the ordinary class teacher, was a very interesting experience. I am used to groups like 2 set 7, where the ability is low and the behaviour often disruptive, and have become used to using traditionally 'safe' activities to control the class. Rhys was keen to experiment with new learning strategies . . . which has had wide-reaching beneficial effects on the pupils and my work with them since . . . and it has had a most salutary effect upon their attitudes which is still noticeable some months later. And the pupils' experience of English was certainly enriched.

(Year 8 teacher, Pemburton)

In this chapter I have sought to show what pupils think about the ways in which they learn. The conclusions that must be drawn are both inspiring and discouraging. It is heartening that pupils (and teachers) respond positively to the much greater demands that independent learning makes upon them than does the National Curriculum, with its typical presentation via the didactic class lesson and its concomitant assessment of individuals via timed tests of memory. It is even more encouraging that teachers and pupils declare that independent learning generates opportunities for educational advance in both the affective and cognitive domains, fostering the pupil's development as an autonomous, socially aware and critically reflective learner–citizen. On the negative side, it is galling to report that both pupils and teachers feel constrained to reject the obvious benefits of independent learning in favour of the National Curriculum – not because of any educational advantages, but from the perfectly understandable pragmatic expediency of passing Key Stage tests at the ages of fourteen and sixteen.

7 National Curriculum: National Disaster

In Chapter 1, I sought to trace the development of state secondary education in the United Kingdom from its confused beginnings to the National Curriculum of the present day. I have argued that, throughout that time, education has been characterized by stasis rather than change, and that the National Curriculum, far from being the maelstrom of 10 years of constant change as claimed by the teachers' unions, has actually consolidated a type of education and a concomitant pedagogy that has hardly altered at all in nearly 130 years. Neither have the twin purposes of a state education: to prepare the school-leaver for her cultural and economic roles in a democratic society based upon a capitalist economy, that is, to equip her with the skills of citizenship and the workplace.

In Chapters 2 and 3 I offered evidence to show that the typical school experience of secondary school pupils falls far short of fulfilling these twin aims of the state educational system, as delineated in the Education Reform Act of 1988 and represented by the 10 subject syllabuses of the National Curriculum. In Chapters 4, 5 and 6 I drew upon the opinions and experiences of pupils involved in independent learning projects that were intended to develop the likely attributes of third millennial citizenship, in a way that the present system does not. I concluded that, given the opportunity, secondary school pupils across the full age and ability range were able to organize teams for specific purposes, to plan and conduct research, to solve problems, to use a variety of learning strategies as appropriate to different situations, to work purposefully in a self-motivated and self-disciplined manner in largely unsupervised conditions, to distinguish between 'factual knowledge' and opinion, to investigate topical social and ethical issues, to weigh evidence and to present their research findings in different ways to different audiences. Released from the strictures of a prescribed, knowledge-based curriculum and a didactic instructional pedagogy, school pupils almost naturally began to acquire and develop the social and workplace skills required in the increasingly complex and sophisticated world which they will inhabit as adults.

In this final chapter I want to examine more fully how an educational system that is manifestly failing its own stated intentions seems to be gaining an ever tighter stranglehold; and to develop my argument that the present system of education is becoming so irrelevant to the reality of life that within the next 30 years or so, the economy of capitalism and the social fabric of democracy may well suffer irreversible damage – National Curriculum: National Disaster, indeed.

It is a military axiom that tactics are more readily discerned and evaluated than strategy. For the generals of education – successive governments since the middle of the nineteenth century – the strategy of state educational policy has been to produce school-leavers who would fit into an appropriate social niche in an evolving social democracy, and adopt a productive role in the workplace of an evolving capitalist economy. Ideally, each cohort of school-leavers would contribute both to the social cohesion of a rigid but not inviolable class system and to the advance of technology (either in its development, management or application) that underpins an industrial capitalist economic system. The original tactics intended to achieve this strategy were the construction of a tripartite system of education based upon a hierarchy of knowledge: a classical education for the aristocratic owners of the means of production, a liberal education for the bourgeois managers of production and a general education for the proletariat workers.

These neat tactics synthesized the twin strategy of social engineering and technical/vocational training and, arguably, were at first highly effective: during the second half of the nineteenth century Great Britain, as Empire, reached its zenith of social influence and economic power. However, the Victorian *zeitgeist* of permanence and stability was exposed as a chimera by the First World War. By its end, many were questioning the old values of capitalism and its concomitant class system structured around monarchy, the Church of England and traditional paternalist government. Returning members of the forces (amongst them, my paternal grandfather and several of his brothers), had met and talked with allied comrades from the diverse cultures of France, America, Canada, New Zealand, South Africa and Australia and also with German prisoners of war, and found that they could no longer believe in the simplistic jingoism of 'my country, right or wrong' or, having experienced the blunders of the generals and politicians (and by implication the monarchy), the diktat 'to serve and obey'. Women who had worked in factories and on farms, confidently and competently carrying out traditionally male tasks, were not content to retreat to the scullery. The intricate, interwoven and incestuous system of European monarchy had been shattered and in the United Kingdom dynastic aristocracy had been decimated by the loss of fathers and sons. Further afield, the great but terminally flawed experiment in a communist system that aspired to reject capitalism and classism was developing in the USSR, whilst across the Atlantic the pluralist society of the United States, impelled by the American Dream, was establishing itself as a world power. In the United Kingdom, the post-war rejection of traditional acceptances of nationalism, working class labour, the ruling class and the role of women were exemplified in the following decade by the ceding of Home Rule to Ireland (1920), the appointment of the first Labour government (1924), the rise of syndicalism and the National Strike (1926), and the extension of the franchise that gave women the vote (1928).

Although the nature of democratic citizenship and the role of the capitalist worker and manager were changing, it would be fair to say that the original strategy of the state educational system was still relevant: to equip school-leavers for society and the workplace. What were no longer effective were the original tactics employed to achieve this strategy, for as a rigid class system became more flexible, and women began to exert a more powerful influence at home and in the workplace, as industry adapted to Fordian methods of production, and national economies became subject to international pressures (such as the Wall Street crash of 1929 and the European and American depression of the 1930s) so both the demands of democracy and a capitalist economy were becoming consistently more complex. Yet a tripartite system of education remained in place, and indeed was strengthened by the 1944 Education Act. The piecemeal comprehensive reorganization of the 1950s–80s, which remains uncompleted as we enter the twenty-first century, was an attempt to restructure a tripartite system in more socially equitable circumstances, rather than to dismantle it.

The post-First World War citizen and worker is of historic interest but has no concordant identification with the citizen and worker of the third millennium. Yet the school state system has continued to promulgate a hierarchy of knowledge as the one tactic for achieving the strategy of equipping the school-leaver with the sophisticated social and technical skills that are required of the contemporary citizen and worker. This tactic has culminated in the National Curriculum which effectively demands that 11 years of state education are devoted to learning by heart bits of 'knowledge' that can then be examined by written tests of memory and the school-leaving cohort graded from A–G. As democracy and capitalism have developed since the mid-1860s, there has been an ever-widening gulf between the original, still relevant, strategy of a state educational system intended to prepare the pupil for later life as worker and citizen and the development of effective tactics for the achievement of that strategy. Essentially, although British and global society has changed hugely since the Victorian era, the tactics for preparing pupils for life in the twenty-first century are exactly those used 130 years ago.

The main campaign continues to be directed via a knowledge-based curriculum, with occasional skirmishes on the flanks intended to more properly address the needs of the citizen (via personal and social education) and the needs of the worker (via technical and vocational education). Some examples of post-Second World War developments in technical and vocational education since the short-lived experiment with technical schools are the Technical and Vocational Education Initiative (1983), the British Technology and Education Council (1983), the Certificate of Pre-Vocational Education (1985), the establishment of the National Council for Vocational Qualifications (1986), the emphasis upon technology as a cross-curricular dimension of the National Curriculum (1988), and the introduction of General National Vocational Qualifications (1993). Examples of attempts to develop personal and social education are the drive towards comprehensivization begun in the 1950s, the Agreement to Broaden the Curriculum (ABC) in the 1960s, the pastoral care initiatives of the 1970s, counselling, profiling and Records of Achievement in the 1980s and the recently mooted suggestion of the Government Task Force on Citizenship that lessons in citizenship should utilize 5 per cent of lessontime (1998). These initiatives have had little impact upon the entrenchment of a knowledge-based curriculum. Thus, we have an educational system that polarizes and marginalizes the skills of the citizen and the worker in bolt-on courses that have low status and are not part of National Curriculum assessment. Ironically, this is happening at a time when there is a growing synthesis between the attributes of the contemporary citizen and the contemporary worker, that is to say that the personal and social skills of the confident citizen accord very closely with the technical and vocational skills of the successful worker: adaptability, flexibility, the ability to work in teams, a capacity for self-reflection, an ability to get on with others from diverse backgrounds, to see the other's point of view, to negotiate to find solutions, to manage time, to handle stress, to defuse conflict, to set and achieve personal targets. These are the skills of independent learning as exemplified in Chapters 4, 5 and 6. This seems to me to be the folly of the National Curriculum. We are pushing to the very borders of the curriculum the skills that are central to life in the twenty-first century in favour of a nineteenth century model of the rote-learning of arcane and arbitrarily chosen chunks of 'knowledge'.

The current construct of a liberal education and a knowledge-based curriculum as experienced by pupils regards knowledge as existing independently of space and time, ahistorical, neutral, factual, value free. Knowledge is 'out there', waiting for mankind to discover it, like a diamond, immutable and eternal. This was the view promulgated by a trio of educational philosophers (some say the inventors of the discipline) who held great prestige during the 1960–70s and whose influence is still felt today: R.F. Dearden, P.H.

Hirst, and R.S. Peters. They promoted the concept of the *logic of education* (Hirst and Peters, 1970) and their central idea was that it is through certain bodies of knowledge (rather than intercourse and activity) that we develop a critical disposition – the premise upon which the National Curriculum is based. The logical structure of existing knowledge was 'one of distinct, unique, irreducible forms' (Hirst, 1973, p. 137). Seven forms of knowledge were defined: the physical sciences, mathematics and formal logic, the human sciences and history, moral understanding, religion, aesthetics and philosophy.

This Kantian view of enlightenment – the pursuit, via rational thoughts, of universal objective truths, that, if searched for diligently may be found, interpreted and understood – has a certain noble attraction, I suppose, a sort of dome-headed academic Arthurian quest for the grail. It conjures up images of earnest students in Rodinesque postures asking Socratic questions which they then ponder with recourse to *The Boys and Girls Bumper Book of Amazing Facts*. Nevertheless, I am in full agreement with the intention of such a curriculum, explained as follows:

> This constitutes a liberal curriculum, liberal in the sense that its successful transmission will provide the learner with the wherewithal to distinguish true propositions {. . .} from false, valid arguments from invalid, and correct judgements from erroneous ones.
> (Pring, 1993, p. 49)

My disagreement with the Peters' trinity is that their advocated curriculum is unlikely to realize its intentions, and certainly has not in its transmogrification to the National Curriculum. There are several reasons for this.

The first is the superficiality of the kind of knowledge that Hirst *et al.* identify, particularly in its prescribed form, the 10 subject syllabuses of the National Curriculum. It is superficial in that it consists of many bits of unrelated information that do not coalesce into a coherent body, as has been shown in Chapters 2 and 3. It is superficial in that it promotes only one type of knowledge: that which can be discovered by the processes of rational thought, effectively excluding from the learning process the affective domain, a capacity for reflexivity, the ability to mount a critique and to theorize, in short, the intellectual ability to look through and beyond the immediately observable, to see the underlying structure concealed by the facade (as independent learning encourages pupils to do). The Hirst viewpoint appears to be that these high order skills will somehow manifest themselves spontaneously once the learner has assimilated the various Hirstian forms of knowledge.

The second reason for doubting the Peters–Hirst–Dearden concept of the logic of education is that it is untrustworthy, in that it assumes that discovered human knowledge is uncontaminated by contact with human minds, which it is not. All discovered knowledge is open to interpretation and to value judgments that may differ from culture to culture and era to era. This is as true of the physical sciences as it is of the human sciences and aesthetics, as such figures as Columbus, Galileo and Einstein have demonstrated. It is untrustworthy in that there are few tests of the validity of knowledge in the Hirstian forms, that is, that the knowledge has been discovered rather than socially constructed – this criticism applies particularly to the human sciences and history, moral understanding, religion, aesthetics and philosophy, but also to the physical sciences, mathematics and formal logic. It is untrustworthy in that not all knowledge can be accommodated in either Hirst's forms or the subjects of the National Curriculum, therefore someone has to make selections, to decide which bits shall and shan't be learnt. The National Curriculum does not cover all knowledge: it selects certain areas of knowledge (the 10 National Curriculum subjects) but excludes others; and then makes finer selections within the subjects to construct syllabuses;

and then prescribes certain parts of these syllabuses to different groups of children using markers of age, ability, gender and faith. Even if one were to concede that there may be a body of uncontaminated knowledge, this selection process contaminates knowledge by organizing it into a hierarchy based upon human – value – judgments. Ironically, the clearest admission that knowledge is not value-free can be found in the rubric of the government-produced text *The National Curriculum: A Consultative Document*:

> Cross-curricular themes, including personal and social education, *are by their nature rooted in subjects*, [my italics: RG] and where courses are offered they need to be planned and developed in relation to subject teaching.

> (DES, p. 5, 1987)

This leads on to my third objection, for if it is accepted that at least some of the forms, disciplines or subjects into which we organize knowledge are not value-free then a knowledge-based curriculum is likely to play a significant role in the social conditioning of the future citizen. A curriculum containing subjects such as history, music, literature, social geography (as does the National Curriculum) can implant powerful notions of cultural heritage. If pupils accept unquestioningly certain beliefs, interpretations of events or value judgments as incontestable truths then the learning process, intentionally or unintentionally, is moving away from the inquiring nature of education and closer towards the passive acceptance of indoctrination (Spiecker and Straughan eds., 1991). Of course, the United Kingdom is not alone in this; any state educational system that bases itself upon a knowledge-based curriculum and an assessment system that requires that knowledge be accepted and memorized rather than challenged and discussed is open to such a charge of indoctrination. The indoctrination may be implicit, even unintended but will exist. The saluting of the American flag and the singing of patriotic songs such as *America The Beautiful* or the national anthem *The Star Spangled Banner* is the traditional way of starting the day in many American schools. More overt programmes of civic instruction and historic interpretation were a common part of the curriculum of eastern European countries until the revisionism of the 1980s, and continue to exercise a powerful effect in the state educational systems of communist China and the religiously fundamental cultures of the middle east.

In this country there is some evidence to suggest that the National Curriculum intentionally promotes an Anglocentric view of the world. As Secretary of State for Education, John Patten insisted in 1992 that National Tests for fourteen-year-olds must include questions on a Shakespearean text. A booklist prepared by one of his predecessors, the self-proclaimed bibliophile Kenneth Baker, was felt by many to champion English rather than world literature, and in particular the classics: nineteenth-century works by *dwhimms* – dead white middle-class men. In his book *A Lesson For Us All – The Making Of The National Curriculum* Duncan Graham, the ex-Chief Executive of the National Curriculum Committee, relates the direct editing of the music and history syllabuses by Secretary of State for Education Kenneth Clarke. In two articles (*Daily Telegraph*, 19 July and 19 August, 1995) the Chief Executive of the School Curriculum and Assessment Authority, Nicholas Tate 'urged head teachers to instil a sense of British identity into all pupils, irrespective of their ethnic background' (Hartley, p. 57, 1997). John Clare, the *Daily Telegraph* Education Editor, wrote that 'Tate had reportedly said that "factual knowledge was being sidelined, narrative neglected, heroes and heroines debunked, and nationalism regarded with distaste"'.

(Hartley, p. 57, 1997)

I do not regard the above examples as evidence of some clandestine political conspiracy intended to brainwash the school population. Quite clearly they are evidence of the opposite: an overt and public political policy intended to brainwash the school population. With increased devolution to the Celtic nations and other British regions and a greater respect for the diversity of indigenous culture and their historicity within those areas, Tate's notion of Britishness seems naively simplistic in its inclusiveness. What precisely is, or was, the Britishness to which he refers, other than the imposition of imperial Englishness? More importantly, though, in a discussion of a knowledge-based curriculum, is the misunderstanding that lies at the core of Tate's remarks: his insistence that heroes and heroines, nationalism and narrative constitute knowledge when in fact the pageant approach to history is a huge distortion of 'fact', presenting history as being created and controlled by the enactments of a series of noble heroes from whom we supposedly derive our cultural heritage. The truth that Tate sees in this approach is a social construction, not an empirical fact.

Fourth, irrespective of the debate about the quality and selection required to construct a knowledge-based curriculum, and the possibilities of indoctrination, I suggest that the uncritical learning of 'knowledge' as a route to becoming an educated person, what Lawrence (1992) terms a 'civilised generalist', is redundant. Knowledge is proliferating so quickly (some sources claim that it is doubling every year), and hence existing knowledge is becoming obsolescent at almost the same pace, that the notion of a good education comprising memorizing some selected bits is risible. The traditional idea of an educated person as someone funded with the general knowledge that typifies an outdated concept of a liberal education (little more than an ability to identify literary quotes, historical dates, capital cities and snatches of classical music) seems laughably quaint.

In short, the National Curriculum predicates an outdated, exclusive and incomplete epistemology, or *way of knowing*. The past two millennia can by and large be characterized by two different epistemologies: faith, in the first millennium, and reason in the second. But as we approach the third millennium, both systems of knowing, whilst not discredited, are viewed as incomplete. Postmodernist approaches to epistemology vary in two major ways, the second rather more pessimistic than the first. The first holds that there may be universal, objective truths, but they are beyond present human knowing; and if we are to know them it may be through different forms of knowing than the certainty of rational thought (Giroux, 1981). The second holds that there are no universal, objective truths: all human understandings are consensual and impermanent; reality is what local groups consider it to be at a particular time (McLaren, 1989).

> We have ceased to see knowledge in any sphere as fixed, static, God given, eternal, unchallengeable, unproblematic, and have begun to recognise it as fluid, tentative, hypothetical, necessarily open to constant questioning and highly problematic.
> (Blenkin, Edwards and Kelly, p. 21, 1992)

And in this surely lies the greatest irrelevance and the greatest danger to post-millennial citizenship of a liberal education that depends upon a knowledge-based curriculum. To put it simply, the state educational system is based upon something that no longer exists in the postmodern world: we have no knowledge. The National Curriculum is essentially a modernist curriculum unsuitable to a postmodern or high-modern age and its construction seems in part to be a classic reaction to the uncertainty of postmodernism, a retreat to the remembered, or imagined, comfort of modernist certainty: Empire, God, Class,

Heterosexuality, Monarchy. This was the mind-set that led Prime Minister John Major to launch his 'Back to Basics' campaign in 1993. The rose-tinted nostalgia for a mythic golden educational age was typical of a prime minister who fondly imagined an England still existed in which the thwack of leather on willow could be heard on the village green, spinsters cycled to church and there was warm beer, drawn from the hand pump, to be supped in the village pub. Maybe John Major's Huntingdon constituency exists in this comfortable time-warp, but I don't think there'd be room – or a welcome – for most of us there.

If we can no longer trust old definitions of knowledge, how can we know – and therefore teach and learn – anything? Developing from the earlier work of philosophers such as Wittgenstein (1990), Habermas (1971), and Foucault (1990), researchers in the 1980s, notably Cohen and Manion (1980) and Reason and Rowan (1981) questioned the exclusive nature of positivist research that requires empirical scientific proofs, the purpose of which is prediction and control. They questioned first the exclusiveness of this epistemology, which rejected all other ways of knowing, and second the internal validity of positivist research itself, claiming that there must always be an interaction between the researcher and the researched and that this relationship should be recognized as a valuable part of the research process. This led to a recognition of the legitimacy of different ways of knowing – different epistemological systems. For instance, philosophers use logic and language to scrutinize the semantics of ethical statements, scientists conduct controlled experiments, sociologists use observation as a basis for hermeneutic understanding, children know because they are told. Religious faith or vision, instinct and intuition, premonition, cultural heritage and tribal consciousness, and political dialectic are all legitimate epistemologies (ways of knowing) within their own ontologies (views of the world). Rational thought is neither exclusive nor situated at the apex of a hierarchy of epistemologies. In this way, Piaget's theory of genetic epistemology (which underpinned the Plowden Report of 1967) – that the child develops naturally, in linear stages, from emotionality to rationality – has been criticized by feminists and also regarded as a construct of western culture which wrongly values abstract logical thought as the most powerful epistemic process (Burman, 1994, Kincheloe, 1993, Walkerdine, 1994).

Not all epistemologies demand positivist proofs: some may instead rely upon consensual understanding. But the more powerful do require some form of justification, a personal authentication, an internal exploration or dialogue that leads to the agents being able to state why they know something. The least powerful may be termed the epistemology of acceptance, where the individual makes no personal exploration, but placidly accepts the authority of a didact, an instructor, an authoritarian teacher, priest or political figure. It is the least powerful epistemology, not only because the knowing has no internal validity but because that form of knowing is reliant on other agents – which raises two obvious doubts about the validity of the knowledge. First, the didact's own epistemology, which must be taken on trust, may be flawed – and an acceptance epistemology generates no processes by which flaws may be identified and questioned. Second, the acceptors are unequipped in life to learn for themselves – their knowing is reliant on an external authority. To relate this to schooling: pupils may be told things as facts which are really opinions and they would not recognize the difference; and once they left school their capacity for learning would effectively come to a halt. This is the 'Because I say so' knowing, the acceptance epistemology, that underpins the dependent learning of the National Curriculum.

Epistemologies inform ontologies, an ontology being a view of the world. A positivist ontology is that the world is governed by immutable scientific laws and the corresponding epistemology is based upon a conviction that controlled experiments to discover these laws will lead to the formulation of a rational code of natural and human behaviour that can be used to predict and control events. A religious ontology is that the world is governed by a benign supernatural force, and the corresponding epistemology is founded upon religious faith. The ontology that is formed by an acceptance epistemology is a view of the world in which the individual compliantly accepts her place in life, relinquishing major decisions and agency to a higher human authority. This is itself a form of secular faith, the belief that led to British supremacy during the Victorian era and the construction of a communist empire in eastern Europe during the twentieth century. But what happens when that faith is lost? There are surely two consequences: the disintegration of the social system in which faith has been lost and then a long and troubled period of reinvention as people who have rejected their ontology and epistemology search for new definitions of self and new ways to organize themselves as societies. During this transition a society can turn on itself in bitterness and confusion and split into opposing factions as the social structure collapses. In the last 30 years we have seen this process miserably vivified in post-colonial Africa, in post-Shah Iran, in eastern Europe, particularly Russia, and most vividly in Tiananmen Square, China. Germany and Japan appear more successful examples of redefinition, perhaps because both countries seemed to have discovered a unity of purpose (a shared ontology) following defeat in war and so were enabled to embrace their reinvention as international powers via industrial competition rather than territorial conquest (a shared epistemology).

Like all organisms, human cultures must evolve to survive and the process of redefinition, if gradual and consensual, is essential to the well-being of any social group. It seems to be that when a country loses its belief in itself (its ontology) and can find no consensus for reconstruction (a common epistemology) that things fall apart. We should not be complacent about the future stability of the United Kingdom.

The collapse of the manufacturing base of the British economy in the 1960s effectively ended the traditional concept of a subservient but satisfied working class that had been withering since the end of the First World War. Greater tolerance of gays, lesbians and transsexuals, allied to the rise of feminism in the 1970s, forced a reassessment of gender stereotyping. With growing unemployment in the 1980s, more young people were diverted from the dole queue into further and higher education, which encouraged social mobility. As the second and third generations of 1950s immigrants from India and the West Indies became established, so British society became more multicultural. As has been argued in Chapter 1, class, ethnic and gender distinctions are becoming more flexible. The 1990s have witnessed, via computer technology, an explosion of information and news that is accessible to people around the world. Internet publication makes it almost impossible for governments or multinational cabals to control and censor the flow and presentation of information to the public. Medical advances have blurred the distinctions between life, death and biological procreation. The great institutions of parliament, the monarchy and the Church of England no longer command the respect they once did. There is an energy and diversity about these social changes which is exciting, but motion is more unstable than rest and change more volatile than stasis. The personal confidence to make meaning of one's own place in today's fast-changing, pluralistic, global society requires a more sophisticated way of knowing than the acceptance epistemology offered by state education via the National Curriculum. The old ontology is weakening and unless we move beyond an acceptance epistemology we will not be equipped as citizens to redefine and reinvent ourselves in a peaceful, ordered way:

to acknowledge change in society and to resist it in education is a very odd position to adopt intellectually.

(Blenkin, Edwards and Kelly, p. 18, 1992)

In a constantly changing world, education needs to be about much more than memorizing things for tests. Trivial Pursuit is a game and life is not a quiz show. Real life requires the ability to make connections, to interpret, to understand, to make things meaningful.

> The real power of hermeneutic consciousness is our ability to see what is questionable . . . Reflection on a given pre-understanding brings me something that otherwise happens behind my back.
>
> (Gadamer, p. 38, 1997)

Contemporary pupils, citizens and workers need a critically reflective epistemology. Such an epistemology would not reject other ways of knowing, but rather, would use them selectively as appropriate to different circumstances. Habermas (1971, 1990) suggested three categories of human cognitive interests: the technical, relating to the world of work and requiring an empirical and analytical form of knowledge; the practical, referring to the polity, the way in which society understands itself, requiring an interpretive form of knowledge; and the emancipatory, relating to the matter of power, and requiring a critical form of knowledge. Habermas warns of category error: for instance seeking a technical solution to an emancipatory problem (which I think is exactly what has happened with political change – rather than educational reform – and the construction of the National Curriculum).

> Habermas sets out a case for what he calls communicative rationalization: that is to say, we can reach agreement or consensus through open dialogue, freely arrived at. The centrifugal and fragmentary forces in postmodernist culture can therefore be avoided.
>
> (Hartley, p. 35, 1997)

The three characteristic features of a critically reflective epistemology are a capacity to consider and reflect, rather than to accept unquestioningly; to employ different analytical procedures to different problems, and perhaps to combine procedures; and to seek consensus, to test the validity of one's own conclusions against the opinions of others. It is a critically reflective epistemology that informs the ontology of the global citizen and the pedagogy of independent learning as defined in Chapter 1 and described in Chapters 4, 5 and 6.

However, at a time when the social and professional demands on the citizen and the worker are becoming more complex, the education intended to prepare pupils for these demands is becoming more simplistic. The National Curriculum with its prescriptive syllabuses and methodology, restrictive teacher training courses, a relentless campaign by the Chief Inspector of Schools for back to basics, front-of-class, chalk and talk teaching is leading to a deskilling of teachers, the direct consequence of which is that pupils' education is dumbed down. Learning becomes a technical rather than an intellectual process, teaching a form of instruction rather than a programme of enlightenment. Professor Paul Black, former Chairman of the Conservative government Task Group on Assessment and Testing (TGAT) and Vice-Chairman of the National Curriculum Council became so alarmed at the government's dismissive attitude to the opinions of teachers and other educationalists, and its legislative programme of centrally imposed restrictions upon the practice of teachers, that he had this to say:

> If the teaching profession's practices and judgements are no longer to be trusted, then the fault cannot be corrected simply by giving them new orders. All who care for education should not want them to be robots. To treat them as if they were robots is to run the risk that they will soon start to behave like robots should.
>
> (Cited in NATE, 1992)

Jean-Francois Lyotard (1984) predicted the dumbing down of educational institutions and the instrumentalization of knowledge, so that the purpose of state education would be functional, technical, practical (but not in the Habermas sense) rather than reflective, inquiring, critical, valuable of itself. That is the kind of knowledge that is being crammed into children in British schools. The purpose of knowledge is utilitarian rather than intrinsic: its use is to pass tests in the National Curriculum. The reduction of teachers to technicians is noted by Giroux (1989), Giltin (1987) (in America on an imposed curriculum with the kind of simple testing that characterizes the National Curriculum) and Hargreaves (1989), writing about the introduction of the National Curriculum. Hargreaves makes the point that the imposition of curricula, the technicizing of the teachers' skills, the removal of LEA inset, means that teachers lose the ability to query their own practice. If Hargreaves is right, and I think he is, then a climate is created in which a critically reflective epistemology cannot exist, let alone be promulgated to pupils. If teachers can't think for themselves, how can they teach their pupils to do so? Blenkin *et al.* also draw attention to the instrumentalization of both teachers and pupils:

> During the 1980s and continuing into the 1990s, Britain has witnessed a marked swing to the right of the political spectrum in both social and educational policy-making. This appears to be consistent with a general trend within Western capitalist societies as they endeavour to readjust to the demands of an emerging post-industrial social and economic order. Across the Western world, political parties, conservative and socialist alike, are now defining education primarily in terms of producing an 'educated' and flexible workforce through the inculcation in young people of those skills and dispositions which are perceived to be necessary in order for them to respond to post-Fordian modes of production and consumption. Central to these policies are discourses which objectify the human subject as producer and consumer and reduce education to a marketable commodity.
>
> (Blenkin *et al.*, 1992, p. 61)

Stenhouse (1975, 1980, 1983) and Elliot (1981, 1991) have been for a long time front runners against the instrumentalization of teachers. Both regard education as to do with the making of meaning rather than the memorization of discrete bits of knowledge. To this end, education for both teachers and pupils is a form of research, an enquiry, a process of making connections rather than rote learning. This point is also raised by Grundy (1987) who draws a direct connection between this way of learning and the demands of contemporary society, so linking the learner with the citizen, the guiding principle of my idea of educational citizenship:

In emancipatory action research the guiding ethic extends beyond the individual level to the social. In addition to respect for individuals, symmetrical communication (a requirement of emancipatory action research) presupposes a common striving for consensus. True consensus, moreover, is possible only in conditions of equality for participants. The guiding ethic of emancipatory action research, therefore, embodies the social and political ideals of freedom, equality and justice.

(Grundy, 1987, p. 155)

Thus at a time in history when there has never been a greater need for an educational service to equip its pupils with the attributes of global citizenship, there has actually been a remorseless reductionism of education and authentic assessment to training, rotelearning and crude tests of short-term memory. Yet there has been an awareness of the need for affective, as well as academic, education since the inception of secondary education in this country – and well before. Writing in 1531, Sir Thomas Elyot (1962) saw learning as an all-embracing affair that went beyond schooling. He maintained that practical arts (what current writers sometimes refer to as 'life-skills') were as important to the wholeness of being educated as classical studies. In 1605, Francis Bacon elaborated this theme in his *Advancement of Learning*, complaining that the practical nature of education was being ignored for the theoretical: 'words and no matter' (p. 69, 1975). In 1778, Joseph Priestley, in *An Essay on a Course of Liberal Education for Civil and Active Life*, wrote that the purpose of liberal education – as he called it – should be 'to qualify men [sic] to appear to advantage in future life' (Priestley, 1778, p. 9). Rousseau (1762) believed that learning is a natural and joyous process, Froebel (Hayward, 1979) that young children learn through play. Dewey (1900, 1916) recognized the need for pupils to experience whole-person growth and social interaction. John Stuart Mill's complaint of 1832 could be applied to the present National Curriculum:

> Modern education is all *cram* – Latin cram, mathematical cram, literary cram, political cram, theological cram, moral cram. The world already knows everything, and has only to tell it to its children, who, on their part, have only to hear, and lay it to the rote (not to the *heart*). Any purpose, any idea of training the mind itself, has gone out of the world.

(Mill, p. 99, 1965)

Government reports during the last 50 years have consistently stressed the importance of teaching the child rather than the subject and that education is primarily to do with enquiry rather than instruction. The main conclusion of the Clarke Report (1947) was that secondary pupils benefited from a broadly based education rather than job specific training. The Evans and Aaron Report (1949) recommended that secondary pupils should benefit from a curriculum that was creative, cooperative and inventive. The Crowther Report (1959) emphasized the requirements of adaptability in a changing world and opposed subject specialization in the first years of secondary schooling. The Newsom Report (1963) recommended introducing stimulating, personally relevant and socially oriented courses for secondary modern schools and also the construction of more architecturally adventurous classrooms in which new teaching and learning styles could be developed. The Robbins Report (1964) gave further impetus to the Newsom Report recommendations by exposing the social classism prevalent in the existing secondary school system that adversely affected pupils of higher education potential who came from the lower socioeconomic groups. The Bullock Report (1975) in stressing the responsibility of all teachers to develop 'language across the curriculum' offered an oblique critique of the division of the curriculum into rigid specialist subjects that had no interaction, and hence the report may be considered a contributory factor to the development of cross-curricular and linked modular courses. The Cockcroft Report (1982) recommended that mathematics should be enlivened and made more relevant to pupils via practical projects, problem-solving, cooperative groupwork and discussion. The Swann Report (1985) stressed that it must become a central responsibility of all schools to promote a multicultural society based upon equality and diversity. The Elton Report (1989) into discipline in schools recommended that pupils would benefit from more socially relevant courses that prepared them for citizenship and parenthood, from being given greater responsibility within schools, and from having non-academic achievements more fully recognized and rewarded.

It is as if the political controllers of education since the Second World War have been blind to the changes in society that require progressive not regressive educational policies, and deaf to the counsel of educational philosophers and practitioners – even when they have requested their advice. As Eric Bolton, the last HMI Chief Inspector of Schools before OFSTED reorganization, starkly puts it:

> There is the risk in education that the government is heading in the direction of a closed, darkened room. It listens so selectively and has so firmly closed the windows and curtains that it does not seem to hear, or see, the education scene as most people out in the world experience it.
>
> (Cited in NATE, 1992)

This is one of the penalties of the politicization of education and the centralization of control: if a government is given sound educational advice by a committee of enquiry *which it has established itself*, but that advice does not fit with the broader thrust of party policy, then the advice will be ignored. During the tenure of the last Conservative government, under both Thatcher and Major, there were some staggering examples of this blinkered obduracy that imposes a particular and temporary political ideology upon the long-term development of state education in a supposedly democratic society.

The National Curriculum Task Group on Assessment and Testing (TGAT), chaired by Professor Paul Black delivered its seminal report on assessment procedures for the embryonic National Curriculum in 1987. TGAT recommended that assessment should be sensitive, formative and diagnostic and should be based upon teachers' judgments of the pupils they taught throughout the year. The government should commission a wide series of standardized assessment tasks from which teachers could choose an appropriate selection to check their own assessments. These SATs, as they quickly became known, were to be designed to fit into the normal work routine of pupils as a discreet part of their natural classroom activity. The assessments of individual children should be confidential; if schools or local education authorities wished to publish the results of SATs as a guide to parents of schools' performance, such publication should highlight any socioeconomic or other factors that would have had an influence upon a particular school's results. Such a sensitive approach was unlikely to be accommodated within the competitive, monetarist, business-led ethos of Thatcherism. Teachers' assessments were downgraded to the point of being completely ignored, and the unobtrusive and wide-ranging standard assessment tasks became high profile and uniform summative tests that were administered across the country on the same day amid much media hullabaloo (there was a cynical sleight of-hand in this political manoeuvre: the acronym of SATs was retained, but an entire educational philosophy was significantly changed in the transition from 'standard assessment *tasks*' to 'standard assessment *tests*'). Since 1994, the tests' results have been baldly published in the national press as crude league tables with no attempt made to distinguish the catchment or circumstances of one school from another. This was a political decision impelled not by reasonable ideas of fair accountability but by petty and spiteful notions of intentionally misdirected culpability.

In 1988, the Higginson Report into post-16 education that suggested a broadening of courses so offended Prime Minister Thatcher's devotion to the 'gold standard' of A Levels that the recommendations were rejected out of hand on the day the report was published. An incident from 1989, recalled by Professor Brian Cox, Chair of the English working party established to advise upon English in the National Curriculum, illustrates this high handedness:

> When my Report was submitted to Mr Kenneth Baker, Secretary of State for Education and Science, he so much disliked it that he insisted that it be printed back to front, starting with Chapters 15 to 17, which included our recommendations for attainment targets and programmes of study, and relegating the explanatory chapters 1 to 14, which he thought unnecessary, to a kind of appendix. The creation of a National Curriculum in English was influenced by several bizarre incidents of this kind.
>
> (Cox, 1991)

Even this peremptory treatment was mild in comparison to the fate that befell the government-funded LINC project (Language in the National Curriculum) in 1991. The chair of LINC, Professor Ron Carter wrote that:

> Language should be studied in its own right, as a rich and fascinating example of human behaviour. It should be explored in real, purposeful situations, not analysed out of context. Language reveals and conceals much about human relationships. There are intimate connections, for example, between language and social power, language and culture, and language and gender.
>
> (Introduction to the LINC units, 1991; unpublished)

It might have been thought that such self-evident and common-sense views would have been uncontroversial. The response of the Minister of State for Education, Tim Eggar, was to suppress the publication of the LINC materials (after a two-year project costing twenty-one million pounds and involving 150 personnel) with comments that made it clear that the Conservative government viewed its National Curriculum as a curriculum with an instructional pedagogy not just unrelated to, but deliberately separated from the real world. Carter's vision of socially contextualized language study was dismissed as 'a distraction from the main task of teaching children to write, spell and punctuate correctly' (Eggar, TES, 26 June 1991).

Government appointees such as Duncan Graham (1993), Brian Cox (1991) and Ron Carter (1990) have all appeared in print expressing regret about the way in which the Conservative government (1979–97) ignored the advice of its own educational appointees in order to promote policies that fitted the political ideology of the moment.

The politicians were amateurs, instinctively confident that common sense was sufficient to guide them in making judgments.

(Cox, 1991)

Change is so slow in education (the concept of comprehensive schools was first suggested in the Spens Report of 1938; the raising of the school leaving age to sixteen in 1974 was legislated for in the 1944 Education Act) that the state educational service is likely to be saddled with the effects of Thatcherism long after it has been discredited and superseded.

The boundary between the government management of a state educational system and the political manipulation of that system has been steadily eroded since the imposition of a statutory curriculum in the Education Reform Act of 1988. As education has climbed the political agenda, so the quality of serious discussion of educational issues has fallen. Although it is easy to poke fun at John Major's nostalgic simplicity, his Back to Basics speech to the Conservative party conference in 1993 obviously struck a chord with the psyche of the general public, at least insofar as education was concerned. Each 'new initiative' to revive some Victorian practice (the reintroduction of times tables in mathematics, a literacy hour in English, the Tate approach to history referred to earlier, an abandonment of groupwork in favour of the old style whole-class lesson, homework set for all primary school children, and test after test after test) is greeted with popular approval. I suspect that this is because such measures have the smack of firmness about them, a common-sense approach that cuts through the mad theorizing of numbskull educational boffins and the dangerous beliefs of revolutionary left-wing teachers, to restore calmness and order to the classroom.

What is remarkable is the way in which these regressive policies, so redolent of education in the last century, have been promoted so successfully as a new and dynamic form of education suited to the next century. Back to Basics is simultaneously The Way Forward. Because educational debate has largely been replaced by political sound bite, much of what is claimed about schools is no more than the suave rhetoric of the showroom, yet it is nevertheless highly persuasive. Starkey has written that 'The school is no longer the information-rich, action-poor, isolated institution that Torsten Husen described' (Starkey, 1991, p. 16), a comment that seems to me as far wide of the mark as Hartley's assertion that 'the old didacticism no longer holds sway. A new learner-centred pedagogy is being ushered in. Much is made of empowering the learner who can take responsibility for his or her own learning' (Hartley, 1997, p. 149). I cannot share Professor Lawton's optimism that:

> The standards of the state education service are central to the whole question of quality of life for the entire community. There are signs that at last this message is beginning to be understood.
>
> (Lawton, 1992, p. 143)

Three years before the 1988 Reform Act, the Department of Education and Science issued a report that enumerated six principles of state education that could, with a few minor amendments, inform a pedagogy of independent learning and a policy of educational citizenship:

i   To help pupils to develop lively, inquiring minds, the ability to question and argue rationally and to apply themselves to tasks and physical skills.

ii To help pupils to acquire understanding, knowledge and skills relevant to adult life and employment in a fast-changing world.

iii   To help pupils to use language and number effectively.
iv   To help pupils to develop personal moral values, respect for religious values, and tolerance of other races, religions and ways of life.
v   To help pupils to understand the world in which they live, and the interdependence of individuals, groups and nations.
vi   To help pupils to appreciate human achievements and aspirations.

(Better Schools, DES, 1985)

This wish-list does not describe the lived reality of the National Curriculum at a classroom level. Go and ask Josie and Emily.

With national tests for all pupils at the ages of seven, eleven, fourteen and sixteen (and plans to introduce 'baseline' testing for four and five-year-olds) it is inevitable that the 'old didacticism' will continue to hold sway, because, as any teacher knows, the most effective way to prepare children for tests of memory is to drill the facts into them via repetitive exercises and crib sheets and to reinforce this rote learning with a series of preparatory tests before the day of the Big Test. This is the process my elder daughter went through in June as a Year 6 pupil in her last year at primary school. Despite my strong philosophical objections, I found myself colluding with the whole sorry business, helping Jo revise in the evenings. The reason for this was that the local secondary school had abolished its mixed-ability policy and had written to parents stating that they intended to set pupils in groups of graded ability by their Key Stage 2 test results. Jo, her teacher and I each had our own perspective: Miss Price felt under pressure as her class' results would be scrutinized by the headteacher and governors; Jo wanted to do as well (or as badly) as her friends so that she'd be in the same sets as them the following term; I wanted to support my daughter in the best way I could, although I was confused as to what 'best' could mean in such circumstances. Whilst we had different viewpoints, the three of us shared a common conviction: we thought the tests were a complete waste of learning time. It was hardly the joyful partnership between pupil, practitioner and parent that we had experienced in the past. As I write this, my daughter is just finishing her first full week in secondary school and has been placed in Set One for English and French (even though she had no French lessons in primary school), Set Two for maths and Set One for science. The area in which we live introduced comprehensive schools in 1980, but Jo's just passed her eleven-plus.

The point to be drawn from this family experience – one that I am sure was replicated in thousands, if not hundreds of thousands, of homes – is that despite the rhetoric of emancipation, political control is strangling real educational opportunity in favour of the specious but plausible trappings of the National Curriculum. Political interference of what happens in classrooms is now just about complete, for once a statutory curriculum has been imposed with a mandatory reductive system of assessment in its train (that government inspectors use as the main criterion to judge the success or failure of a school), then a reversion to didactic teaching styles is inevitable, because this is the most efficient way of getting pupils to pass the tests. Clause Five of the 1988 Education Act stipulates that no qualifications can be given in public exams without Department for Education and Employment approval: if you control the assessment, you control the curriculum and its presentation. All that remains is to institute the present government's proposed legislation for performance related pay and the reversion to a Victorian educational system will be complete. The whole edifice of the National Curriculum – syllabuses, assessment, pedagogy – is a precarious house of cards in educational and citizenship terms, but has the spurious patina of neatness and efficiency that is so attractive to the quick fix, brand image, business-oriented, spin-doctored politics of the 1990s.

But at what cost to the quality of the school experience? You can pick up a local or national newspaper most days of the week and find some new horror story to do with schools: rising truancy rates and expulsions, increased teacher absence due to stress-related illnesses, vindictive bullying (often race or gender motivated), the rise of gang culture and the carrying of weapons, the commonplace of drug taking, the haemorrhage of teachers taking early retirement (many on health grounds), the desperate shortage of newly qualified teachers, vandalism on school premises, the decaying fabric of many school buildings, violent attacks upon teachers by pupils and parents.

No-one seems to know what to do. Government sets up yet another spurious task force to advise on this or that initiative, teachers' unions lose all dignity and advise teachers to 'bash and dash' if confronted by an aggressive parent, the media throws up its hands in despair, social think tanks pontificate from the safety of their ivory towers, but nothing effective is done to reverse the decline in state schools. The general line taken by talking heads on radio and TV is that 'there are no simple answers to complex problems'. Fingers in dykes everywhere. Don't panic. Chicken Little is in charge.

But what is wrong with schools *is* a very simple matter. As a teacher, head of department, LEA adviser and INSET provider for 25 years I know that the key to a successful school is not what is promulgated on the cover of a glossy prospectus (pictures of smiling pupils who seem to spend all their time fencing, swimming, surfing, on foreign exchange trips or in lessons that involve computers, musical instruments or interesting scientific apparatus) but what really happens in lessons. An enjoyable and well-disciplined lesson is not characterized by heavy-handed authoritarianism, but by a curriculum that is relevant to the pupils. The key to success is so simple: if pupils are given the opportunity to learn what they want to learn, then they learn in a self-motivated and enthusiastic way that means that discipline problems just cease to exist – as Chapters 5 and 6 seek to show. Learning is a natural activity, but the passive memorization of the National Curriculum is neither natural nor active and pupils will rebel against it.

This rebellion may be as innocuous as pushing the boundaries of school uniform or hair-length, as opportunistic as Emily capitalizing upon a timetabling error that allowed her 'time off' in maths lessons, as universal as the societal chat of pupils in lessons; or more destructive: serious defiance, vandalism, violence, and in the tragic case of headteacher Philip Lawrence, death. At whatever level the rebellion has reached in a particular school, it is eroding to some degree the efficiency of the system and the morale of those within it. If the history of the twentieth century has taught one lesson, it is that a population cannot be forced indefinitely to live under a repressive regime. Sooner or later something has to give: either the regime has to adapt to the will of the people or the regime is overthrown. And I think that that is a fair analogy to bring to bear on education. For some time longer we can continue with the repressive regime of the National Curriculum, longer in the rural shires than in the more volatile urban areas. But eventually the National Curriculum will have to go because the school population will simply make it impossible to enforce. Whether this happens in 30 years' time, after an inexorable process of educational ghettoization, or sooner, is going to make all the difference to the kind of society that will be forged by the next three decades. If we continue the steady descent, it is not only within the schools themselves that the rebellion will make itself felt. As schools fail to provide the kind of education that will equip the learner with the skills of citizenship and the workplace, so both democracy and capitalism – the culture and the economy of the United Kingdom – will be increasingly undermined.

Is this decline inevitable? Possibly. Human societies probably have organic lives as do the individuals that comprise them: they grow, wither and die. Is this decline preventable? Again, possibly – there is no reason to believe that democratic capitalism has reached the end of its natural lifespan, indeed it is likely to be the global model during the first century of the third millennium. I am going to close by suggesting seven steps in a strategy that might begin to reverse the decline in the quality of state education in the United Kingdom.

First, discussion about education needs to be depoliticized. It seems to me that the standard of political debate in this country is now so low, so much a matter of polarization of opinions, of combative exchanges, of interviewers as opponents, of a refusal to concede that any viewpoint other than one's own is worthy of merit, that it is impossible to discuss anything meaningful at all. Political talk is suave, persuasive, hectoring, argumentative and emotive. This is not the register of rational debate, and above all, when we discuss education now, it needs to be in a quiet, calm and informed way.

Second, discussion about education needs to be enfranchised. Before politicians took an ideological interest in education as a party political issue (slowly developing from the 1950s but accelerated by Prime Minister James Callaghan's watershed address to the Oxford Union in 1976) most educational debate was at a philosophical level, the preserve of university dons and professors. Neither politicians nor academics are relevant commentators, in the sense of being able to speak as the truly informed and immediately affected. The people with the greatest direct experience of education are hardly ever consulted: most importantly, pupils, and some way behind them, parents, teachers and the many other people who work in schools.

Third, educational debate needs to move up a gear. Instead of tinkering around with cosmetic changes to this or that bit of an antiquated curriculum, we need the breadth of vision to challenge the whole notion of curriculum, in the light of the kind of society we want to be. We must not be afraid to examine new ideas for a new millennium and to question the conservatism that has been the hallmark of the ratchet tweaking of the state system of secondary education in the last 130 years. We need to reject the kind of thinking that goes: 'We've always done things this way so it must be right and we've never done things that way so it must be wrong'.

Fourth, we need to look very closely at the nature of assessment within the educational system. At present, the whole system is assessment led, from the proposed baseline tests for four-year-olds to entrance to university for eighteen-year-olds. As it is easier to test memory of facts rather than the development of personal or social skills or the attributes of citizenship, then a knowledge-based curriculum is legitimated. Thus the primary purpose of education becomes the passing of examinations rather than the quality of the educative experience itself. Assessment should not be the master of curriculum but its servant.

Fifth, in a pluralistic society that is seeing increasing regional and ethnic diversity, we need to question the sacred cow of blanket uniformity. Changes should not be imposed on a national scale, but introduced gradually and voluntarily and suited to the differing requirements of different regions. Sixth, any changes to teaching and learning styles need to be well-researched, well-funded and well-supported at a local level. Seventh, change must be consensual, and the consensus should have at its centre pupils, parents and teachers.

Is there any real hope that this process of educational and social reform may be initiated? Frankly, I doubt it. The present government is committed to the National Curriculum and, having just renewed Chris Woodhead's contract for a further four years, to the entrenchment of the didactic teaching and simplistic testing of a knowledge-based curriculum. I just don't see that there is the healthy intellectual climate required for an objective debate about the purpose of education. The National Curriculum is the one way and that's that. We've been told and we must accept it – which leads to a final gloomy thought. It's not just teachers and pupils who are being dumbed down by an acceptance epistemology. Parents, including myself, are allowing themselves to be, too. National Curriculum: National Disaster? Pretty soon there'll be no way of knowing.

Independent learning project questionnaire glossary

Aspect a major component of an independent learning project, as identified by pupils. Some aspects are part of the process of the project (e.g. group dynamics) and others are part of the product of the project (e.g. videomaking).

Aspect-based profiling the writing of a profile, incorporating all the responses a pupil has made in the questionnaire, for each pupil in a group revealed by interrogation of the database to have mentioned the same aspect of independent learning in their responses to a particular question or questions (for instance all pupils who found collaborative groupwork to be the hardest thing that they had to learn). The purpose of aspect-based profiling is to provide information about any aspect of the project:

1 by setting responses that concern one aspect within the full context of all a pupil's responses to the questionnaire;
2 by reconciling any inconsistencies between a pupil's different responses;
3 by exploring the inter-relationship between a group of pupils' responses to different questions that refer to the same aspect (for instance the group of pupils who found the aspect of videomaking to be what they regarded as most important and most enjoyable).

Choice of subject the aspect that deals with the criteria that pupils suggest for a collaborative group's choice of the subject for the group's research programme and the project outcomes of video, magazine and live presentation.

Collaborative groupwork (Independent Learning Factor One): a small group of pupils working in partnership to complete independent learning project outcomes on a subject of their own choice. Preferably, a collaborative group is self-chosen, using its own criteria of selection, and comprises three to five members of mixed gender.

Cooperative groupwork (Independent Learning Factor Two): non-competitive agreements and exchanges between the collaborative groups that make up the cooperative group engaged in an independent learning project. The boundaries of the cooperative group are more fluid than those of the collaborative groups and may fluctuate during the course of a project to include other classes, other teachers, adults other than teachers, parents, special interest groups and so on. All the members of the cooperative group are people of equal status.

Constituent a component of an aspect, as identified by a keyword or its subsidiary. For instance, a constituent of the aspect of group dynamics is 'team'; a constituent of the aspect of videomaking is 'camera'.

Cross-referenced data-field interrogation a data-field search that refers to more than one field, in an attempt to find an inter-relationship between responses to different questions and to identify any interface groups. For instance, a cross-referenced interrogation of the fields 'hardest' and 'mostenjoy' reveals an interface group of 82 pupils (16 per cent of the questionnaire population) for whom there was an inter-relationship between that aspect of the project which they found hardest to learn and that which they most enjoyed.

Diversity   the element of diversity describes the variety of opinions expressed by pupils, not only from different schools, but from the same schools, classes and collaborative groups, on every aspect of the project and in response to every question.

Educational citizenship   a concept of education that prepares pupils for global citizenship by granting them active, democratic citizen's rights throughout their education; and that uses the curriculum as a vehicle for developing young citizens' explicit awareness of these rights and their ability to act upon them within an ethically informed critical context of distanced reflection.

Element   one of the three rudiments necessary to an understanding of the oblique nature of pupils' responses to the questionnaire (see Diversity, Inconsistency and Inter-relationship).

Eudemonic comments   comments made by pupils expressing enjoyment of an inde-pendent learning project. These comments were unsolicited. There was no question such as 'Did you enjoy independent learning?' Eudemonic comments were offered voluntarily in the Comments section of the questionnaire.

Eudemonic test   an analysis of the number of pupils who expressed enjoyment or lack of enjoyment of an independent learning project, taking into account the variables of gender, age and school. The test is based on the idea that enjoyment is integral to independent learning, and therefore that the percentage of pupils who have enjoyed an independent learning project gives a rule of thumb guide to the pupils' perception of the educational effectiveness of a project in promoting independent learning.

Expertise   a criterion that may be used for the formation of collaborative groups; expertise can apply to the product and process skills required to complete the outcomes of an independent learning project.

Factor   one of the determining characteristics of independent learning, such as collaborative groupwork (Factor One), cooperative groupwork (Factor Two) or the use of a range of language technology (Factor Eight).

Field   a bank in the database that contains all the keyword references to one question. For instance, the field 'different' contains the 514 responses to Question Five: *What would you do differently if you were doing the project again?*

File   each pupil's questionnaire responses are transferred to a database file that contains the keyword abbreviations of their questionnaire responses.

Friendship   a criterion that may be used for the formation of collaborative groups.

Group dynamics   (1) an aspect encompassing the ways in which members of a collaborative group interact (signified by the keyword 'team' as in 'team plus get on with' or 'team plus patience'); (2) the activities of a collaborative group (signified by keyword phrases such as 'putting it all together' or 'off school premises'); (3) influences upon a collaborative group (signified by such keyword phrases as 'getting on with the teacher' or 'freedom'). Group dynamics subsumes within it, the constituent of collaborative groupwork.

Inconsistency   the element of inconsistency describes the apparent or real dissimilarities, contradictions or paradoxes expressed by a pupil in different responses to the questionnaire.

Independent learning the pedagogy of educational citizenship. Independent learning is a way of learning that equips the learner to become independent of the structures and strictures of a statutory curriculum, and aware of the influences of the institutional media and less formal, though influential, social codes and sub-cultures, so that the learner can continue to learn throughout her life. Independent learning inverts the traditional notion that the process of education (the way in which pupils learn) serves its product (subject-based knowledge). Independent learning is intended to develop the attributes of global citizenship, and is skills not content-based. In independent learning, the curriculum has no intrinsic value; it is the vehicle for the development of personal and social skills. Thus, it might be said that independent learning regards the process as the product, the experience as the outcome. Independent learning is defined as 'the pedagogical construct intended to translate a policy of educational citizenship into effective practice. Pupils have the independence to choose how they will learn, and through the development of the qualities of global citizenship, have the opportunity to learn to become independent in their making of decisions, both as pupils and as citizens'.

Interface group any group of pupils that exists on the interface between two questions and which is only revealed by cross-referenced data field interrogation. For instance, there is a group of pupils who least enjoyed videomaking and another group who regarded videomaking as the most important thing they learnt. There is also an interface group of pupils who found videomaking to be the aspect of the project they least enjoyed but regarded as most important.

Inter-relationship the element of inter-relationship describes the principle underpinning interface groups, that pupils' responses to different questions are not always discrete, that there are connections between different database fields, and that to ignore these connections, to make a separate interrogation of each field that does not involve cross-referenced data-field searches, will give a partial and distorted picture of the pupils' opinions.

Keyword the database word or words used to identify a reference made by a pupil, in response to the questionnaire, to any aspect or constituent of independent learning. For instance the keyword 'magazine' signifies a reference to the project outcome, for each collaborative group, of the production of a magazine based upon the subject studied by the group. All keywords, and subsidiary keyword phrases use the words of pupils in their responses to the questionnaire.

Other project outcomes an aspect encompassing the tasks set for each collaborative group other than the video: the magazine, the live presentation, the project diary and the bibliography. Included in this aspect are constituents such as research, writing, drawing, acting.

Process the personal and social aspect of an independent learning project.

Product the palpable evidence of the outcomes of an independent learning project.

Pupil-guided choice a criterion that may be used for the formation of collaborative groups.

Pupil-negotiated parameters a criterion that may be used for the formation of collaborative groups.

Project outcomes (1) an aspect of the questionnaire; (2) the common tasks that each collaborative group, irrespective of its choice of subject, should aim to complete within the time limits of an independent learning project. The outcomes of an independent learning project were: a video, a magazine, a diary, a bibliography, a live presentation. Included in this aspect are also constituents such as research, writing, drawing, acting, the use of language technology.

Reference   the comment within a response that refers to an aspect or constituent of independent learning.

Response   what a pupil has written in answer to a question in the questionnaire. A pupil can only make one response to a question, but this response may contain references to more than one aspect of the project, or more than one constituent of an aspect.

Subject   a criterion that may be used for the formation of collaborative groups.

Subsidiary keyword (or phrase)   a further word or phrase that elaborates upon a keyword. For instance, the keyword 'team' has 75 subsidiaries, each describing a different facet of collaborative groupwork as perceived by pupils in their questionnaire responses.

Task   a section of work related to any independent learning project outcome.

Task allocation   one or more members of a collaborative group taking on the sole responsibility for one aspect or outcome of an independent learning project.

Task sharing   the responsibility for each aspect or outcome of an independent learning project is rotated, is capable of being carried by any member of a collaborative group, so that, for example in a group of four, one pair may spend one lesson writing for the magazine whilst the other pair use the videocamera, and then swap roles in the next lesson.

Time management   the management of time, by collaborative groups, within the time limits of the project set by teachers.

Videomaking   one of an independent learning project's five outcomes, but regarded as an aspect in its own right in the questionnaire. There were so many positive references to videomaking, but negative references to the other project outcomes, that to have absorbed them all under the aspect 'project outcomes' would have confused the data.

References

AGIT (1994) *Equal Opportunities in School: Sexuality, race, gender and SEN*, London: Longman.

Andrews, G. (1991) (ed.) *Citizenship*, London: Lawrence and Wishart

Arblaster, A. (1994) *Democracy*, 2nd ed., Buckingham: Open University Press

Ashdown, P. (1989) *Citizen's Britain*, London: Fourth Estate

Bacon, F. (1975) *The Advancement of Learning* (1605), Book 1, (ed.) W.A. Armstrong, London: The Athlone Press

Bagnall, R.J. (1990) 'Lifelong education: the institutionalisation of an illiberal and regressive ideology?' *Educational Philosophy and Theory*, **22**, 1, March, 1–7

Baker, M. (1994) *Who Rules Our Schools?* London: Hodder and Stoughton

Balfour Act (1870) London: HMSO

Ball, S.J. (1994) *Education Reform: A Critical and Post-structural Approach*, Buckingham: Open University Press

Barton, L., Meighan, R. and Walker, S. (1980) (eds) *Schooling, Ideology and the Curriculum*, Lewes: Falmer

Beehler, R. (1985) 'The schools and indoctrination' *The Journal of Philosophy of Education*, **19**, pp. 261–72

Blenkin, G.M., Edwards, G. and Kelly, A.V. (1992) *Change and the Curriculum*, London: Paul Chapman Publishing

Bowles, S. and Gintis, H. (1976) *Schooling in Capitalist America*, New York: Basic Books

Bruner, J. (1990) *Acts of Meaning*, Cambridge, Massachusetts: Harvard University Press

Bryce Commission (1895) London: HMSO

Burman, E. (1994) *Deconstructing Developmental Psychology*, London: Routledge

Bullock Report (1975) London: HMSO

Butler Act (1944) London: HMSO

Carr, W. (1991) 'Education for Democracy? A philosophical analysis of the National Curriculum' *The Journal of Philosophy of Education*, **25**, 2, pp. 183–90

Carr, W. and Kemmis, S. (1986) *Becoming Critical: Education, Knowledge and Action Research*, Barcombe: Falmer Press

Carter, R. (1990) (ed.) *Knowledge About Language and the Curriculum: the LINC Reader*, London: Hodder and Stoughton

Central Advisory Council For Education Report (1954) Chair: Gurney-Dixon, F., *Early Living*, London: CACE

Chapman, J.D. and Aspin, D.N. (1997) *The School, The Community and Lifelong Learning*, London: Cassell

Clarke Report (1947) London: HMSO

Cockcroft Report (1982) London: HMSO

Cohen, L. and Manion, L. (1980) *Research Methods in Education*, London: Croom Helm

Corrigan, P. (1990) *Social Forms/Human Capacities: Essays in Authority and Difference*, London: Routledge

Cox, B. (1991) *Cox on Cox: An English Curriculum for the 1990s*, London: Hodder and Stoughton

Crowther Report (1959) London: HMSO

Darling, J. (1994) *Child-centred Education and its Critics*, London: Chapman

DCI and UNICEF (1988) *The UN Convention on the Rights of the Child: A Briefing Kit*

Dearden, R.F., Hirst, P.H. and Peters, R.S. (1975) (eds) *A Critique of Current Educational Aims*, London: Routledge and Kegan Paul

Dearing, R. (1993) (chair) *The National Curriculum and its Assessment: an Interim Report*, York: NCC

Department for Education (1994) *Our Children's Education: The Updated Parents' Charter*, London: HMSO

Department of Education and Science (1985) *Better Schools*, London: HMSO

Department of Education and Science (1985) *Education for All (the Swann Report)*, London: HMSO

Department of Education and Science (1987) *The National Curriculum: A Consultative Document*, London: HMSO

Department of Education and Science (1991) *Your Child and the National Curriculum*, London: DES

Department of Education and Science and the Welsh Office (1989) *English for Ages 5 to 16*, York: NCC

DES and the Welsh Office (1989) *Mathematics in the National Curriculum*, HMSO

DES and the Welsh Office (1989) *Science in the National Curriculum*, HMSO

Dewey, J. (1897) 'My pedagogic creed' in Archambault, R.D. (1974) (ed.) *John Dewey on Education*, Chicago: University Press

Dewey, J. (1900) *The School and Society*, Chicago: University Press

Dewey, J. (1916) *Democracy and Education*, New York: Macmillan

Doll, W.E. Jnr (1993) *A Post-modern Perspective on Curriculum*, New York: Teachers College Press

Education Reform Act (1988) London: HMSO

Edwards, G. (1983) 'Processes in the secondary school: MACOS and beyond' in Blenkin G. M. and Kelly A.V. (eds) *The Primary Curriculum in Action*, London: Harper and Row

Edwards, J. and Fogelman, K. (1993) *Developing Citizenship in the Curriculum*, London: Fulton

Edwards, T., Fitz, J. and Whitty, G. (1989) *The State and Private Education: An Evaluation of the Assisted Places Scheme*, Lewes: Falmer Press

Eggar, T. (1991) TES: 26 October 1991

Elliott, J. (1981) *Action Research: A Framework for Self-evaluation in Schools*, Schools Council Programme 2 Teacher–Pupil Interaction and the Quality of Learning, Working paper 1

Elliott, J. (1991) *Action Research for Educational Change*, Milton Keynes: Open University Press

Elton, Lord (1989) (chair) *Discipline in Schools: Report of the Committee of Enquiry.* HMSO

Ely, M. (1991) *Doing Qualitative Research: Circles Within Circles*, London: Falmer

Elyot, T. (1962) *The Book Named The Governor* (1531) (ed.) Lehmberg, S.E. London: Everyman's Library

Encouraging Citizenship: Report on the Speaker's Commission on Citizenship (1990) HMSO

English in the National Curriculum (1989) DES and the Welsh Office: HMSO

Evan and Aaron Report (1949) London: HMSO

Fogelman, K. (1991) *Citizenship in Schools*, London: Fulton

Forster Act (1870) London: HMSO

Foucault, M. (1990) *Archaeology of Knowledge*, London: Routledge

Franklin, B. (1986) *The Rights of Children*, Oxford: Blackwell

Franklin, B. (1992) 'Children and decision making: developing empowering institutions' in

Fortuyen, M.D. and de Langen, M. (eds) *Towards the Realizations of Human Rights of Children; Lectures given at the Second International Conference on Children's Ombudswork*, Amsterdam. Children's Ombudswork Foundation and Defence for Children International-Netherlands

Freeman, M.D.A. (1988) 'Taking children's rights seriously' *Children and Society*, 1, 4

Freire, P. (1972) *Pedagogy of the Oppressed*, London: Penguin

Freire, P. (1976) *Education: the Practice of Freedom*, London: Writers' and Readers' Publishing Cooperative

Gadamer, H.G. (1977) *Philosophical Hermeneutics*, (trans. Linge, D.) Berkeley: University of California Press

Gelpi, E. (1984) 'Lifelong education: opportunities and obstacles' *The International Journal of Lifelong Education*, 3, 2, pp. 79–87

Giddens, A. (1991) *Modernity and Self Identity: Self and Society in the Late Modern Age*, Oxford: Oxford University Press

Giddens, A. (1994) *Beyond Left and Right: The Future of Radical Politics*, Cambridge: Polity

Gilligan, C., Ward, J.V.and Taylor J.M. with Bardige, B. (1988) (eds) *Mapping the Moral Domain*, Cambridge, Massachusetts: Harvard University Press

Gilligan, C. and Brown, L.M. (1991) *Meeting at the Crossroads*, London: Harvard University Press

Giltin, A.D. (1987) 'Common school structures and teacher behaviour' in Smyth, J. (ed.) *Educating Teachers: Changing the Nature of Pedagogical Knowledge*, London: Falmer Press

Giroux, H. (1981) *Ideology, Culture and the Process of Schooling*, Barcombe: Falmer Press

Giroux, H.A. (1989) *Schooling for Democracy: Critical Pedagogy in the Modern Age*, London: Routledge

Giroux, H.A. (1991) *Postmodernism, Feminism and Cultural Politics: Redrawing Educational Boundaries*, Albany, New York: State University of New York Press

Goetz, J.P. and LeCompte, M.D (1984) *Ethnography and Qualitative Design in Educational Research*, Orlando, Florida: Academic Press

Golby, M. (1994) *Case Study as Educational Research*, Exeter University: Monograph

Graff, G. (1990) 'Other voices, other rooms: organizing and teaching in the humanities conflict' *New Literary History*, 21, 4, pp. 817–39

Graham, D. with Tytler, D. (1993) *A Lesson For Us All – The Making Of The National Curriculum*, London: Routledge

Gray, J. (1983) *Mill on Liberty: A Defence*. London: Routledge & Kegan Paul

Griffith, R. (1996) 'Transforming Power Relationships' in (ed.) John, M. *Children In Our Charge: The Child's Right to Resources* London: Jessica Kingsley

Griffith, R. (1998) *Educational Citizenship and Independent Learning*, London: Jessica Kingsley

Grundy, S. (1987) *Curriculum: Product or Praxis?* London: Falmer Press

Guba, E.G. and Lincoln, Y.S. (1982) 'Epistemological and methodological bases of naturalistic inquiry' *Educational Communication and Technology Journal*, 30

Gutmann, A. (1990) *Democracy and Democratic Education*, Paper presented at the International Network of Philosophy of Education Conference. London: University of London

Habermas, J. (1971) *Towards A Rational Society*, London: Heinemann

Habermas, J. (1990) *Moral Consciousness and Communicative Action*, (trans.) Lenhardt, C. and Nicholsen, S.W., Cambridge: Polity Press

Hadow Report (1926) London: HMSO

Hammersley, M. (1993) (ed.) *Social Research: Philosophy, Politics and Practice*, London: Sage

Hargreaves, A. (1989) *Curriculum and Assessment Reform*, Milton Keynes: Open University Press

Hart, R.A. (1992) *Children's Participation: From Tokenism to Citizenship; Innocenti Essays No 4*, Florence: UNICEF International Child Development Centre

Hartley, D. (1997) *Re-schooling Society*, London: Falmer Press

Hayward, F.H. (1989) *Curriculum and Assessment Reform*, Milton Keynes: Open University Press

Herbert, C. (1992) *Sexual Harrassment in Schools*, London: Fulton.

Higginson Report (1988) London: HMSO

Hirst, P.H. (1973) *Knowledge and The Curriculum*, London: Routledge and Kegan Paul

Hirst P.H. and Peters R.S. (1970) *The Logic of Education*, London: Routledge and Kegan Paul

HMSO (1926) (chair) Hadow; Report of the Consultative Committee of the Board of Education entitled *The Education of the Adolescent*

HMSO (1991) *The Parent's Charter*, Bristol: HMSO

Hutton, W. (1995) *The State We're In*, London: Jonathon Cape

Jeffs, T. (1995) 'Children's educational rights in a new era' in (ed.) Franklin, B. The Handbook of Children's Rights: Comparative Policy and Practice, London: Routledge

John, M. (1993a) 'Children with special needs as the casualties of a free market culture' *The International Journal of Children's Rights*, **1**, Netherlands: Kluwer Academic

John, M. (1993b) 'Children's rights and new forms of democracy' in Fortuyen, M.D. and de Langen, M. (eds.) *Towards the Realizations of Human Rights of Children; Lectures given at the Second International Conference on Children's Ombudswork*, Amsterdam: Children's Ombudswork Foundation and Defence for Children International-Netherlands

Jones, N. (1990) 'Reader, writer, text: knowledge about language and the curriculum', in Carter, R. (ed.) *The LINC Reader*, London: Hodder and Stoughton

Kincheloe, J. (1991) *Teachers as Researchers: Qualitative Enquiry as a Path to Empowerment*, London. Falmer

Kincheloe, J. (1993) *Towards a Critical Politics of Teacher Thinking: Mapping the Postmodern*, Westport, Connecticut: Bergin and Garvey

Lawrence, I. (1992) *Power and Politics at the Department for Education and Science*, London: Cassell

Lawton, D. (1992) *Education and Politics for the 1990s – Conflict or Consensus?* London: Falmer Press

Lynch, J. (1992) *Education for Citizenship in a Multicultural Society*, London: Cassell

Lyotard, J.-F. (1984) *The Postmodern Condition*, trans. Bennington, G. and Massumi, B., Manchester: Manchester University Press

Mackinnon, D. and Statham, J. with Hales, M. (1996) (revised ed.) *Education in the UK: Facts and Figures*, London: Hodder and Stoughton

McLaren, P. (1989) *Life in Schools: An Introduction To A Critical Pedagogy in the Foundations of Education*, New York: Longman

Measor, L. and Sykes, P. (1992) *Gender and Schools*, London: Cassell.

Meighan, R. (1993) *Theory and Practice of Regressive Education*, Nottingham: Educational Heretics Press

Meighan, R. (1995) *The Freethinkers' Pocket Directory to the Educational Universe*, Nottingham: Educational Heretics Press

Mestrovic, S.G. (1994) *The Balkanisation of the West: The Confluence of Postmodernism and Postcommunism*, London: Routledge

Mill, J.S. (1965) 'On Genius' (1832) in (ed.) Scheewing J.B. *J.S. Mill, Essays on Literature and Society* New York and London: Collier-Macmillan, pp. 87–101

Murgatroyd, S. and Morgan, C. (1993) *Total Quality Management and the School*, Milton Keynes: Open University Press

NATE (National Association for the Teaching of English) (1992) *Made Tongue-tied by Authority? A Response by NATE to the Review of the Statutory Order for English*, York: Longman

National Curriculum Council (1987) *The National Curriculum: A Consultative Document*, London: HMSO

National Curriculum Council (1989) *Consultation Report: English*, York: NCC

National Curriculum Council (1990a) *Curriculum Guidance 3: The Whole Curriculum*, York: NCC

National Curriculum Council (1990b) *Curriculum Guidance 8: Education For Citizenship*, York: NCC

National Curriculum Council (1991a) *Teaching Talking and Learning in Keystage 2*, York: NCC

National Curriculum Council (1991b) *Teaching Talking and Learning in Keystage 3*, York: NCC

Newson Report (1963) London: HMSO

Nixon, J. (1992) *Evaluating The Whole Curriculum*, Milton Keynes: Open University Press

Norwood Report (1943) London: HMSO

Peters, R.S. (1983) 'Philosophy and Education' in (ed.) Hirst P.H. *Education Theory and its Foundation Disciplines*, London: Routledge and Kegan Paul, pp. 30–62

Plowden Report (1967) London: HMSO

Pollard, A., Purvis, J. and Walford, G. (1988) (eds) *Education, Training and the New Vocationalism*, Milton Keynes: Open University Press

Preece, J. (1991) *The Enterprising Classroom*, Manchester: Trafford

Priestley, J. (1778) *Miscellaneous Observations Relating to Education. Most Especially as it Respects the Conduct of the Mind. To Which is Added, An Essay on a Course of Liberal Education for Civil and Active Life*, Bath: R. Cruttwell

Pring, R. (1993) 'Liberal education and vocational preparation' in Barrow, R. and White, P. (eds.) *Beyond Liberal Education, Essays in Honour of Paul Hirst*, London: Routledge

Reason, P. and Rowan, J. (1981) *Human Enquiry: A Sourcebook of New Paradigm Research*, Chichester: John Wiley

Riddell, S. (1992) *Gender and the Politics of the Curriculum*, London: Routledge

Riding, R. and Raynor, S. (1998) *Cognitive Styles and Learning Strategies*, London: David Fulton

Rogers, R. (1980) *Crowther to Warnock: How Fourteen Reports Tried To Change Children's Lives*, London: Heinemann

Robbins Report (1964) London: HMSO

Rousseau, J-J. (1762) *Emile* (trans.) Foxley, B. (1911) London: Dent

Ruddock, J. (1984) 'Introducing innovation to pupils' in Hopkins, D. and Wideen, M. *Alternative Perspectives on School Improvement*, London: Falmer Press

Schempp, P.G., Sparkes, A.C. and Templin, T.J. (1993) 'The micropolitics of teacher induction' *American Educational Research Journal*, **30**, 3

Schofield, J.W. (1993) 'Increasing the generalizability of qualitative research' in (ed.) Hammersley, M. *Social Research: Philosophy, Politics and Practice*, London: Sage

School Curriculum and Assessment Authority (1993) *Keystage 3 School Assessment Folder*, London: SCAA

School Curriculum and Assessment Authority (1994) *Keystage 3 Sample Test Materials English*, London: SCAA

School Examinations and Assessment Council (1991) *Teacher Assessment in Practice*, London: SEAC

School Examinations and Assessment Council (1992) *Pupils' Work Assessed: English Keystage 3*, London: SEAC

School Examinations and Assessment Council (1992) *Teacher Assessment in the Classroom*, London: SEAC

School Examinations and Assessment Council (1993) *Children's Work Assessed: English, Mathematics and Science*, London: SEAC

Shotton, J. (1993) *No Master High or Low: Libertarian Education and Schooling 1890–1990*, Bristol: Libertarian Education

Siegel, H. (1991) 'Indoctrination and education' in (eds) Spiecker, B. and Straughan, R. *Freedom and Indoctrination in Education: International Perspectives*, London: Cassell

Smethurst, J. (1995) 'Education: a public or private good?' *The Royal Society of Arts Journal*, **CXLIII** (5465) December, pp. 33–45

Spens Report (1938) London: HMSO

Spiecker, B. and Straughan, R. (1991) (eds) *Freedom and Indoctrination in Education: International Perspectives*, London: Cassell

Stake, R.E. (1978) 'The case study in social inquiry' *Educational Researcher*, 7

Starkey, H. (1991) (ed.) *The Challenges of Human Rights Education*, London: Cassell

Stenhouse, L. (1975) *An Introduction to Curriculum Research and Development*, London: Heineman

Stenhouse, L. (1980) (ed.) *Curriculum Research and Development in Action*, London: Heinemann

Stenhouse, L. (1983) *Authority, Education and Emancipation*, London: Heinemann

Stock, J. (1991) *Case Studies in English*, Manchester: Trafford

Sullivan, M. (1991) *Marketing Your Primary School* London: Longman

Swan Report (1985) London: HMSO

Taunton Commission (1864–9) London: HMSO

United Nations General Assembly (1948) Official Records, Resolution 217, 3rd Session, Part 1, *The Universal Declaration of Human Rights*, New York: UN

United Nations General Assembly (1989) Official Records, Resolution 25, 44th Session, *The United Nations Convention on the Rights of the Child*, New York: UN

Walkerdine, V. (1994) 'Reasoning in a post-modern age' in Ernest, P. (ed.) *Mathematics, Education and Philosophy*, London: Falmer Press

White, J. (1997) *Twenty-first Century Schools: Educating for the Information Age*, Whitaker (UK)

Whitty, G. (1989) 'The new right and the national curriculum: state control of market forces?' *The Journal of Education Policy*, **4**, 4, pp. 329–41

Whyld, J. (1983) (ed.) *Sexism in the Secondary School Curriculum*, London: Harper and Row

Wittgenstein, L. (1990) *Tractatus Logico-Philosophicus*, London: Routledge

Wolcott, H.F. (1973) *The Man in the Principal's Office: an Ethnography*, New York: Holt, Rinehart and Winston

Wolcott, H. F. (1990) *Writing Up Qualitative Research*, London: Sage

Woodhead, C., Rose, J. and Robin, M. (1992) *Curriculum Organisation and Classroom Practice in Primary Schools: A Discussion Paper*, London: HMSO

Yin, R.K. (1989) *Case Study Research: Design and Method*, New York: Sage

Index